just10

GOD'S TIMELESS VALUES FOR LIFE TODAY

J.John

First published as *The Ten Commandments* in 2020 by Philo Trust
Witton House, Lower Road, Chorleywood, Rickmansworth,
WD3 5LB, United Kingdom

www.jjohn.com

Paperback edition published as *just10* in 2023

The right of J.John to be identified as the author of this work has
been asserted by him in accordance with the Copyright, Designs and
Patents Act 1988.

British Library Cataloguing in Publication Data
A catalogue record for this book is available from the British Library

Hardback ISBN: 978-1-912326-10-5
Paperback ISBN: 978-1-912326-24-2

Cover design: John West

Print Management by Verité CM Ltd
www.veritecm.com

Printed in England

CONTENTS

INTRODUCTION

The Ten Commandments – has so much ever been based on so little? Barely 300 words long in English, enshrined in the heart of our governmental structures they form the foundation of the legal systems of the western world and set out the values at the very core of our civilisation. In words so few they would fit into a tweet or condense into an Instagram story, this great arch of law encompasses family rights, property rights, the rights of the individual and even the rights of God.

Now some people might agree that the Ten Commandments are of great historical and cultural significance, but at the same time deny they have any other significance to us today. They would argue that while they might be honoured, they need not be obeyed. So do these ancient commandments still apply to us personally? At first glance it seems unlikely. What can the moral code of nomadic, late-Bronze Age peasants teach us in our politically correct, app-filled twenty-first-century world? Well, I have taught on these commandments for twenty years and I believe that they do still speak to us today. I believe the Ten Commandments come from God and express his guidelines for how all human beings, of whatever century and whatever culture, are to live. And precisely what these guidelines are is the central theme of this book.

WHAT THIS BOOK IS (AND ISN'T)

I began teaching on the Ten Commandments at the beginning of the twenty-first century. I then turned the talks into a book entitled simply *Ten*. Now, many years on, I have realised that it is time to revisit the manuscript because things have changed. Not, I hasten to add, either the Ten Commandments or my view of them, but our world. We cannot compartmentalise our private ethics from our public practice. Therefore, I believe it is imperative to see the relevance of the commandments for how we live our lives today and tomorrow. The rules are in the context of a relationship with our rescuer – Jesus – not detached from it.

Let me also say here what this book is not.

First, because of a number of contentious issues, there is a widespread belief today that Christian ethics is only about issues of human sexuality. It isn't. I hope that this book reflects the true balance of the Ten Commandments, where only one actually deals with this area. There are many other important matters to discuss which encompass a myriad of principles pertaining to living our lives well.

Second, this is not a 'feel bad' book, delivering a burden of relentless condemnation or designed to get us into the cul-de-sac of guilt. Although the commandments do judge us, they do so in order to turn us to God's forgiving grace found in Christ. When we have received that grace, the commandments – and the Old Testament law in general – acquire a new role: they become our guide and guardian. They encourage and inspire us to remember that who we start out being does not determine who we end up becoming. This is a book of blessing and hope. We can often confuse conviction with condemnation. Conviction leads us to a place of deliverance and change; condemnation leads us to the gallows of despair and hopelessness.

Finally, this is not some analytical intellectual study on the Ten Commandments. What I have written here has been hammered out in countless seminars, discussions and speaking events to over one million people. Many people I speak to are struggling with issues of right and wrong. When we grapple with the commandments, we are forced to come face to face with the painful implications of our moral failure. Indeed, the commandments challenge me whenever I turn to them. If you think of life as a battle, this book is not a theoretical study of military strategy or a forensic examination of how a soldier has fallen and failed; it is a blood-stained message from a fellow soldier on the front line.

THE TEN COMMANDMENTS – SOME BACKGROUND

Because of the practical focus of this book, I have chosen not to go into great historical and theological details on how the Ten Commandments were given. If you want to know the background, any good Bible dictionary, Bible study plan or phone app will help. I do, however, need to make some brief comments.

The Ten Commandments occur in two places in what Christians call the Old Testament part of the Bible. Exodus 20 is an account of how they were given to Moses on Mount Sinai, and Deuteronomy 5 repeats them in the introduction to the laws for the Jewish people.

This is the Exodus 20 version:

And God spoke all these words:

'I am the LORD your God, who brought you out of Egypt, out of the land of slavery.

'You shall have no other gods before me.

'You shall not make for yourself an image in the form of anything in heaven above or on the earth beneath or in the waters below. You shall not bow down to them or worship them; for I, the LORD your God, am a jealous God, punishing the children for the sin of the parents to the third and fourth generation of those who hate me, but showing love to a thousand generations of those who love me and keep my commandments.

'You shall not misuse the name of the LORD your God, for the LORD will not hold anyone guiltless who misuses his name.

'Remember the Sabbath day by keeping it holy. Six days you shall labour and do all your work, but the seventh day is a sabbath to the LORD your God. On it you shall not do any work, neither you, nor your son or daughter, nor your male or female servant, nor your animals, nor any foreigner residing in your towns. For in six days the LORD made the heavens and the earth, the sea, and all that is in them, but he rested on the seventh day. Therefore the LORD blessed the Sabbath day and made it holy.

'Honour your father and your mother, so that you may live long in the land the LORD your God is giving you.

'You shall not murder.

'You shall not commit adultery.

'You shall not steal.

'You shall not give false testimony against your neighbour.

'You shall not covet your neighbour's house. You shall not covet your neighbour's wife, or his male or female servant, his ox or donkey, or anything that belongs to your neighbour.'
(Exodus 20:1–17)

The Bible tells us that the Ten Commandments were given to the people of Israel after their liberation from slavery in Egypt as they journeyed under Moses' leadership to the Promised Land. As such, it may be helpful to think of them as part of the constitution of God's Old Testament people, the nation of Israel.

The date for that event – the Exodus – is 1450 BC. By anyone's standards, that makes the Ten Commandments very old.

Over 3,500 years have passed since these commandments were written. The Bible describes the commandments as being engraved on stone; a compelling image of their enduring nature. Prosperity and adversity, catastrophe, wars and civilisations, kings, queens and emperors have come and gone but they have had no more impact on the permanence of the Ten Commandments than a few raindrops on a granite slab. As we go through these commandments you will find that, despite their origin in a nomadic culture so long ago, very few clarifications or concessions need to be made today. There is an extraordinary clarity and timelessness to these words; it requires no great mental acrobatics or no new self-help 'hack' to believe that they are indeed God-given, universal values and instructions for all people and all time, with the intention of enriching our lives rather than eroding our contemporary progress.

THE TEN COMMANDMENTS IN A CHANGING WORLD

I believe the Ten Commandments are God-given and relevant for all races and forever. Nevertheless, I believe that we need to think about how to apply them to the culture in which we live. One reason for rewriting this book is that the modern world is changing so fast that today's culture becomes yesterday's at an unprecedented rate, with over 2 million new articles being published on the internet every single day specifically focusing on changes in cultural traits, trends and tendencies.

Only forty years ago the world was a larger, less crowded, less complex and less fluid place. There were still countries that were distant and different, and who knew nothing – except perhaps by rumour – of Apple, let alone keeping up with today's global networks and the shifting technological landscape. Interconnected networks spanning the globe were only fantasies in novels and film directors' imaginations. Pornography was only accessible in seedy bookshops but is now just one click away.

In most of the western world the majority of people were still defined by culture, race, language or class. There was a formality and structure to the way we lived. This has all changed and, if anything, the pace of change has increased. We now have the makings of a global culture. Everybody seems to be everywhere. We are now interconnected: we use the same phones and watch the same films. We don't even need to be in the same room to conduct a meeting, with the emergence of Skype, Zoom Calls and FaceTime. Watching pornography, gambling and the buying and selling of almost anything, legal or otherwise, can be done by pulling our phones from our pockets. Informality and flexibility are the rules, whether in office clothes, language or sexual relations.

There are other differences. Towards the end of the last millennium there was a general optimism about the future. The world's economies were expected to continue to grow, there were moves to pay off the debts of the developing world, there was a vague expectation that the poor might become less poor and the West still exported things to China. Indeed, if memory serves me correctly, we still respected bankers! *No longer*. We have developed a distinct distrust for those in leadership, and scepticism has spread like a virus that has contributed to the erosion of trust and unity within our culture.

Some of the most visible changes have been brought about by technology. Even as the new millennium dawned, cameras still used film, recorders used tape and mobile phones were weighty bricks that ruined the line of your suit and did no more than make and receive calls. There was no Facebook, Twitter, Instagram, Google, Skype, Wikipedia or Kindle, and no one had heard of social networking. Amazon was merely a blue line on a map of South America. Music was stored on discs or tape and films on bulky video cassettes.

Books, television, radio and newspapers were the sources of all our information. If you needed to know something, you went to the library or pulled out an encyclopaedia.

In less than two decades there has been a total transformation in technology. We now live in what is optimistically called a 'connected society'. This change has had both spectacular and subtle effects. The World Wide Web is like a vast, sprawling garden, full of endless promise and opportunity. Yet it's a garden where harmful snakes slither.

It has made distant people close but – as anybody who has been ignored by a friend tapping at their smartphone knows – it has also made the close distant. It has allowed anybody to publish lies around the world and has offered the cloak of anonymity to those who seek fulfilment for every kind of desire. We become the stars of our own self-made reality show, with each of us broadcasting our opinions, knowing that people will engage with us, for better or for worse.

Social media, an incredible tool, makes a wonderful supplement to human interaction and relationship, but a terrible substitute. We have become a society living for 'likes' but longing for love. Sending a 'tweet' or posting a photograph with a filter has become the native tongue of every culture. Social media has become as ubiquitous as television in our everyday lives, and research shows that social media can be as addictive as drugs, alcohol and chemical substance abuse.

Though we have become more interconnected than ever we are lacking intimacy, with anxiety levels at an all-time high as we try to process so much information competing for our attention. According to a new report, the more social circles a person is linked to, the more likely social media will be a source of stress. A study in 2018 reported over a third of British residents feel stressed for at least one full day per week. That equates to four days in a month at minimum. However, it doesn't end there: when taking into account the entire study group, Brits feel stressed for an average of nine days per month. Those who don't feel stressed at all are very much in the minority, coming in at around 15 per cent of all participants. That means that the remaining 85 per cent are regularly experiencing a clearly recognisable level of worry.[1] 'Fear of Missing Out' is now a medical condition that doctors can prescribe drugs for as people are inundated with requests and expectations from other people.

One of the themes of the last twenty years has been an increasing uneasiness about our own security and identity. In an age when reality is adjusted and manipulated, in which cameras watch our every move and sophisticated programs track our Web visits, we find ourselves threatened. Technology was supposed to liberate us but instead we find ourselves less free. With the advancement of artificial intelligence, our future, though advancing, can be vulnerable as we try to keep up with the sheer volume of information being created and directed towards us.

In those linked areas of belief and morality surrounding the Ten Commandments there have been other profound changes. In both Britain and the United States we have seen an erosion of the Christian framework that once upheld our culture. The recent rise of the New Atheists has, despite their claims, almost certainly had little to do with this. They are most probably an effect rather than a cause.

Many commentators suggest that in both Britain and the United States there was once a uniform society bonded together by Christian belief, and that this 'Christian society' has collapsed or eroded over the last few decades. I think the reality is more complex. My belief is that in both Britain and the United States there have always been 'cultural Christians' alongside believing, committed Christians. These 'cultural Christians' are happy to sign up to a modest form of churchgoing, tick 'Christian' on the census boxes and give roughly Christian answers when asked about moral decisions. It has produced a culture of church consumers rather than contributors. People become someone in a crowd, rather than part of the core which is committed to building the kingdom and the church.

'Cultural Christianity' makes few demands on its adherents and gives, in return, a sense of identity. In the past, cultural Christianity was very popular; many people on both sides of the Atlantic have found it a convenient spiritual badge to wear. From the 1960s onwards, however, new pressures on culture emerged and, under the influence of materialism and a growing tendency to make personal happiness and fulfilment a priority, cultural Christianity lost its ability to retain followers and began to ebb away. The result is that although the core of 'committed believers' has probably remained steady, the statistics on such things as churchgoing have shown a sharp numerical decline. In England alone, church membership is forecast to decline to 2.53 million (4.3 per cent of the population) by 2025.[2] According to the UK Census, between 2001 and 2011 the number of Christians born in Britain fell by 5.3 million – about 10,000 a week. With a continued rate of decline at this level, the number of UK-born Christians would reduce to zero by 2067.

Now if this analysis is correct, in one sense it suggests that what has happened in western Christianity is not particularly serious. Jesus himself appears to have preferred quality over quantity when it came to followers and had no unease about discouraging casual followers (Luke 14:25–35; John 6:60–71). Nevertheless, this narrowing of the 'support base for Christianity' has had two important effects on how we live and how we relate to the Ten Commandments.

Firstly, it has contributed to a culture of ignorance about what Christianity actually teaches. To have a Christianity that is only cultural is problematic, but it does at least allow some exposure to the teachings of the Bible. The waning of cultural Christianity has removed that exposure to biblical values. We are also living in a more pluralistic society where no 'moral absolutes' are propagated, tolerance has been elevated to a place of virtue, and standing firm to orthodox Christian values and ideologies has been seen as 'religious fundamentalism'. In speaking on the Ten Commandments I have been amazed at the ignorance that now exists about them. In this 'post-Christian' culture we have a rising generation whose morality is derived from those forces that shout loudest, such as Hollywood, YouTube bloggers, and those with the most social media followers who are able to be re-tweeted and reach a larger audience than the average individual. In this kind of environment it is vital that we set out once more the guidance that the Ten Commandments offer.

Secondly, the weakening of a biblically informed culture has created an environment in which head-on challenges to Christian beliefs and practices now exist. The Ten Commandments are so deeply embedded in western culture that, until recently, it was extremely rare for anybody to feel the need to defend them. They were taken for granted to the extent that 'everybody knew' that stealing, adultery and lying were wrong. Yet we now have a culture in which such actions are not simply defended but actively promoted. Affairdating.com receives 34,000 website visits a day. Indeed, so radical have the changes been that biblical positions on marriage, family and work ethics are now taken by an often-unpopular minority. It is vital we affirm that God has spoken and given us guidelines for what is good and right to live by. People have started to stand over the Bible and its teachings in judgement, as opposed to sitting under the Bible as their ultimate authority. As the world becomes more sophisticated, the Bible is being seen as too simple an answer. However, the message is timeless and more needed than ever before.

Where We Are Now

Some people think that losing the influence of the Ten Commandments in our society is a good thing. Many who might term themselves atheists or agnostics are saying, 'It's good for us to be set free from such superstitious ancient bondage.' Well, we have now had an entire generation who have indeed been set free from the influence of the Ten Commandments. So how do things look?

The answer is not very good. No one likes moralists who turn around and say, 'Well, I did warn you.' Yet I am afraid to say that the neglect of biblical morality has indeed given rise to major problems.

In Britain, it seems that on the basis of almost every social criterion, the nation is in deep decline. We are being confronted with a rise in crime, family breakdown, personal debt and drug abuse. This does not diminish the older people get. In fact, the number of people aged above fifty receiving hospital treatment after taking drugs has more than quadrupled in the past decade.[3] The Royal College of Psychiatrists reports NHS services are struggling to cope with a huge increase in older drug users, particularly driven by baby-boomers continuing the hedonistic lifestyles of their youth.

Once proud and historic city centres are now all too frequently places from which people flee before nightfall. Some academic research carried out in 2018 showed that while our contemporary cultural climate may be fraught with racial tensions and intense discussions about inequalities for women and minorities, recent surveys have concluded that over the past thirty years we have actually become a more tolerant nation than ever before.[4] Britons are less honest than a decade ago. British people today are also 'more likely to tolerate extramarital sex, drink-driving or failing to leave a contact after damaging a parked car than those of 2001'.[5]

The United States is experiencing a similar decline in morality. According to its findings, not only have Americans become more tolerant on the whole, but individual generations, especially Baby Boomers (born 1946–1964), have each shown increasing tolerance regarding multiple social issues.[6]

Interestingly, the two most common moral problems listed were 'consideration of others/compassion/caring/tolerance/respect' and 'lack of family structure/divorce/ kids' upbringing'. There are other troubling social statistics: out-of-wedlock births have increased in the United States so that at least four in ten children are now born to unmarried women. Evidence shows that such children tend to do worse later in life in terms of health, education and income.[7]

Other areas of morality are not easy to quantify; how do you put a numerical value on 'political corruption' or 'pornography on the internet' for example? One interesting study used the enormous archive of literature in Google Books to look at how language had changed from 1901 to 2018. The authors of the study found an overwhelming decline in the use of words related to personal morality, virtue and care for others.[8]

In fact, many social commentators believe that tolerance is now the virtue our society needs to uphold above all others and words such as acceptance, liberalism, diversity and complexity are used in our vocabulary more than at any other time. I think that on both sides of the Atlantic there is a recognition that we are in trouble. It is dangerous to generalise about the past, but I feel that for Britons the 500 years running up to the year 2000, and for Americans the 250 years before the millennium, were times when everybody knew who they were and what their respective nations were about. There was a common purpose (often lost), a common morality (often ignored) and a common identity (often forgotten). But the fact was that when someone said 'be good', 'that is wrong' or 'they are decent people', everybody knew what they meant. There was, if you like, a 'standard standard'. That is no longer the case; we no longer sing from a common hymn sheet. We now determine what's right or wrong based on the information we choose to read, which has been filtered through a particular leaning or worldview. Unity has become misunderstood and identified with uniformity and anything that looks like it can inhibit our freedom is dismissed as primitive or irrelevant. Not realising that unity doesn't erase difference but it does erase division.

Mind the Gap

Any user of London's Underground is constantly reminded when boarding the trains to 'mind the gap!' Something of a moral equivalent has opened up in our society. It is not just nature that abhors a vacuum, but also culture. If we abolish the Ten Commandments, what do we fill the gap with? Self-help books? The latest inspirational article from the Huffington Post?

There have been two responses, the first of which is to modify them. The new world of the twenty-first century needs a new ethic. But as to what sort of ethic, there is no agreement. Various modifications to the commandments are proposed: the deletion of some, the replacement of others. The tone is also changed. Because this is the age of democracy and personal autonomy and no one wants to be pushed around by commanders or commandments, you end up with something that might be called the 'Ten Suggestions' – really good ideas that are laced with biblical morality, unfortunately focused on what we can do as individuals, rather than receiving the help we need outside of ourselves in Christ.

A second response has been to completely jettison the Ten Commandments and try to create an alternative. Some have tried to develop a modern, secular, more twenty-first-century set of Ten Commandments. One recent attempt was that of Jordan Peterson, whose book *The Twelve Rules for Life: An Antidote to Chaos* became a *New York Times* Best Seller. This shows people are hungry to discover practical tools to give them a guide to a better life. The reviews have coined this book 'the modern-day commandments' as critics send the biblical commandments to the gallows and call them not just unfamiliar but obsolete. Peterson's commandments are as follows:

1. Stand up straight with your shoulders back.
2. Treat yourself like you would someone you are responsible for.
3. Make friends with people who want the best for you.
4. Compare yourself with who you were yesterday, not with who someone else is today.
5. Do not let your children do anything that makes you dislike them.
6. Set your house in perfect order before you criticise the world.
7. Pursue what is meaningful.
8. Tell the truth, or, at least, don't lie.
9. Assume that the person you are listening to might know something you don't.
10. Be precise in your speech.
11. Do not bother children when they are skateboarding.
12. Pet a cat when you encounter one on the street.

Let's just say I don't think the original Ten Commandments have much competition.

The fact is that for all our technology and knowledge, human beings remain stubbornly the same. We may live in apartments and houses rather than tents, we may have a thousand friends on social media, we may fly 100,000 miles a year, we may have modified our appearance but, beneath all that we appear to be, we are no different to those people who first heard Moses read out God's Ten Commandments. All our ancient literature, biblical or otherwise, shows that in terms of ethics, humans have not changed in the slightest in 4,000 years. We have the same vices as our ancestors. And we need the same rules.

No, the Ten Commandments are not obsolete, but they are *absolute*. They were not made for any particular period in history. They were made for human nature and therefore were commandments for all seasons, all centuries, all cultures. They are as universal and perpetual as honour and truth. No nation can survive without a moral base built on them.

There is a savage irony here. We have got rid of the Ten Commandments in the name of freedom, yet the price we have paid is our own liberty.

We are no longer free to venture out at night, no longer happy to let our children play on the street or spend time in internet chatrooms, no longer able to have cars and homes without equipping them with alarms and hi-tech locks or security systems.

Law and liberty are not in opposition. In fact, law is at the heart of liberty; laws do not restrict us, they free us to live in order and harmony. It is not to be seen as the enforcer of rules as much as they are an outpost of grace. This is true for societies and it is true for individuals. St Augustine paraphrased the Christian law as 'Love God and do what you like'. Many people have gone for a different motto: 'Do what you like and, soon after, rush to a psychoanalyst to find out why you no longer seem to like anything.'

We have come to realise that nothing is quite as enslaving as total freedom.

A Renewed Interest

Despite this rejection of the Ten Commandments and attempts to create some sort of alternative, I have also detected a surprising renewed interest. Again and again I find myself being asked to run teaching series on them. I think there are two reasons for this demand.

The first is quite simply the recognition that western culture is in a mess. We are part of a generation that has lost its fixed standards. For all its claims, New Atheism can offer us nothing to hold on to, guide us or challenge us. In throwing out God, they have also thrown out any guidance on how to be good. The reality is that, on whichever side of the Atlantic we live, our society is not simply a ship that has slipped loose from its moorings; it is a ship that has lost its compass and rudder too. The Ten Commandments hold out the promise of being a landmark, a GPS to navigate us and even an anchorage.

The second reason for this renewed interest is that deep down inside all of us is an ingrained recognition that we were made to operate under these ancient rules. They are the maker's instructions for those he has created. They and we belong together and for us to operate without them is an act of the highest stupidity.

I believe passionately that we need to recover the Ten Commandments for our society. The idea that God has rules for the way we live may sound uncomfortable to us today. Yet if there is a God who has made us and if he has spoken, then it makes a lot of sense to listen to what he has to say about how we live our lives. I come across many people who believe *in* God, but don't believe God; they believe in the maker but do not accept the maker's instructions. That, of course, is nonsense. God himself is the source of the Ten Commandments, and because the maker of the Ten Commandments is the one who created the human race, his commands work.

ABOUT THIS BOOK

The title of each chapter expresses the heart of each commandment in a contemporary, positive way. I have chosen to start with the tenth commandment and end with the first. When these commandments were first given, it was to people who already knew something about God and who he was. We are very different today. The first commandment is the dazzling heart of the law, like some fiery star in the centre of a planetary system. It's the equivalent of a 'pinned tweet' on a profile page. The first thing we want people to see before we explain all other things. I think it is easier for us today to spiral slowly in through the outer laws before we come face to face with the scorching incandescent glow of the first commandment.

For each commandment, I consider the issue that it addresses and look at the heart of the problem and then present a series of suggestions on how we can help keep the commandment in the twenty-first century. Again, I remind you that this is a practical book. There are lots of technical questions I have avoided. There is, for instance, very little here on the relationship of the sixth commandment ('you shall not murder') to warfare or capital punishment. A major reason for these omissions is the tendency for human beings to occupy their minds with intriguing abstract problems they do not face in order to avoid dealing with the real ones they do face.

There are many quotes in this book and I have tried to give due credit to their authors. The eighth commandment applies to words as well as things. However, in some cases they have been bouncing about my brain (or my study) for so long their sources have become worn away. For the unconscious use – or abuse – of any such material I ask forgiveness.

Finally, let me also say a word about the quotations from the Bible here. Most of the verses cited are in either the New International Version or the New Living Translation. However, having grown up as a Greek speaker, I have been unable to resist occasionally making my own translation of the New Testament where I felt the published versions didn't reflect the best meaning of the text.

I pray this book inspires you and infuses you with faith, hope and love.

J.John
Reverend Canon

---

1   https://www.forthwithlife.co.uk/blog/great-britain-and-stress/

2   www.faithsurvey.co.yk/uk-christianity.html

3   https://www.thetimes.co.uk/edition/news/doctors-see-huge-rise-in-drug-abuse-by-over-50s-70x02mk07

4   https://journals.sagepub.com/doi/full/10.1177/1468796817723682

5   https://www.theguardian.com/commentisfree/belief/2012/jan/30/re-moralise-society-less-honest

6   https://mic.com/articles/113164/new-study-shows-america-has-become-more-tolerant-than-ever-before#.EFcRFi4qW

7   http://www.economist.com/blogs/democracyinamerica/2012/03/morals

8   http://www.theatlanticwire.com/entertainment/2012/08/moral-decline-words-we-use/56142/

1

HOW TO FIND TRUE CONTENTMENT

COMMANDMENT TEN: YOU SHALL NOT COVET

You shall not covet your neighbour's house. You shall not covet your neighbour's wife, or his male or female servant, his ox or donkey, or anything that belongs to your neighbour. (Exodus 20:17)

SO, WHAT'S THE PROBLEM?

Coveting may not be a word we use a lot today. It means the uncontrollable desire to acquire. The concept of wanting what is not ours is well known. In fact, the problem the tenth commandment addresses is so familiar, it is expressed in popular sayings:

> *The grass is always greener on the other side.*

> *God made us a little lower than the angels, but most of us want to climb a little higher than the Joneses.*

> *Our yearnings will always exceed our earnings.*

Whether it is clothes, houses, salaries, talents, lifestyles or cars, we want what other people have – what we haven't got.

Not all desire is wrong, of course. Some of our deepest desires are for good things: pleasure and joy, belonging and security, comfort and safety, excitement and adventure. After all, God gives us the desires of our heart (Psalm 37:4). We want to be well respected, to be loved, and to have some meaning in our lives. Those are all good things. Indeed, you could argue that many of the great explorations and discoveries that have advanced the human race have come from desires, whether for money, security or glory. Human beings dream of things we do not have from the moment we are born to the moment we die.

Yet if we have good desires, we also have bad ones. When we see a friend or a colleague with something better than we have – whether more social media followers, a better car, or we see someone upload a photo from a luxurious holiday destination, or check in on social media somewhere abroad – we find ourselves wanting the same. In the 1920s the psychiatrist Sigmund Freud wrote a book called *Civilisation and Its Discontents* in which he identified many of the problems of human society but – famously – attributed most of them to sex. A far wiser book on universal discontent would have focused on covetousness. At the very deepest level, all our personalities have become distorted so that our desires are excessive. We have become covetous.

Matters are made worse because what we consider to be *our* desires are not entirely ours. From the moment we are born, our desires are encouraged and moulded by the world around us. Soon we start to believe that the fulfilment of those good and natural desires to be loved, to belong, are to be found in obtaining material things. We live in a world that seeks to fulfil its internal appetite with a cup of externals. Our restless hearts seek contentment; we come to believe that the only way of achieving this is by acquiring things that we don't already have. The compass needle of our hearts has shifted away from pointing true north and is now pointing elsewhere. We have become lost in the wilderness.

The result of this combination of our own desires and the influence of advertising is the mess that we are in. The moment we browse a website for something we are interested in purchasing, algorithms and cookies make it possible for websites to entice us from then on with similar items. We no sooner buy something than we want the next best thing: the upgrade, the next model up, the special edition. Production lines are four-times faster at creating new products than they were ten years ago.

It is not surprising that in a desperate but futile attempt to satisfy the insatiable thirst that covetousness produces, our favourite national pastime is shopping. Napoleon famously accused the British of being 'a nation of shopkeepers'; two centuries on, they would be better labelled as 'a nation of shoppers'. Actually, these days, most countries are nations of consumers. You can see it in the architecture. In medieval times the focal point of a European city was often the soaring spires of the cathedral; in the twenty-first century it is the gleaming glass and steel of the shopping mall.

No one is exempt. In our idealistic youth we think that we will be content with a small house, a modest car, a nice holiday once a year and a few possessions. In middle age, we suddenly find that our desires have expanded. We want a bigger house, a better car, at least two holidays abroad a year. We long to find fulfilment. Either through:

- Pleasure
- Power
- Prestige
- Popularity
- Possessions
- Promotion
- Prosperity

The weeping Old Testament prophet Jeremiah put it this way:

> 'My people have committed two sins: they have forsaken me, the spring of living water, and have dug their own cisterns, broken cisterns that cannot hold water.' (Jeremiah 2:13)

Unmet appetites are all ways of telling us 'I'm thirsty'. Being thirsty is hardly a heinous crime. Surely the other commands are more obviously wrong? We agree that people can, and should, be prosecuted for stealing or murder. But it is not against the law to covet. Indeed, our society is built around wanting or acquiring things. In this age of recession, the government desperately hopes that the nation will spend its way out of trouble and every month casts anxious glances at the growth in retail sales. So what's the big deal? What's wrong with a bit of dreaming, a bit of desiring? The problem is it doesn't satisfy our deepest need.

The lyrics from a song from the film *The Greatest Showman* are a powerful indictment and exposition of our culture at large. We could hold the whole world, we could have everything, but it 'will never be enough'. There is a global desire and quest for fulfilment. We are plagued with a sense of 'not-enoughness'; a desire to acquire more and more. Everything we observe and are exposed to suggests to us that we can find complete and total fulfilment in acquiring and accumulating more. However, nothing seems to be enough. We are a generation swiping from left to right, scrolling up and down, searching our own name on Google, selecting memes to point out other people's deficiencies. None of this coveting will satisfy.

It is true that nobody has been imprisoned for the crime of 'coveting'. However, the effects that wrong desires have on people's actions are clear to see. We might not choose to act on all of our desires, but all of our actions are the result of our desires. Every act of theft starts with someone's desire to have something that they have no right to. Every act of adultery begins with someone's desire for a person to whom they are not married. Once we recognise the part that desire plays in our actions, we can deal with what is underneath the surface.

The writer of Ecclesiastes warned:

> It is better to be satisfied with what you have than to be always wanting something else. (Ecclesiastes 6:9 GNB)

Covetousness might be unseen and impossible to prosecute but its effects are everywhere, and they can be devastating. Many of the darker events in human history have resulted from covetousness. Throughout history, rulers and nations have coveted the land, resources and wealth that belonged to others. Their actions in pursuit of these desires have caused invasion, poverty and war. Coveting is also one of the key factors behind the global environmental crisis. In the last twenty years, the population of planet Earth has risen by 1,000 million people. Moreover, the population in the United Kingdom is expected to rise by over four million over the next few years.[1] That would be difficult enough to handle but it is made far worse by the fact that everybody, everywhere, seems to want more. Covetousness has the potential to ruin the planet.

Covetousness also breeds exploitation and unrest. We are all familiar with the cycle of wage increases, whereby one group of people in an industry gets a pay increase and then others in the industry demand one too. When they get one, the first group needs another one in order to keep pace. And so the cycle goes on. But interestingly, no one uses words like greed or covetousness. Instead they use noble words such as 'parity', 'equality', 'harmonisation' and 'justice'.

One relatively recent feature of the business world is the growing gap between the salaries earned by chief executives and those who work under them. Paying management disproportionate amounts, whether as salaries, shares, bonuses or other perks, has always happened but has become more widespread in recent years. This has been epitomised in the gender gap disputes of the last several years. The UK gender pay gap is now at its lowest level ever – just over 18 per cent. But it hasn't always been that way. A salary of £1 million a year is now quite common in large firms. A 2019 *Wall Street Journal* analysis found the median salary for 132 CEOs in the S&P 500 was $12.4 million in 2018, up from $11.7 million in 2017. According to the journal, Iger earned $66 million in 2018, which made him the highest-paid CEO on their list of companies disclosing salaries.[2]

The sense that things are going very well for the 1 per cent has fuelled protests all over the world, many under the banner 'We are the 99 per cent'. The argument is often made that such salaries are performance related. Yet evidence from many countries suggests they are not. Whether the various economic indices, such as the Dow Jones or FTSE, go up or down seems to be irrelevant; the salaries of the few men and women at the top continue to rise.

These figures demonstrate something very significant about covetousness: it is subtly and dangerously contagious. When you read the previous paragraphs, you were no doubt struck by how unjust those salaries were. Yet I am positive that, mixed in with that defensible indignation, came the wish that we could be sharing in something of that wealth. It may be righteous indignation that opens the door, but covetousness slips in just behind. We are all prone to covetousness.

Our natural tendency to covet, bad enough as it is, is manipulated and heightened by society. Encouraging coveting is a major national industry: we call it advertising or marketing. The total UK advertising spend is expected to grow by 4.6 per cent in 2019 – a slight fall from an estimated 6 per cent growth last year. Total UK advertising spend in 2017 was £22.1 billion, which included internet ad spend of more than £11.5 billion.[3] The equivalent US figure for 2019 is around $129.34 billion.[4]

These billions of dollars and pounds are spent with the express purpose of trying to enlarge and direct our desires. Fuel is poured upon the fire. Once, advertisements might have been created with no other goal than the modest desire to inform the public; now they clearly set out to manipulate existing desires and create new ones. Through advertising, the world and all its goods make a plea for space in our hearts. Whether we are sitting in front of our televisions, reading magazines, surfing the internet, or even just driving down the road, we are bombarded by subtle attempts to direct our desires. Adverts and digital marketing skilfully entice us to buy a faster car, a smarter phone, a more fragrant perfume or simply another type of coffee. We read articles on the possessions and lifestyles of the rich and famous and scroll through our phones as they advertise the latest product (for which they are paid money to advertise) and we can't stop ourselves wanting what they've got and what they are. Advertisements are intended to create dissatisfaction. A car, house, kitchen or sound system that we have been content with for several years suddenly, under the onslaught of advertisements, seems old, shabby and in need of urgent replacement.

This is what the tenth commandment tackles. It addresses the longing, craving, yearning, desiring – call it what we will – for what we want but cannot have.

Before we look more deeply at covetousness and how it can be remedied, let's just pause for a moment and look at the commandment itself. I believe all the commandments are of universal value, but this is the one that appears most linked to its culture and time. So we smile slightly at the idea of coveting our neighbour's donkey, ox or servants. And as for coveting his wife, isn't adultery covered in the seventh commandment? And isn't it a bit sexist to talk about wives in the same breath as property and livestock? However, it is a good rule never to ignore difficulties in the Bible. Sometimes great gems can be hidden in the deepest undergrowth.

In fact, what we read here is surely a commandment ('do not covet anything that belongs to your neighbour') and examples (his home, possessions, wife). We have no liberty to change the commandment, which is for all time, but the examples are something else. The commandment is that we should not want what our neighbour has. You may ask 'who is my neighbour?' and in the New Testament Jesus answers that very question in the Parable of the Good Samaritan (Luke 10:29–37). A neighbour is anyone with whom we come into contact.

The examples (donkey, ox, servants and wife) are set in the culture of the time: an agricultural, male-dominated world, not far from what we would call the poverty line. The examples listed are surely meant to cover everything that makes our neighbour wealthy or brings them joy.

The reference to the wife is interesting. The fact that adultery is covered in the seventh commandment suggests that there is something else going on here. Although our culture majors on sexual desire, there are in fact many other reasons why a man or woman might want someone else's spouse. For example, a woman might wish her husband was the thoughtful, sensitive, good listener that her friend's spouse is. A man might wish his wife was the athletic, adventurous, outdoor personality that his friend is married to. Whatever good things our friend or neighbour has, whether people or possessions, we are not to desire them.

Let's begin below the surface of our lives, in the place where it all begins – our hearts.

THE HEART OF THE MATTER

So, why do we always want more? Why is it a universal truth that men and women desire what they haven't got?

We all have desires that are God-given. I believe that the desires to be loved, to feel valued, to belong, to feel secure and to be happy are from God. They are good and natural desires in exactly the same way that feeling hungry for food is good and natural. The problem comes because the only satisfaction for these desires lies in the God who has revealed himself in Jesus Christ. Just as it would be a very unwise solution to satisfy the desire of hunger by stuffing your stomach with paper, so covetousness encourages us to try to satisfy our needs in the wrong way. 'How can I be satisfied in life?' is a good question; the problem with covetousness is that it points us to the wrong answer. Instead of trying to find fulfilment for our legitimate desires by going to our creator God, the one who made our hearts and all we seek, we go elsewhere. J.R.R. Tolkien, author of *The Lord of the Rings*, said, 'We are soaked with a sense of exile, a desire to find our way home, lost and unsure how to get back to where we truly belong, we get distracted en route, focusing on unhealthy things.'

Let me give an example of how covetousness misleads us. I believe that the desire to feel significant is a good, God-given desire. We have value and we need to know that we have value. I believe the only real and lasting fulfilment of this desire is to come to know that we are loved children of a heavenly Father. But many people try to satisfy this desire in other ways: having the most likes on their social media page, having the smartest phone or wearing the 'right' clothes with that subtly visible designer logo. Encouraged by advertising, we can come to believe that by being popular, having the phone or wearing the clothes, this significance is transferred to us. Advertising says 'you are what you have'! The message of the advertisements is that buying the right product will turn a nobody into a somebody. Yet a moment's thought will reveal that this is futile. If I buy a new phone or car this week to give me significance, what happens next month when the new model comes out? Or even worse, when everybody else gets one too? To seek significance with physical things is like filling up a petrol car with diesel. In seeking to fulfil our needs through material things, we fail to recognise what we truly do need. Why is this?

One person who succinctly explained the human dilemma, nearly five hundred years ago, was the Christian leader Martin Luther. He said that the basic human problem is that our hearts are 'curved in on themselves'. His diagnosis holds today. The people we are most concerned about in the world are ourselves. All over our radio and TV airwaves, people are opening their hearts on talk shows. If you watch programmes hosted by Oprah Winfrey or Graham Norton, what do people talk about all the time? Themselves. Few people can resist it, a weakness that can end up in embarrassing revelations. This has been made worse with our social media profiles replicating our own online reality TV show. Instagram TV allows us to capture everything we are doing 'live' and in 'real time'. We can 'add to our story' which allows us to broadcast our own opinions and block those who disagree or criticise us. And if we were there behind the microphones, would we be different? I fear not. We are all self-obsessed. The root of covetousness is selfishness; living in a universe which orbits around you.

Early in the last century the question was raised in *The Times*, 'What is wrong with the world?' One writer wrote the following response:

Dear Sir,

I am.

Yours faithfully,

G.K. Chesterton

Why is this? Is it that when God made us we were deliberately constructed to be more concerned for ourselves than anyone else? Or is it some accidental design flaw with our species? Are we like the Samsung smartphones that had to be recalled in 2018 by the makers because of a construction fault?

No, we can't blame God. At the beginning of the Bible in Genesis 1 we are told that God made the world and 'God saw that it was *good* . . .' Man and woman were also made good, designed to enjoy the world and live together contentedly under God's rule.

Unfortunately, trouble soon came. We read in Genesis 2 how God gave humankind freedom to eat from any tree in the Garden of Eden. There was just one restriction given: 'You must not eat from the tree of the knowledge of good and evil.' The Bible then describes how the devil, in the form of 'a serpent', tempted Adam and Eve to break this restriction. Eating the fruit, he suggested to Eve, would give the power to be 'like God'. The desire to covet – to want what was not hers to have – was sown in Eve's heart. It was an attractive offer. Imagine it – being like God and having all that power, all that authority. We would be able to make all the decisions in our life, we would not have to do what anyone else said, we would not have to live in the way that someone else told us; we would have total freedom.

It was too attractive an offer and Eve and Adam took it up and disobeyed God. The promised liberty became imprisonment. The result of their disobedience lives on with us today. What they did then, we continue to do. We, too, push God off the throne and plant ourselves firmly there instead. We do what we want, we make our own decisions, we live as rulers of our own lives.

The result is the tragedy of the human species. Our hearts were made to love God and to love others as we love ourselves. Instead we choose to love only ourselves. As a result, God and the rest of the world, has to fall into place behind us. The effects of this distortion are massive.

Jesus' brother James wrote to a church that was going through difficulties:

> Those conflicts and disputes among you, where do they come from? Do they not come from your cravings that are at war within you? You want something and do not have it; so you commit murder. And you covet something and cannot obtain it; so you engage in disputes and conflicts. (James 4:1–2 NRSV)

It has been wisely said that the heart of the human problem is the problem of the human heart. Our hearts – the centres of our affection and motivation – have turned away from what God desires. Cut loose from God, we now desire all sorts of things, in all sorts of ways that are bad for us. In the Old Testament God addresses his people saying, 'The heart is deceitful above all things and beyond cure. Who can understand it?' In the next verse God answers his own question: 'I the LORD search the heart and examine the mind' (Jeremiah 17:9–10).

Nearly sixteen hundred years ago, a young man called Augustine, who had grown up in a Christian home, rebelled against everything he had been brought up to believe in and embraced wild living. It wasn't long before he turned again to God and then was able to say, 'You have made our hearts, Lord, and they are restless until they find their rest in you.' We've all got restless hearts; it is the heart disease – or dis-ease – that is universal. One of the most famous poets of the last century, T.S. Eliot, wrote a poem called 'Choruses from the Rock' which describes how a desert is not just a region of dry scrubland but a condition of our hearts. Recognising the desert in our heart, we try and pour water into it. Much of what we desire is a desperate misplaced attempt to try to irrigate our internal wasteland. Yet what we moisten our land with is not water. Far from curing the problem, it makes it worse. This is the case in three specific areas: money, things and fame.

Money

We earn more now than we ever have. Wages and the standard of living go up and up. Yet as they rise, so do our expectations. We live at a time when people seem more covetous for money than at any other time in history. Today, those who set the trends in our society are earning extraordinary sums, recession notwithstanding. Some footballers earn £500,000 a week. In the United States some NBA players are earning similar amounts, with annual salaries of $35 million. The demand for ever higher salaries in sport is causing enormous difficulties. To find the money to fund the salaries, ticket prices rise and many people, including the young – the fans of tomorrow – are squeezed out of watching the game. In some cases, clubs are going bankrupt.

Coveting today is facilitated by easily available credit. Items that, fifty years ago, a family would have had to save up for over the course of many months can now be bought instantly, creating instant debts. 'Buy now, pay later' is the invitation and '52 easy payments' the slogan. I've never met an easy payment in my life! The shift from free university education to payment of tuition fees has also given rise to a new problem in Britain. In the past, graduates often avoided debt but now most young people come out of the university system owing the government £30,000. While there are many questions about how we fund university education, my point here is simple. The old wisdom in society was that you should avoid being a debtor; unfortunately it now seems you have no option. If you are already in debt then borrowing a little more to fund whatever you want seems to be no big deal. Moreover, now that we can 'swipe' or 'tap' our cards on a pad, we do not feel the full weight of paying for items.

The result of the debt crisis is that people can increasingly be divided into three groups: the 'haves', the 'have-nots' and the 'have-not-paid-for-what-they-haves'. Everything is faster in today's society, especially getting into debt. *The Guardian* gives up-to-date statistics:

> *Britain's household debt mountain has reached a new peak, with UK homes now owing an average of £15,385 to credit card firms, banks and other lenders, according to the TUC.*

> *The trade union body said household debt rose sharply in 2018 as years of austerity and wage stagnation forced households to increase their borrowing.*

The TUC said in its annual report on the nation's finances that the amounts owed by British households rose to a combined £428bn in the third quarter of 2018. Each household owed £886 more than it did 12 months previously, it said. The figures do not include outstanding mortgage debts but do include student loans.[5]

The current recession was largely brought about by covetousness, by the greed of those in the financial world who wanted to multiply what were already more than adequate salaries. The response to the financial crisis has been utterly contradictory. On the one hand, our governments are trying to impose cutbacks and restraints on their own spending. On the other, they hope that personal spending will somehow buy us out of the recession. So if you are the state, financial restraint is good; if you are an individual, it is bad. I wish I could believe that it made sense.

In the US gambling profits are currently at least $126.2 billion a year according to H2 Gambling Capital. And in some states, such as Nevada, gambling is a major source of state income. Gambling highlights the futility of covetousness. One of the intriguing features is seen not in the fate of the losers, but the winners. Statistics show that most of those who win continue to gamble. No win is a big enough win. If all that money had made them content and satisfied, why would they keep on playing? John D. Rockefeller – at one time the richest man in the world – learned the grim answer. 'How much money does it take for a person to be really satisfied?' he was asked. His reply said it all: 'Just a little bit more.'

Things

One of the big changes in our culture in the last quarter of a century has been the rising number of 'things'. We have more 'stuff' now than we ever had. Ten years ago most of us did not know what a GPS was; now we have navigation devices in our pockets on our phones. Similarly, even a decade ago, if a household had a computer at all, they had just one. Now most houses will have two or three: a desktop, a laptop, an iPad and/or a tablet. Despite the increasing price of petrol, cars have got both bigger and more numerous. Not only do we have more things, we change them more regularly. Most mobile phones come with a two-year contract because people get bored with them.

The industry is very happy to oblige. I suspect that most garages now are not actually used for housing cars, but for storing the boxes from our purchases!

We do not just want things; we want more things and better, newer things. This, of course, exacts a toll. We spend hours reading about 'stuff', researching on websites, comparing models and reading reviews. We spend hours more working to earn the money to buy the things. And when we get the thing, we find it to be as demanding and troublesome: there are the manuals to read, software to upgrade, batteries to charge, the maintenance and backup routines to complete. Things erode our lives away.

Here, too, there is a tragic irony: the more things we have, the greater the hold they have on us. We have all met people who were so busy interacting digitally on their phones with virtual friends at a distance that they failed to interact with the real ones sitting just in front of them. There is now a phrase, registered in the *Oxford Dictionary*, which is used to describe avoiding your loved ones because your attention is on your mobile phone: 'Phubbing'. Things are not the answer.

Fame

In addition to money and things, fame also holds the illusion of being an answer to our deepest needs. In a confusing, materialistic world dominated by the brutal artificiality of television, young people increasingly imagine that fame equates to success. You can hardly blame them. Social media exposes us to people's successes and lifestyles in a way we weren't aware of ten years ago. Moreover, every newsagent or supermarket has shelves of glossy magazines that parade, in multi-page photo spreads, the lives and deeds of celebrities who are mainly famous merely for being famous. (When was the last time you saw a school teacher, a surgeon or a scientist in the pages of those magazines?) As we look at them, they ask us the question, 'Do we belong with these people?' Deep down we would like to be there. If only, we think, I was appearing in that big photo spread of the latest television or sports celebrity's wedding, then I would know for certain that I was something. I would have made it. To be receiving phone calls from other famous people, to be invited to their parties and dinners – surely that would mean the hunger of my heart would be filled? The logic seems inescapable: become a household name and you are a success, and success means happiness. Therefore, fame equals happiness. The converse is also believed to be true. To be unknown is to be a failure and to be a failure is a disaster. Our celebrity culture has created an obsession with fame which is potentially very damaging.

In October 2009 a survey on the aspirations of British youngsters was carried out for the TV series *Tarrant Lets the Kids Loose*.[6] The results were troubling. Career aspirations have shifted significantly within the space of a single generation and over a third of the younger generation were looking for careers that involved fame and fortune.

The top career choices for pre-teens (aged 5–11) in 2015 were:

1. Education 12%
2. Professional, scientific and technical activities 10%
3. Arts, entertainment and recreation 9.5%
4. Financial and insurance services 8.5%
5. Information and communication 7.6%
6. Human health and social work 6.3%
7. Construction 5.3%
8. Public administration and defence 4.5%
9. Water supply and waste management 2.7%
10. Real estate 2.6%; manufacturing 2.6%[7]

What is particularly interesting is to compare this with the top-ten ambitions of pre-teens twenty-five years earlier:

1. Teacher 15%
2. Banking/finance 9%
3. Medicine 7%
4. Scientist 6%
5. Vet 6%
6. Lawyer 6%
7. Sportsman 5%
8. Astronaut 4%
9. Beautician/hairdresser 4%
10. Archaeologist 3%

I hardly have to point out the seriousness of this shift. We can live without sports personalities and pop stars; we cannot live without teachers, doctors and scientists. Equally, I do not need to list examples demonstrating the bitter truth that fame is perilous. Fame is fleeting, fails to satisfy and frequently destroys. It is fleeting because to become famous is like surfing on the crest of a wave. You are either high, visible and glorious, or you are out of sight under the waves. So, writers of successful books or artists with a hit album become enticed by the challenge of the sequel. Is there anything crueller than being a one-hit wonder? Other people have found that to gain fame does not satisfy. They have stood there in the spotlight, realised that it is all empty and walked quietly away. Perhaps the saddest are those whom fame has destroyed. The history of popular music in particular is studded with premature obituaries: Elvis Presley, Jimi Hendrix, Jim Morrison, Janis Joplin, Michael Jackson, George Michael and Amy Winehouse.

Fame and fortune are now considered central goals of society. Yet the sad reality is that neither will permanently refresh the desert or create a reformation in the human heart.

COUNTERING COVETOUSNESS

So how do we respond? Let me suggest several lines of defence against covetousness.

Beware and Be Realistic

Never underestimate the dangerous power of covetousness. The Bible is brutally honest about the effects of wrongful desire and the fact that it can run rampant in all of us. The classic case is of that mighty figure of the Old Testament, David: a great psalm-writer, noble warrior and king who had, it might seem, everything that he could want. Yet a single case of unchecked illicit desire almost destroyed his kingship and led to untold grief. The account (in 2 Samuel 11) tells how one day David saw a woman bathing and, even though both of them were married, he desired her. From this act of covetousness things spiralled downwards in a tragic pattern of escalating sin. Acting on his desire, David sent for the woman, Bathsheba, and slept with her. She became pregnant and as her husband Uriah had been away for months at war, this threatened

David with a considerable scandal. David, desperate for a cover-up, sent for Uriah on the assumption that he would sleep with his wife and the baby could be passed off as his. However, as a man of honour in a time of war, Uriah refused to go home to his wife. David, now in a real corner, was forced to get himself out of the mess by arranging for Uriah to be killed on the battlefield so that he could marry Bathsheba and legitimise the baby. Inevitably, the result was a disaster. David was judged by God and the ensuing problems overshadowed David's entire reign. David committed adultery, abused his position, lied and eventually murdered, all because he let his covetous desires for another man's wife overtake him. Breaking the tenth commandment resulted ultimately in David breaking the sixth, seventh and ninth commandments as well.

Not only is covetousness powerful, it is also subtle. In fact, it can enter into almost every area of life. The Bible talks a lot about coveting, not just of things and money but also of other people's gifts or responsibilities. Covetousness, it seems, can easily turn followers away from Jesus and his words. In one of Jesus' stories, the sower and the seed, he talks about how people do not allow God's word to work in their lives because they let the word become choked by 'life's worries, riches and pleasures' (Luke 8:14).

There is even a story in the Bible which tells how, in the days of the early church, a man called Simon so coveted the apostles' miraculous gifts of the Holy Spirit, that he tried to buy them with money (Acts 8:4–25).

We need to be aware that covetousness is powerful and subtle and can entice us in all sorts of ways. We need to be on our guard in every area of our lives.

See Through the Illusion

To be on our guard about covetousness we need to keep reminding ourselves that it is based on an illusion. Covetousness promises contentment and fulfilment. Yet few, if any, of the things we covet bring us either.

Ironically, this is something that, deep down, we know. In the case of money, the spectacular tales of quarrels, depression and suicides that have resulted from big lottery wins are so widespread that some people fear winning.

So widespread are lottery disasters that in 2012 *BusinessWeek* ran an article with the bitter headline, 'With Any Luck, You Won't Win the Lottery'. The limitations of material wealth have been well stated by an anonymous poet:

> *Money can buy medicine, but it cannot buy health.*
> *Money can buy a house, but not a home.*
> *Money can buy companionship, but not friendship.*
> *Money can buy entertainment, but not happiness.*
> *Money can buy food, but not an appetite.*
> *Money can buy a bed, but not sleep.*
> *Money can buy a crucifix, but not a saviour.*

We need to remind ourselves of this: covetousness promises but fails to deliver. In fact, it does the opposite: it traps. Covetousness is deceitful; it says that if you desire things, people, lifestyles or fame, once you get them you will be satisfied. Actually, once you get them you still want more. 'Shop until you drop' has become a grim reality: the admission of the power of an inescapable compulsion. In 1851 the German philosopher Schopenhauer wrote that coveting 'is like sea water, the more we drink the thirstier we become'.

Above all, we need to remember that *things* are temporary. They are not real riches. In warning his followers about covetousness, Jesus told a chilling story.

> *A rich man had a fertile farm that produced fine crops. He said to himself, 'What should I do? I don't have room for all my crops . . . I know! I'll tear down my barns and build bigger ones. Then I'll have room enough to store all my wheat and other goods. And I'll sit back and say to myself, "My friend, you have enough stored away for years to come. Now take it easy! Eat, drink, and be merry."' But God said to him, 'You fool! You will die this very night. Then who will get everything you worked for?' Yes, a person is a fool to store up earthly wealth but not have a rich relationship with God.* (Luke 12:16–21 NLT)

Jesus pointed out how the man in this story had concluded that material possessions could satisfy all his needs. Suddenly, without warning, he was called to account and it was all taken from him.

Covetousness can damage our health. We need to remember that.

Realise That Fear Feeds Covetousness

We may think that covetousness is simply the product of greed or desire. The truth is the roots are deeper. Strange as it may seem at first, one of the most fertile soils for covetousness is fear.

In today's world, fear is like the air we breathe, it's everywhere. Whether we identify it as fear or just consider it as worry, uncertainty or unease, it is universally present. We fear all sorts of things, some big, some small. We fear some things that are real threats and some that are not. There is a multitude of things that keep people awake at night but the number-one worry for many people is money. Either we worry we don't have enough or we worry about keeping what we do have. One of the lies of money is that if we have enough of it we are immune to life's problems. Of course, we are not. Even the richest people die.

When we face the future, we need to have something to hope for, something that will offset the grim prospect of ageing and death. Things in general and money in particular offer apparent security. Here again we find another problem with covetousness. The only lasting security is to be found in God. Covetousness focuses us away from God. Covetousness makes us live as if our survival depended on our own efforts. We take our lives into our own hands. Unfortunately, in doing so we find that we have taken our lives out of God's hands.

Jesus points out the absurdity of the situation.

> *Therefore I tell you, do not worry about your life, what you will eat or drink; or about your body, what you will wear. Is not life more than food, and the body more than clothes? Look at the birds of the air; they do not sow or reap or store away in barns, and yet your heavenly Father feeds them. Are you not much more valuable than they?* (Matthew 6:25–26)

Jesus encourages people, time and time again, to trust in God because he is faithful and true. If he looks after the birds, then of course he will look after those people who trust in him. Things provide only an illusion of security, not the reality.

Do you know which commandment is most frequently given by God to his people in the Bible? Interestingly enough, it is not one of the Ten Commandments. It is the command, 'Do not fear, do not be afraid.'

Over 370 times, God says to his people – in various ways – that they needn't fear. Why? Well, obviously, not because bad things don't and can't happen, but because he is the Lord and they can trust him with their lives. As my friend the Christian writer and scholar Tom Wright says, this is the best news in the world because it's what we most need to hear: God addressing our fears and telling us we needn't be afraid because we can trust him.

If we knew God better, I believe we would be less tempted to be afraid. And that would cut at the very root of covetousness.

CULTIVATE CONTENTMENT

The old saying 'the grass is always greener on the other side' isn't true. The problem is that we have been watering it. Maybe it's time we started watering the grass on *our* side.

Let me offer you some guidelines for contentment.

Keep Your Heart in Shape

The first way we find lasting contentment is by letting God, not the world, shape our desires. God wants us to know that he desires us and that we can trust him. Then, if we let him, he will get to work on shaping our desires so that what we want is what he desires for us and is best for us. From the opening chapters of the Bible to the last, it is clear that God wants our love and our friendship. God is a loving, caring, forgiving, kind and personal God who will settle for nothing less than the closest of relationships with us. We need to embrace his love.

The first thing that we must straighten out is the state of our hearts, something that no fitness regime or self-help programme can do. What we cannot do, God can. There is a wonderful promise made by God through the Old Testament prophet Ezekiel: 'I will give you a new heart and put a new spirit in you; I will remove from you your heart of stone and give you a heart of flesh' (Ezekiel 36:26).

This heart transplant is exactly what happens when we come to know Jesus. He removes from us our old hearts, curved in on themselves, self-obsessed and selfish. In their place, he gives us his own heart. It is an extraordinary exchange. If your heart feels tired and self-obsessed, perhaps you need this heart transplant? Whoever we are, we need to ask him to take our old, hard heart from us and give us his heart instead.

We also need to realise that the fulfilment of our desires, even those that are God-given, can only come from God himself. In chapter 4 of John's Gospel we read how Jesus once sat by a well with a woman and told her he was the one who could give living water that would cause anyone who drank it never to thirst again. Jesus alone satisfies our deepest needs. If you have become aware that you are thirsting for all sorts of things on offer in the world, it might suggest that you are drinking from the wrong sources.

The first key of contentment is to have and maintain a friendship with God through Christ. We need to guard this friendship, protectively nurturing it and taking care that it grows and flourishes. That must be our number-one priority.

Adopt an Attitude of Gratitude

As we have seen, coveting does not lead to contentment, only dissatisfaction with what we already have. We read repeatedly in the Bible that God desires his children to be content. Listen to the apostle Paul, writing from prison: 'I have learned the secret of being content in any and every situation, whether well fed or hungry, whether living in plenty or in want' (Philippians 4:12).

A major part of contentment is having a positive attitude to the situation we are in. That is not easy to do in our modern society because coveting plays on our dissatisfaction. God, however, does not want unhealthy complaining from us. Rather he seeks the opposite outlook, what we can call 'an attitude of gratitude'.

Alphabetise your blessings. Rather than catalogue your burdens, itemise benefits. The sure cure for a grumpy spirit is gratitude. To say thanks is to cross the tracks for have-not to have-much, from the excluded to the recruited. Thanks proclaims, 'I'm not disadvantaged, victimised, forgotten or ignored. I am blessed.' Gratitude is a dialysis of sorts. It flushes the self-pity out of our systems.

In the Bible the idea of giving thanks is not a suggestion or a recommendation; it is a command. More than 100 times, the Bible commands us to be thankful.

It is amazing to hear Paul (again from prison) saying that he can rejoice and then go on to tell his friends to 'Rejoice in the Lord always' (Philippians 4:4). How could he do this in such a miserable situation? One reason was that he knew that everything he had was a gift from God. One of the problems that we have in the western world is an assumption that we deserve everything, that it is owed to us and that we have a right to it. What we fail to see is that everything we have is a gift from God. We deserve nothing.

As a starter, think about all you have:

- You are alive.
- You live in a beautiful world.
- You live in one of the few very prosperous countries in the world.
- You have greater freedom and more security than the majority of people in the world.
- Almost certainly, you have friends or family who care about you.
- Above all, God loves you and desires that you come to know him.

And that's just a start. Coveting makes us long for more; thankfulness enables us to see how much we already have. As someone once said, 'A man had no shoes and complained, until he met a man who had no feet.' Ingratitude is a devil's brew: it will kill you.

Be a Wise Steward

God calls us to be thankful for what we have. He also calls us to responsibly manage what he has given us. And that is no light matter. God has entrusted humanity with the creation he has lovingly made, with each other, and with our own abilities and resources.

We need to remember that the things that we want, that we set our hearts on, are not ours by right. We have done nothing to deserve them. We cannot even keep them; death strips us of all our possessions. At best, God loans us our wealth for a little while, and we are accountable for our use and abuse of his property.

Jesus told the following story about a servant to whom the master had given the responsibility of managing his household and feeding his family.

If the master returns and finds that the servant has done a good job, there will be a reward. I tell you the truth, the master will put that servant in charge of all he owns. But what if the servant thinks, 'My master won't be back for a while,' and he begins beating the other servants, partying, and getting drunk? The master will return unannounced and unexpected, and he will cut the servant in pieces and banish him with the unfaithful. And a servant who knows what the master wants, but isn't prepared and doesn't carry out those instructions, will be severely punished. But someone who does not know, and then does something wrong, will be punished only lightly. When someone has been given much, much will be required in return; and when someone has been entrusted with much, even more will be required.
(Luke 12:43–48 NLT)

This is a sobering rebuke to covetousness. The more we have, the more we are responsible for. It is as if every possession we have comes with an audit slip upon which God marks how we have used it.

The whole principle – that we are stewards not owners of what we have – has enormous implications and we in the wealthy West need to think much more about it. We have a higher standard of living than almost any other people who have ever lived and we control so much that happens across the planet. As a result, we have an enormous responsibility to be wise and trustworthy stewards. We have – quite literally – been given the earth.

Focus on Relationships Not Things

In the pursuit of riches, things and fame, relationships can pay the price. In the race for prosperity, people are easily crushed in the rush. Children and families can be sacrificed on the altar of overtime. Friends can fall by the wayside because of our desire for possessions or power.

God wants us to have good relationships and coveting does no good to friendships. It takes away time and opportunity, it makes us competitors not friends and it makes us envious of each other. God's call to us is to love people and use things. Covetousness inverts this disastrously so that we end up loving things and using people.

How are your relationships? Are any of them suffering because you covet, because you desire things that aren't yours? If someone looked at your priorities, what impression would they get about your life? Would they think that relationships were your number-one priority, or would they think it was money or things? If money has taken over, it's always better to spend the time repairing broken relationships than replacing them with money.

The book of Proverbs in the Old Testament sums this up well: 'Better a little with the fear of the LORD than great wealth with turmoil. Better a dish of vegetables with love than a fattened calf with hatred' (Proverbs 15:16–17).

People matter. After all, they are eternal; things aren't.

Be a Giver

Perhaps the best antidote for coveting is to be generous with what we have. Instead of being concerned to amass things we should be concerned about giving them away. Generous giving will break the grip of greed on your life. Our life isn't to be measured in terms of the harvest we reap, but by the seed we have sown. One of the saddest outcomes is that since the lottery began, giving to charity has gone down. In percentage terms, giving in Britain has actually been going down for the last twenty-five years. This is remarkable given that salaries and personal wealth have increased. For instance, the number of people who gave to charity either via donations or sponsoring someone in 2018 decreased from the previous decade – led by the decrease in sponsorship.[8] In the US there is a long and solid tradition of generous charitable giving, aided by helpful tax legislation, and that appears to be continuing.

The evidence suggests that in Britain, as we get wealthier, we get stingier. The principle is clear: covetousness turns us inward. It is bad for us and for our society. The world lives from the outside in, but we are called to live from the inside out.

Covetousness can be seen as one of the causes of the recession, and as a major factor in making the rich richer and the poor poorer. This increasing wealth gap seems to be a global phenomenon. In 2019 the richest man in the world had a net worth of £87.9 billion, a figure almost twice as large as the combined GDP of the poorest 40 countries.

Now it is very easy to focus on the super-rich, but in global terms. The website Givingwhatwecan.org charts exactly where you are in terms of the world's population.[9] My guess is that you find yourself in the top 5 per cent, and that if you give away 10 per cent of your income your position will not change very much at all. Instead of grasping for more, we need to learn to give it away.

Jesus talked a great deal about giving. Why? Because giving is the antidote to materialism and the cure for covetousness. Jesus said, 'It is more blessed to give than to receive' (Acts 20:35). The great Christian writer C.S. Lewis succinctly stated that biblical charity should be more than just giving away that which we can afford to do without.

Let's do something for somebody who can never repay us. We need to live simply so that others can simply live. We need to learn again the gift of giving.

Evaluate Our Priorities

We make decisions based on a system of priorities in our life. It is often times when order is restored, that blessing is released. However, complacency is dangerous. It is a wise policy to check ourselves once in a while and make sure we haven't lost the things that money can't buy. Jesus himself said, 'Beware! Guard against every kind of greed. Life is not measured by how much you own' (Luke 12:15 NLT). We all need to make priorities. Remember, if you don't live by priorities, you will live by pressures.

Devoting a little of yourself to everything means committing a great deal of yourself to nothing. It would serve us well to focus on what brings addition to our lives, rather than adding on more accessories!

Let me suggest some simple questions for you:

- What do you like to think about most?
- What do you like to talk about most?
- What do you invest most of your time and energy in?
- What do you spend your money on? (Your bank account is your theology in numbers.)
- Is there anything that you would find hard to give up to save your closest relationships?

Covetousness seems the least deadly of all the Ten Commandments; it seems the most soft-centred, the one that we can live with most easily. That is why it is so perilous. There is a story that if you drop a frog into a saucepan of hot water it will leap out. But if you put a frog in a pan of cold water and increase the temperature slowly, the frog stays there until it is boiled alive. The frog cannot sense a threat in the slow but ultimately deadly rise in temperature. I often wonder if that's what is happening to us today. All around us the temperature is going up, yet we simply sit there, oblivious to our impending fate. When contentment in God decreases, covetousness for gain increases. The fight of faith is the fight to keep your heart contented in God. Let's take this commandment to heart and not get boiled alive.

1   https://www.theguardian.com/world/2015/oct/29/uk-population-expected-to-rise-by-almost-10-million-in-25-years

2   https://www.wsj.com/articles/many-s-p-500-ceos-got-a-raise-in-2018-that-lifted-their-pay-to-1-million-a-month-11552820400

3   https://pressgazette.co.uk/publishers/nationals/uk-advertising-spend-grew-to-record-22bn-in-2017-as-duopoly-prosper-and-newsbrands-are-squeezed/

4   https://www.emarketer.com/content/us-digital-ad-spending-2019

5   https://www.theguardian.com/business/2019/jan/07/average-uk-household-debt-now-stands-at-record-15400

6   https://www.telegraph.co.uk/education/educationnews/6250626/Children-would-rather-become-popstars-than-teachers-or-lawyers.html

7   https://www.telegraph.co.uk/education/educationnews/11461047/Teaching-revealed-as-top-career-choice-for-teenagers.html

8   https://www.cafonline.org/docs/default-source/about-us-publications/caf-uk-giving-2018-report.pdf

9   www.givingwhatwecan.org/why-give/how-rich-am-i

2

HOW TO HOLD TO THE TRUTH

COMMANDMENT NINE: YOU SHALL NOT LIE

You shall not give false testimony against your neighbour.
(Exodus 20:16)

SO, WHAT'S THE PROBLEM?

We are surrounded by words: from TV and radio, in books and newspapers, on emails, text messages, the internet and tweets. Words are everywhere, words are vital but, all too frequently, the words we speak are not true. In fact, we are beginning to lose the expectation that words will be true. For example, it is hard to resist smiling when we hear any of the following:

- 'The cheque is in the post.'
- 'I'll start my diet tomorrow.'
- 'I have absolutely no recollection of that.'
- 'This questionnaire will take just two minutes of your time.'
- 'Open wide, this won't hurt.'

The loss of truth in the public world is well known and barely a week goes by without a trial involving claims and counter-claims of lying. We have replaced truth with tolerance.

The career of Lance Armstrong, the former world-champion cyclist, collapsed. The fact that he took banned substances is bad enough, but it was made worse by the fact that he lied about taking them. Another example is the fiddling of MPs' expenses over the last few years which has caused a deep distrust to be woven throughout the fabric of our society.

In the 2016 US election there were widespread allegations from both sides, each accusing the other of corruption, lying and illegal interference. Whether it was computer hacking or the deletion of emails on private White House servers, deception has been the focus of the media and the key story throughout the presidential elections. Lies and the allegations of lies are universal.

People lie in politics, in sport, in the media – everywhere. No one is surprised. After all, we have now reached the stage where it is considered naive to believe that anybody in the public sphere will tell the truth. Lying is so prevalent that we now doubt almost any claim, especially made by politicians. We have reached a crisis state when we cannot trust those who are supposed to govern us.

But the problem of lying is that a deceptive heart becomes a divided heart. It is not just in the world of the elite; it is at all levels and we have many euphemisms for it. People are 'economical with the truth', statistics are 'massaged', dates are 'adjusted', qualifications are 'enhanced', expenses are 'inflated', work history is 'padded', alibis are 'invented', product defects are 'overlooked', excuses are 'manufactured', promised deadlines 'slide' and difficult issues are 'evaded'. In fact, things have got so bad that we now lie about lying.

We lie at work (over our hours, expenses, lunch breaks and who really broke the copier). We lie to the taxman ('necessary expenses'), we lie to the doctor ('I do take regular exercise') and we lie to the traffic police ('Speed limit? I had no idea'). We've become experts at lying.

The explosion of digital technology and the internet has opened up a whole new territory for lies. Since what happens on the internet is not real, it seems you are allowed to be more dishonest than you are in reality. So fabricating who you are on social media is considered normal, web pages omit inconvenient facts and emailed documents are selectively edited. Digital technology has its own problems. We no longer trust what we see; the verb 'to filter' has passed into general use to indicate the wholesale digital manipulation of an image. There is suspicion about everything from war footage to wildlife programmes.

In fact, lies are so universal that to tell 'the truth, the whole truth and nothing but the truth' appears almost impossible. In the film *Liar, Liar* Jim Carey played a lawyer whose son makes a wish that one day, just for twenty-four hours, his dad will tell the truth. As his wish is fulfilled, the film shows the hilarious disruption that occurs when the protagonist is forced to tell the truth in his personal relationships, in his work, in his family and in the run-of-the-mill comings and goings of the day. He loses a court case, offends work colleagues, makes his secretary quit and his mother vow never to talk to him again. And that's just the result of a single day of telling the truth. Being honest, it seems, only results in trouble.

The ninth commandment tackles the whole issue of truth and lies, and their effect on those around us. It states, 'You shall not give false testimony *against your neighbour.*' Our use and abuse of truth affects our relationships with others. Lies are not simply wrong; they hurt people.

The Cost of Lying

The financial costs are astonishing. In Britain, the official figure for Social Security benefit fraud in 2017/2018 was £2.2 billion.[1] Tax losses to the Inland Revenue due to undeclared incomes were even larger at an estimated £35 billion a year.[2] In the United States it has been estimated that the $385 billion shortfall in tax revenue is mostly from 'underreported income'.[3] Notice, incidentally, the use of words: to 'underreport' your income sounds so much better than to lie about it. Insurance companies now assume that most claims involve some element of dishonesty. Insurance fraud is estimated to cost the UK over £2 billion, with 125,000 dishonest insurance claims valued at £1.3 billion.[4] The annual cost of insurance fraud in the US is $40 billion.[5]

Of course, no one knows for certain; it is hard to get to the truth about lying. The actual cost to society is even higher as more and more is spent trying to prevent fraud by using investigative teams. The ultimate burden falls on the taxpayer who must cover both the cost of the missing revenue and the preventative measures through higher taxes and insurance premiums. There are subtle costs to this epidemic of lying. Increasingly governments are less concerned about how things really are and more concerned about how they appear to be. We have seen the rise of those whose task it is to manage the reputation and image of politicians, parties and products. Such 'spin-doctors' are entrusted with massaging and manipulating the way that events and trends are perceived by the public. One tragic irony of their work is that whereas we used to believe politicians, at least some of the time, we now believe them none of the time.

This atmosphere of 'truth decay' has had an enormous impact on society. Lies breed cynicism and cynicism corrodes trust, whether at work or at home. Is it any coincidence that this epidemic of lying has been accompanied by unprecedented levels of breakdown in families and marriages? I think not. All our social relations are founded upon openness and trust and where lying occurs neither can last long. People tend to exaggerate their success and minimise their failures or deficiencies. They live according to Ruckert's Law, believing there is nothing so small that it can't be blown out of proportion. Except when it costs them personally, at which point we play down what we owe and, at times, what we earn.

The chairman of a local Chamber of Commerce had to introduce the speaker at the organisation's annual black-tie dinner. 'The man who I am about to introduce,' he said, 'is someone I know you'll enjoy listening to. He is a gifted businessman. He has made one hundred million dollars in California oil.' The speaker, embarrassed, came to the podium. 'Thank you for your kind introduction, Mr Chairman,' he said. 'However, the facts need some clarification. It wasn't oil, it was coal. It wasn't California, it was Pennsylvania. It wasn't one hundred million, it was one hundred thousand. It wasn't me, it was my brother. And he didn't make it, he lost it.'

More things depend on honesty and trust than we would imagine. Finance at every level, whether personal, national or global, depends on honesty. A very large factor in the economic collapse of 2008 was the way that property had been bought at unrealistic prices and given dishonest valuations.

The whole area of honesty has been badly affected by the internet and in particular social media sites. Many people now exist in two worlds – the real and the virtual – and there is increasingly a gap between the two. In the virtual world, freed from the constraints of reality, truth dissolves as fantasy is allowed to take over. In cyberspace, you can be whoever you want to be. People have imaginary partners, illusory skills, phoney achievements and fake personalities. As a result, we now find it hard to believe anything we read on the internet. Society pays a high price when people lie.

One of the alarming aspects of lying is the way in which it accelerates other evils. Whether it is theft, marriage breakdown or violent crime, lying is often a major factor and always makes things much worse. Where there is truth, evil can be exposed and dealt with. Where truth has been displaced, every sort of evil can survive and flourish. Lies are not just evil in themselves; they encourage other wrongs. In contrast, truth is like an antiseptic, often painful to apply but effective at stopping disease.

Is There Any Truth About Truth?

Truth is in peril. If the very concept of truth is sliding down the slippery slope, some philosophers have helped to grease its progress. 'There is no truth,' say some of them, 'there is only what you think of as truth.' Instead of absolute truth, they propose that there are as many relative truths as there are people on the planet. The truth is simply 'how you see things'. In such a relativist, 'postmodern' view, 'truth' is private, personal and individual – what is true for you may not be true for me. There are no real facts, only differing opinions. The only difference between truth and lies is your viewpoint. Each person is entitled to their own opinion. And for each individual that opinion is perfectly valid. Because, for them, it is true.

A parable, composed by the eighteenth-century German philosopher Gotthold Lessing, is used to justify the current attitudes to truth. A father has a magic ring that he must bequeath to one of his three sons. Since he loves them all equally and does not want them to accuse him of favouritism, he makes two imitation rings so they can all have one. The result is that each son thinks his own ring is magic and that the others are not. They have an argument in front of a wise man called Nathan who says, 'Let each one think his own ring true and in the meantime show forth gentleness and heartfelt tolerance.' The heart-warming message is that the only thing that matters is you believe your own ring is true and are tolerant of other people's claims. Yet a moment's thought shows the fallacy of the whole story. The reality is that, however much tolerance and gentleness we show, only one ring is magic. Many commentators on religion in a multi-faith age take this view. For them, all religions are to be considered 'right', despite the fact that they contradict each other. They believe that if there is no ultimate truth then who is to say which of them is wrong? One of the many flaws of this view is the paradox that to make relativism an absolute truth is to deny relativism. Practically, this philosophical undermining of truth has helped create a climate in which it does not really matter if you alter the truth to suit you because there is no 'truth'.

It is significant that science, engineering and medicine have remained entirely immune to relativism. Scientific theories are proved true on the basis of experiments, not simply because we wish them to be true. We are given medicines because they have been demonstrated to work, not because of the hopes of doctors. Equally, engineers rely on more than wishful thinking when it comes to assembling bridges. The witness of science confirms that of the Bible: the truth is that truth exists.

THE HEART OF THE MATTER

The Bible pulls no punches about lying. God is *truth*, it says, but men and women naturally prefer lies.

The God of Truth

The Bible tells us about God's character and at the very centre of it is truth. God is true and there is nothing at all false in him. Throughout the Bible, we see the contrast between light and darkness, goodness and evil, right and wrong, love and hatred, truth and lies. It is not just that God possesses the characteristics of light, goodness, love and truth. God *is* light, goodness, love and truth.

Several times the Bible speaks of God in terms that link him with truth (for example Psalm 86:11; 119:160; John 17:17). God is true to his word, true to his character, true to his nature. This is something unfamiliar to us. We are inconsistent and our good character may often only be skin deep. It is not uncommon to hear in a courtroom, 'I don't know what came over him' or 'She acted completely out of character.' In contrast, you can never look at one of God's actions and say, 'That's so unlike him.' He is always true to himself; he is completely, utterly, consistently and wonderfully true. It is interesting that Jesus (in John 8:44) refers to the devil as the 'father of lies', as if to point out the contrast with his heavenly Father.

We know that God is truth, not just because the Bible says so but because in Jesus we have seen God. And in Jesus we see a man who – unlike any other who has ever lived before or since – never lies. In the gospels, Jesus began many of his statements with the phrase 'In truth, I tell you', emphasising that what he was saying was completely and utterly trustworthy.

In the life of Jesus we see a truth that goes beyond mere words. This was a man who practised what he preached. He told his followers to turn the other cheek, and when he was brutally beaten he did exactly that. He told his followers to forgive those who persecuted them, and when his executioners drove nails into his wrists he did just that – he prayed for their forgiveness. Jesus spoke about a God of love who accepted sinners and he showed it in his life. He spoke about a God of life who was stronger than death and he rose from the grave himself. This man shows us the truth of God. Now in heaven, Jesus has not changed; he is still the truth personified.

As well as being truth himself, God knows everything. Our law courts spend much of their time trying to find out the truth of events; God already knows them. There is nothing hidden before him; every word, every action, every thought is done before him. He knows the truth of everything about our lives. One of the terrifying things Jesus said is that 'all that is secret will eventually be brought into the open, and everything that is concealed will be brought to light and made known to all' (Luke 8:17 NLT). One day, we are promised, the complete truth will be made known. Is it any wonder that a world that has denied God his rightful place as Lord over all is now engulfed by lies?

The idea of God overseeing all that we do and say may seem uncomfortable. Yet without this understanding, lies will flourish. It is rather like playing football, deciding to get rid of the referee, and then wondering why the game degenerates into a senseless riot. We need God who will stand over all that we are and do. It is fascinating to note the widespread use of surveillance cameras in Britain. Although we have less than 1 per cent of the world's population, we apparently have 10 per cent of the world's surveillance cameras. If you remove God from society in the way that we have done in Britain, you have to find some other way of ensuring truth.

Many people choose to acknowledge they have done wrong and to offer an apology only *after* their wrongdoing has been publicly exposed, which suggests they are sorry because they got caught! Until then they are quite happy with what they had done. There is a belief that once something is forgotten, it never happened. God tells us that it is otherwise. It is not a question of whether we will be found out or not. We have already been found out by God. One day everybody else will find out too.

People of Lies

If God is a God of truth, it is a sad reality that we are a people of lies. We may not lie all the time about everything but we frequently modify the truth. Truth has become somewhat flexible today.

One reason for this is that we 'lie to deny'. We use lies to cover up who we really are and what our problems genuinely are. We often think about lying in terms of deceiving other people, but one of the biggest problems is that liars deceive themselves. We refuse to see our own guilt. It is always someone else's fault. The British press reported that a woman paralysed in a car crash after a night of underage drinking was suing a bar for not checking her ID. Sadly, she exemplified the way in which we are reluctant to take responsibility for our own actions. Almost anything is preferable to admitting that we are guilty. We shift responsibility to 'my parents', 'my school', 'my genes', 'my hormones'. Of course, we are all products of our environment and background; some people have been through the most appalling circumstances and we need to take account of that. But sometimes people don't face the truth of who they are and what they have done simply because they don't want to take responsibility for it. 'It's not *my* fault!' is an ancient plea.

Anna Russell wrote:[6]

> *I went to my psychiatrist to be psychoanalysed,*
> *To find out why I killed the cat and blacked my husband's eyes.*
> *He laid me on a downy couch to see what he could find.*
> *And here is what he dredged up, from my subconscious mind.*

When I was one, my mummy hid my dolly in a trunk,

And so it follows naturally that I am always drunk.

When I was two I saw my father kiss the maid one day,

And that is why I suffer from kleptomania.

When I was three I had the feeling of ambivalence towards my brothers,

And so it follows naturally I poisoned all my lovers.

But I am happy, now I've learnt the lesson this has taught –

That everything that I do wrong is someone else's fault!

Where does this universal temptation to evade responsibility come from? It is fascinating to see just how early on in human history such sentiments can be found. In the last chapter we looked at how Adam and Eve were tempted into coveting God's position and his authority. If we jump a few verses on, we can see what happened just after they had disobeyed God.

> *Then the man and his wife heard the sound of the LORD God as he was walking in the garden in the cool of the day, and they hid from the LORD God among the trees of the garden. But the LORD God called to the man, 'Where are you?'*
>
> *He answered, 'I heard you in the garden, and I was afraid because I was naked; so I hid.'*
>
> *And he said, 'Who told you that you were naked? Have you eaten from the tree from which I commanded you not to eat?'*
>
> *The man said, 'The woman you put here with me – she gave me some fruit from the tree, and I ate it.'*
>
> *Then the LORD God said to the woman, 'What is this you have done?'*
>
> *The woman said, 'The snake deceived me, and I ate.'*
> (Genesis 3:8–13)

This story illustrates the heart of the problem of humanity. Adam and Eve have done something wrong so they hide – trying to get away from the consequences of what they've done. When God asks the man if he has done the one thing he had been instructed not to do, instead of owning up Adam tries to pin the blame on Eve – 'the woman you put here with me'. Rather than take responsibility himself for his own actions he blames *her*. Then, as the questioning shifts to the woman, she doesn't take responsibility either but blames the serpent – it was *his* fault. What Adam and Eve failed to do was admit their fault and their guilt. And so there, in the very first breaking of a command given by God, it all starts – the great human trait of trying to duck responsibility. Blame it on someone else, something else, anything else but me.

The power of the temptation to lie comes from our desire to protect ourselves from the truth that shows us what we really are. The Bible repeatedly compares truth and falsehood with light and darkness. To face the truth is the moral equivalent of walking out of darkness into sunlight. Jesus himself puts it bluntly as he speaks of his own ministry: 'The judgement is based on this fact: God's light came into the world, but people loved the darkness more than the light, for their actions were evil' (John 3:19 NLT).

The Confrontation of Truth and Lies

If we want to know what God is like we need to look at Jesus. In Jesus' life we see God. As we read the accounts of his life in the gospels, we also see the truth about human beings. At Jesus' trial and crucifixion, we see that as human beings we dislike the truth and often refuse to face up to our own responsibility.

A hastily convened assembly of the religious authorities summoned the arrested Jesus. They wanted to get rid of him and pass a suitable sentence on him. But to do that they needed charges of wrongdoing. It was not easy trying to pin a charge of wrongdoing on Jesus, the Son of God! The way they achieved it was the only way possible: they lied. False allegations flew across the chamber about things that he had said and about the claims that he had made; we read that 'many false witnesses came forward' (Matthew 26:60) and that Jesus' words were misreported and misrepresented. When confronted with the one human being who was completely true – who was in fact *the* truth – human beings told lies about him.

Shortly after this, Jesus was summoned before the Roman Governor Pontius Pilate, a man who had the power of life and death over him. All four gospel writers indicate that Pilate was unnerved by Jesus, who refused either to answer his questions or plead for his life. At one point, responding to Pilate's question of whether he was a king, Jesus said, '"In fact, the reason I was born and came into the world is to testify to the truth. Everyone on the side of truth listens to me." "What is truth?" retorted Pilate' (John 18:37–38).

Pilate's question echoes down through the ages. For all his words, he didn't really want to know the truth. Jesus, the one who was by his own admission 'the way, the truth and the life', is right in front of him, staring him in the eyes. Yet Pilate is so blinded by lies that he cannot recognise the truth when it is standing before him.

There is a story about a man who was in court on a charge. At the start of the trial he pleaded not guilty but, at the end of the first day, he asked the judge if he could change his plea to 'guilty'. 'Why didn't you say that earlier?' came the question from the judge. 'Well, I didn't realise I was guilty until I heard all the evidence.'

Pilate famously washed his hands, as if shedding blame for a judicial murder was of no more importance than a trip to the bathroom. 'It's not my fault,' he said, in effect. 'Don't blame me.' We have said the same ever since.

Yet if, at the trial and the crucifixion, humanity tries to *deny* responsibility, we see on God's side something else altogether. On the cross, God in Jesus *takes* responsibility for the bad things we have done. The one innocent party in the history of the human race becomes guilty so that we might be spared guilt. It is the exact opposite of our actions. Pilate washes his hands to desperately cleanse them of his own guilt, while Jesus extends his hands to take on the guilt of others. As the Old Testament prophet Isaiah predicted centuries earlier, 'All of us, like sheep, have strayed away. We have left God's paths to follow our own. Yet the LORD laid on him the sins of us all' (Isaiah 53:6 NLT).

We might not want to take responsibility for our sins, but Jesus does. Pilate washed his hands of the situation; Jesus went to the cross, took responsibility and washed our sins away.

FIGHTING LIES

So how do we combat our tendency to lie? Let's start with some suggestions on how to deal with the sin itself and then move on to some ways in which we can positively affirm truth.

Beware the Power of the Tongue

In the coral reefs of the Caribbean lives a small fish known as the kissing fish. It's only about three inches long. It's bright blue and quick. Most fascinating is its kiss. It's not uncommon to see two of these fish with lips pressed and fins thrashing. They give the appearance of serious underwater romance. You would think the species would be an aquarium lover's dream. They look energetic, vivid, illuminant and affectionate. But looks can be deceiving, for what appears to be a gentle friend in the sea is actually a bully of the deep. Ferociously territorial, the kissing fish has laid claims to its camp and wants no visitors. His square foot of coral is his and no one else's. He found it, he staked it out, and he wants no other of his kind near it. Challenge his boundaries and he'll take you on, jaw to jaw. What appears to be a romantic rendezvous is actually underwater martial arts. Mouth pushing. Lip locking. Literal jawboning. Power moves with the tongue.

Mouth-to-mouth manipulation isn't limited to the Caribbean! Look closely at the people in our world (or the person in our mirror). You might be surprised how fishy things get when people demand their way. Kissing fish aren't the only ones to use their mouths to make their point. We, too, use our tongue.

Firstly, we need mouth management – the ability to manage our mouths well and wisely. Just because we could say it doesn't mean we should say it. The mouth is the door to whatever is in the heart. Whatever is living in our heart walks out the front door of the mouth. We can try to tie the tongue all we want to but the mouth only speaks what the heart is full of.

Jesus' brother James tells us in the Bible that the tongue is 'a restless evil, full of deadly poison' (James 3:8). He also says that the tongue is like the rudder of a ship in that, though tiny, it steers the course and sets the direction.

Our tongues take up less than 0.04 per cent of our body weight, but they can be both our greatest asset and our most destructive possession. Aesop, the famous teller of fables, was asked, 'What is the most powerful thing in the world?'

'The tongue,' he replied.

'And what is the most harmful thing in the world?' he was asked.

Once more he replied, 'The tongue.' It has been said that the tongue is the only tool that grows sharper with constant use.

The fact that words are so easily spoken also means they can spread quickly. And in spreading they become irretrievable. There is a story of a man who confessed to a monk that he had sinned because he had been spreading rumours about someone in the community. What should he do? The monk told him to go and put a feather on every doorstep in the community. The man rushed away, fulfilled his penance as quickly as possible and returned to the monk. To his surprise, the monk now told him to go back and pick up all the feathers. The man protested that by now they would have been blown by the wind and would be miles away. That, the monk said, was exactly what had happened with his careless words. It is not just true of rumours but of all words, and even more so with the internet. A lie on Twitter can be around the world within minutes.

We all know the power of the tongue; we have all, at some time, been wounded by harsh and cruel words. If we knew how potentially damaging our words are we would keep quieter. As one proverb goes, 'Don't talk unless you can improve the silence.' During the Second World War there was a poster which warned 'Careless talk costs lives'. That is not just true in wartime – it is also true in peace.

As the remark goes, there must be a reason why God made us with two ears but only one mouth. Listening is more important than speaking, but when we do talk we need to make sure that we do so truthfully.

Remember the Cost of Lying

Even at the simplest level, lying causes problems. Telling lies often gets us in more hot water than if we had told the truth. A lie may take care of the present, but it stores up trouble for the future. For one thing, you have to remember what it was that you actually said. As Abraham Lincoln put it, 'No one has a good enough memory to be a successful liar.'

Lies also have an extraordinary habit of growing. As Martin Luther said centuries ago, 'Lies are like a snowball – as they roll, the bigger they get.' To cover up a little lie we need another and then another. Of course, the more lies we tell, the greater the danger that the whole web of deceit may start to unravel.

Lies also affect the liar. They corrode our sense of who we are and what reality is. Today the line between truth and fiction has dissolved. Many people would echo the sentiments of Bette Midler, the American singer and actress, who confessed, 'I never know how much of what I say is true.'

Liars end up unable to trust others. This acid atmosphere of lies and cynicism affects all their relationships. If I lie, they say to themselves, perhaps I am lied to? The liar finds it hard to know what to believe about their friends or their family. Is she telling the truth? Is he? Can I trust them? Is everything lies and illusions, masks and pretences?

Ultimately, the liar no longer knows who they are themselves. Fitting in and becoming part of the scene is so important today that people become like chameleons, changing their personalities, experiences and beliefs to suit the setting in which they find themselves. I remember hearing the story of a person who was very nervous before a major event. 'Don't worry,' someone reassured the star, 'just be yourself.'

'The trouble is,' came the bleak answer, 'I don't know who I am.'

A recent study suggested that honesty may boost your health; the health of people who were allowed to tell lies was compared with that of people who were told not to lie. Significantly, those people who did not lie showed far fewer mental and physical health problems.[7] The comment of a psychologist on the study is revealing: 'When you find that you don't lie, you have less stress. Being very conflicted adds an inordinate amount of stress to your life.'

An even more serious problem is that, by lying, we start to destroy our ability to detect what is wrong in our own lives. The Bible teaches that the only way we can come to know God is by admitting our wrong attitudes and actions and by repenting of them. But if we have fabricated our lives, if we no longer know who we are, then we have become blinded to the fact that we need to repent. Habitual lying about who we are is like disabling the warning signals on a car. It gives a comforting illusion that there are no problems but it also prevents us being warned that we may need to take serious corrective action.

Shun Gossip

It's worth remembering exactly what this commandment says: 'You shall not give false testimony against your neighbour.' In other words, although it is against lying generally, it is specifically against lying which will hurt other people. The context here would be in something like a legal case, where someone lies in such a way that someone else is condemned or punished, as was the case when Jesus was tried. Yet this commandment covers other areas and one of the most important of these is gossip.

The American journalist Earl Wilson once said, 'Gossip is when you hear something you like about someone you don't.' Gossip is repeating private information to someone who is neither part of the problem nor part of the solution. Gossip falls under the ninth commandment because its words are always against our neighbour and are often false. In fact, one of the characteristics of gossip is that whether or not it is true isn't an issue. We pass on a bit of gossip because it is a juicy tale, not because it is true. This commandment speaks out against a love for gossip.

The Old Testament book of Proverbs talks a lot about gossip:

Without wood a fire goes out; without a gossip a quarrel dies down . . . The words of a gossip are like choice morsels; they go down to the inmost parts. (Proverbs 26:20,22)

No doubt we could all name gossips, but I'm sure we would never think of ourselves as one. *We* are simply interested in being kept well informed. Of course, we do sometimes say things that begin with, 'I shouldn't say this to you but . . .', 'Have you heard about . . .?' or 'I am really worried about him; do you know that the other day . . .?'

We need to realise how hurtful and damaging gossiping can be. As I mentioned when talking about the power of our words, gossip can travel as fast and as easily as feathers in a breeze. In fact, rumours and tales are worse than feathers for they multiply in number and size as they travel. The internet adds a whole new dimension; once released onto the Web, even as a blog comment, words may be utterly impossible to ever recall.

We need to be people who do not gossip. There are various guidelines for helping us here. One thing we can do is to monitor what we are saying. Does what I am about to say, we might ask ourselves, include anything that might be termed gossip? If it does, avoid it. Another guideline when tempted to pass on some intriguing but damaging tale is to ask ourselves, 'If this was written down would I be willing to put my name to it?' If not, then we shouldn't share it. Moreover, anyone who has ever talked to you about others will talk to others about you!

Yet another guideline is to ask how we would feel if the person concerned could hear us talking that way about them.

Yet I believe we need to go further. We need to be not only those who do not gossip but also those who *stop* gossip. We mustn't sit quietly by as the tales flow around us. We need to challenge the speaker: 'Are you sure?', 'Have you checked this out?' We might even say bluntly, 'If you don't mind, I'd rather that we didn't talk about this.' We can also walk away or ease ourselves out of conversations that have degenerated into gossip. Even if other people are surprised or put out when we say such things, to become known as people who don't give – or receive – gossip is to earn respect.

In the context of gossiping it may be helpful to remember three things. First, gossips are never trusted because they break confidences. Secondly, in a curious sort of justice, those who are gossips tend to be those who attract gossip about themselves. Thirdly, because gossips cannot be trusted they tend to have few friends. In contrast, those people who are known to be immune to the sin of gossiping may find that they acquire friends. In an age of lying, there is something very attractive about a person who can be trusted to keep a secret.

Avoid gossiping; there are better things to talk about.

BECOME PEOPLE OF THE TRUTH

But it is not enough to reject the bad; we need to take hold of the good. Being known as a man or woman of the truth means more than avoiding lies or gossip; it means affirming truth.

Facing up to the truth means accepting responsibility for our guilt. It means admitting the things that we do wrong. Telling the truth is costly and uncomfortable and it goes against our deepest nature.

Does it mean that we should never have any secrets? Does it mean that if we go to someone's new house and they ask us if we like it – and we don't – that we have to tell them? What about telling 'white' lies? Are there any occasions when lying is the right thing to do? What I want to do now is to suggest some principles so that we can deal with such questions in a way that pleases God.

Be Open

Clearly, most of us would accept that God doesn't want us to be liars. Nevertheless, I suggest most of us could go much further than we do in being open.

As we have seen, our inbuilt human tendency is away from honesty. We always want to blame others, to sweep things under the carpet, to have secrets. Of course there are different types of secrets. Some secrets are good and valid ones: a surprise birthday party, the mobile phone number of the Queen or the President, our medical data, my email password. There is no reason why such things should be circulated. Traditionally, too, it has always been held that it is perfectly correct for such organisations as the military and the police to conceal aspects of their operations.

Yet there are also 'bad secrets'. These are things that are unhealthy or dangerous or things that control and obsess us. Many people have things that happened in their past that continue to haunt and cripple them today. Sometimes these are things they did themselves and sometimes they are things that were done to them. All too often these actions involved someone saying to them, 'This is going to be our little secret,' and extracting a promise of silence. In most cases the 'little secret' involves criminal actions such as the abuse of a child. Such 'bad secrets' should not be kept and need to be resolved. Dealing with such things is a delicate matter and almost certainly will need specialist help, particularly if there are legal issues. If you feel affected by such bad secrets – whether about yourself or another person – then I would advise you to go to someone you trust: a church minister, a teacher, an accredited counsellor or, where a possible crime has occurred, the police, and talk to them in confidence. Where such secrets are brought into the light, by the grace of God healing is often possible. If they remain hidden, it is all too likely that they will continue to fester and cause problems. It may be time to unburden yourself of something you have been carrying for years. There might be things in your past that you need to face up to or be honest about. There are organisations such as the Samaritans that have been set up to give anonymous help and a sympathetic ear.

But we should practise openness before serious problems occur. One useful safeguard is having 'accountability'. Find someone you get on with, preferably older and wiser (and the same sex), and give them permission to ask you difficult questions about your private life. You, in turn, make a pledge not to lie to them and to be open and honest about your weaknesses, temptations and struggles. By being accountable, we can be forced to face up to problems well before they get serious. If we are honest with another person then it becomes harder to lie to ourselves.

Be Wise

Throughout its pages, and nowhere more than in the Old Testament book of Proverbs, the Bible encourages wisdom, caution and careful action. Wisdom is the first spiritual gift mentioned when Paul lists the gifts available to the believer in 1 Corinthians 12. Let me suggest a few aspects of this area of truth and lies where we need to carefully think through how we act.

I have mentioned the internet frequently and with good reason. It has enormous potential for both good and bad and is a rapidly changing feature of our society with many risks. If you are using online sites, you need to think carefully about how you represent yourself. There are dangers that everybody talks about, for example having your identity stolen or having secrets revealed. But there is also the more subtle danger of becoming somebody else in cyberspace. You acquire a persona – an alternative you – which is only distantly related to who you really are. There, safe behind the screen, you can be the happy tweeter, the person with an army of Facebook friends, the witty, caustic blogger. Yet the real you may be someone very different and the result can be a conflict of identity. Some people already struggle to accept who they really are; with the internet it is all too easy for all of us to lie, not just to others, but to ourselves.

A second area where it is tempting to tell a lie is when we think it is our best or only option. Imagine this situation: while a friend is visiting your house, someone angrily knocks on the door asking for them because 'they are going to harm them'. The only sensible thing to do appears to be to lie and say that your friend isn't there. However, there are often alternatives to an outright lie. You could simply refuse to answer and say something along the lines of, 'I am not prepared to tell you.' It is possible, I suppose, that there are times and circumstances where a lie is the lesser of a number of evils, but I think they are very rare. Lying is so contagious an evil and the value of being known as a truthful person so important that I believe we should seek to avoid lying.

Finally, there are some people who, although they technically do not lie, have an amazing ability to distort reality. For example, when someone asks them if they have completed a task they have failed to do, they do not tell an outright lie and say that it's been done; instead they ambiguously reply, 'Well, it's looking good,' which implies that it is done. Here, too, we need the wisdom to be straight talkers. Jesus told his followers, 'All you need to say is simply "Yes" or "No"; anything beyond this comes from the evil one' (Matthew 5:37). Anybody who has employed others will tell you how pleasant it is to have people who will give you a simple, honest answer.

Be an Encourager

One kind word, text, email, call or post can change someone's day, mind, mood, heart or life. Words people say not only have a shelf life but have the ability to shape life. Encouragement is as vital to the soul as oxygen is to the body. Encouragement is the fuel of hope. The apostle Paul counselled the Christians in Ephesus to adopt a policy of 'speaking the truth in love' (Ephesians 4:15) and that balance is a wise one.

I knew a minister whose church was going through a tough time. There were divisions and terrible things were being said behind people's backs. At one meeting the minister said, 'We are going to start an MEF, a Mutual Encouragement Fellowship. We are going to encourage each other, rather than discourage each other. How many want to join?'

Everyone present raised their hand.

'Well then, there's only one qualification for this – you need to *think* before you speak.'

He went on to explain what he meant by giving them an acrostic for the word 'THINK' based on five questions:

T – is it *true*?
H – will it *help*?
I – is it *inspiring*?
N – is it *necessary*?
K – is it *kind*?

In order to make a commitment to telling the truth, we need to make a similar commitment to THINK before we speak.

One thing to be wary of, as we set out to encourage each other, is slipping into flattery. Flattery is insincere praise; we compliment someone – often to try and get something out of them – but we don't really mean what we say. Flattery is an artificial sweetener and of no nutritional value. Flattery is, in its way, just as dishonest as lying and results in the same sort of devaluation of our language. The Bible is very negative about flattery: 'a flattering mouth works ruin,' says Proverbs 26:28. You'll find that although flatterers may be popular in the short term, they aren't trusted in the long term, as they cannot be trusted to tell the truth.

Try to honestly encourage and praise what is good. The apostle Paul provided helpful advice to the church in Philippi that we would do well to heed: 'Fix your thoughts on what is true, and honourable, and right, and pure, and lovely, and admirable. Think about things that are excellent and worthy of praise' (Philippians 4:8 NLT).

Be True to Your Word

Finally, we need to be determined to be people of our word. Whenever you make a commitment to another person, you create hope. When you keep that commitment, you create trust. Psalm 15 starts off with the question, 'Who may worship in your sanctuary, LORD?' In the following four verses, it lists the eleven characteristics of the righteous who can enter God's presence. Interestingly, four of them centre on the right use of words. The final characteristic, though, is challenging: those who 'keep their promises even when it hurts' (Psalm 15:4 NLT).

As people of the truth we are to be people of our word. Jesus encouraged his followers to be people who keep their word whatever the cost. Broken promises break relationships, cause hurt and pain, spread mistrust and generate an unhealthy questioning of everything else that has ever been pledged. To be true to our word means to think carefully about what is involved before we make a promise. It may mean that we need to be prepared to say no now rather than break our word later.

If you were sceptical about the tenth commandment, then this ninth commandment with its reference to abuses of the tongue may seem only slightly less removed from what we think of as 'real sin'. Yet as we journey inwards through the commandments, we can see that both raise very serious issues. The ninth commandment reminds us that speaking is a serious matter. In our modern society, we treat words far too lightly. Honesty in what we say is vital for the health of our society, for our relationships and even for us as individuals. We need to bring before God what we say, so that we may be known as trustworthy men and women whose words are both honest and fair.

1   https://assets.publishing.service.gov.uk/government/uploads/system/uploads/attachment_data/file/762141/fraud-and-error-stats-release-2017-2018-final-estimates.pdf

2   https://www.independent.co.uk/voices/hmrc-tax-gap-avoidance-billions-pounds-a8968591.html

3   https://www.taxresearch.org.uk/Blog/2012/01/10/irs-finds-u-s-tax-evasion-385-billion-per-year-suggesting-tax-justice-network-numbers-are-right/

4   https://www.abi.org.uk/products-and-issues/topics-and-issues/fraud/

5   https://www.fbi.gov/stats-services/publications/insurance-fraud

6   Anna Russell, 'Psychiatric Folk Song'. Copyright © Public Domain.

7   https://usatoday30.usatoday.com/news/health/story/2012-08-04/honesty-beneficial-to-health/56782648/1

3

HOW TO PROSPER WITH A CLEAR CONSCIENCE

COMMANDMENT EIGHT: YOU SHALL NOT STEAL

You shall not steal. (Exodus 20:15)

SO, WHAT'S THE PROBLEM?

Unlike coveting or lying, stealing is a physical action. And it is a huge problem. A report by the World Economic Forum suggested that the cost of corruption is about 5 per cent of the global GDP, and that the cost of bribes each year is $1 trillion.[1] There are even claims that internet-related theft ('cybercrime') alone costs $1 trillion a year.[2]

It has been estimated that 'economic crime' costs the UK around £73 billion.[3] But it is actually very hard to estimate such figures: how can you put a value on the theft of confidential business plans, company reports or software code? If a firm goes out of business because its big invention has been stolen by competitors, the costs are enormous. Many organisations lose money due to inflated expenses, fake bills, 'borrowed' equipment and vanishing computers.

In our own lives we pay the price of theft: the burglar alarm; the insurance cost for car and home; the amount of our taxes that goes to policing; the elevated prices in the supermarket to cover their losses due to shoplifting. As we will see, theft also has invisible costs; it undermines society and creates an atmosphere of fear, unhappiness and suspicion. A survey by the Gallup organisation in 2015 found that three in four Americans last year perceived corruption as widespread in the country's government. This figure is up from two in three in 2007 and 2009.[4] Moreover, majorities in 108 out of 129 countries Gallup surveyed in 2012 see corruption as a widespread problem in their government.[5]

Some theft, like burglary and shoplifting, is blatant and obvious. Much of this, especially where it targets *our* cars, houses, wallets or handbags, seems to be against us as individuals. However, some of it is impersonal, directed against companies or organisations. In recent years, so many road signs have been stolen to be melted down for scrap that most new ones are now made of valueless fibreglass and carry a prominent notice pointing out that it is a waste of time stealing them. Even hospitals are forced to spend vast sums on screwing down or padlocking anything that might be remotely valuable. Even the copper wires carrying signalling and electricity for railway lines are frequently stolen, with an enormous cost to the transport and energy industries. And in a surreal twist, many police surveillance cameras are now surrounded by barbed wire to prevent them from being stolen.

Most of us do not identify with this kind of physical theft. It conjures up cartoon images of the burly, whiskered man with a mask tiptoeing along with a bag of loot swung over his shoulder. Many people view those who carry out such types of direct, unashamed physical theft with contempt. It is easy to sympathise with their demands for stiff sentences for the brutish thugs who ransack our houses or schools, or for systematic burglars who terrorise whole communities.

One of the problems with sin generally is that we create stereotypes of those who commit wrongdoing and ensure that they are not like us. To characterise theft as something carried out by those with a lower social standing than ours is not just unfair but dangerous, because it blinds us to our own potential for stealing. The reality is that an enormous amount of theft is what is called 'white-collar crime', carried out by smooth-talking, smartly dressed, well-educated men and women sitting at desks. It is worth remembering that the largest theft in American history was the 'Ponzi scheme' fraud of the well-spoken Bernard Madoff, in which $65 billion is supposed to have gone missing.

In fact, far more stealing than we would like to think is carried out by apparently respectable and civilised men and women – everywhere taxes are avoided, insurance claims inflated, grant applications faked and business figures adjusted. Tax evasion is an enormous issue today on both sides of the Atlantic. How much goes missing it is impossible to tell, but the figures are huge.

There are many other ways of stealing which are now seen as almost acceptable in our society. The press and consumer affairs programmes are full of stories of mail order firms who never deliver, investments that divest you of your money, workers who never work, special offers that aren't special, price reductions that aren't reductions, 'premium' food that is only mediocre, and dream holidays that are nightmares. Remember, fraud is as much theft as burglary.

Another common way of stealing is in dishonest trading, where things are sold for more than they are worth. Here the line between shrewd marketing and fraudulent misrepresentation is a thin one. Adjusting the mileage of used cars, rebadging computer components so they look 'higher spec' than they are, passing off copied clothing as the real article – these things are in almost every case illegal, always immoral and many of us would despise those who do them.

As with most of the other commandments, our new connected society has created hazards and opportunities in the area of theft. One area of particular concern has been the theft of data. In the past, stealing information used to be not only difficult, but actually quite dangerous. You remember those old spy films, where the hero or villain breaks into an office and then photographs the critical documents page by page with their miniature camera? Today, all you need is access to an open computer, a few clicks on a directory, a quick copy to a 'cloud' and you can walk away with several filing cabinets' worth of information. Indeed, if people are careless enough, you can steal from them by using your computer without ever leaving your house. And as we noted earlier, doing wrong things in the virtual world does not seem quite as bad as in reality. We need to remember that theft is theft in both reality and 'virtuality'. God sees both.

Some acts of theft get ignored because they go under the radar. We make our personal phone calls from the office phone rather than use our own mobiles, 'acquire' paper clips, printer cartridges, pens and photocopies. In a hundred little ways, we justify stealing from our employers.

An AOL jobs survey in the United States revealed that almost half the respondents admitted to taking things from work to keep for personal use, though most of those reported taking only small office supplies of relatively low value. At a time of recession, when wage freezes are in place, it seems to be increasingly common for people in the workplace to supplement their income by helping themselves. 'They owe it to me,' they mutter as they slip another ream of paper into their briefcase. According to a survey by Banner Business Services in the UK, stolen office supplies cost British companies £2 billion per year. What's more, over two-thirds of the respondents freely admitted to stealing from their workplace. Time may be money in business but it is all too easy to ignore that when we want to. So people turn up late, have a 'duvet day' off work and take extended coffee breaks. There are endless excuses to disguise the fact that what we are engaged in is theft.

Some forms of stealing are overlooked because they involve corporate theft. We personally are not involved in making a profit, but our employers are. We are 'just carrying out orders' or 'merely doing our job'. In the recent Libor scandal, some of the world's largest banks manipulated a key interest rate in order to make profits that ran into billions. Presumably, many people knew about this but turned a blind eye to what was going on. People find themselves – perhaps reluctantly, perhaps willingly – engaged in 'creative ways' of enhancing their employer's profitability and maintaining confidence. Doing wrong does not become doing right just because you are ordered to do it.

Theft has always been a problem but the current economic downturn has made matters worse. So in order to avoid the threat of losing investors, companies have exaggerated profits or concealed losses. In Britain there is strong evidence that shoplifting has increased over the last few years. In order to maintain household incomes at a time of inflation, wage freeze and unemployment, many people have turned to supplementing their income in ways that are distinctly dubious. As elsewhere, the new digital culture has made doing evil easier. Now, courtesy of e-commerce sites, the disposal of 'ill-gotten gains' is very easy.

Yet one of the great ironies with the current epidemic of theft is that despite the recession we are more prosperous now in the West than we have ever been. That we have 'never had it so good' is not just political hype, it's true. Our houses are full of electronics, our wardrobes are full of clothes, our roads are full of cars and our shops are full of consumer goods. Many of us have a lifestyle that a generation ago would have belonged to only the very rich. In the western world we earn more and own more than any other people at any other time and place in history. Yet we still want more.

At the start of the twenty-first century, we are a mass of contradictions. John Lennon's song 'Imagine' is consistently high on the charts of people's favourite lyrics. One verse suggests it's easy to imagine having no possessions. It may be popular but there is not the slightest sign that anyone (least of all a rock star) is anxious that such a creed be made the basis of serious economic policy. Realism seems to have triumphed and even in an age of recession most young people still aspire to having a home of their own, to be in a stable relationship, to have money in the bank and to be on some sort of career ladder. 'Having nothing' is not what they, or any of us, want. The problem is that in order to obtain what we want, many of us have no problem in helping ourselves.

Before I conclude, I would like to highlight one particularly unpleasant and troubling area involving theft: people trafficking.

We live in a world where people are moved across borders against their will for the benefit of others. It is hard to see a bigger form of theft than stealing someone's freedom. Pornography and sexual exploitation, too, are not just sins in their own right, but also involve stealing the innocence from other human beings. There are an estimated 30 million slaves in the world today. According to the US State Department 600,000 to 800,000 people are trafficked across international borders every year, of which 80 per cent are female and half are children.[6]

It is a good rule that we should try to go through life seeking to add benefit to others rather than taking it from them. Let us not be those who steal, but those who give.

THE HEART OF THE MATTER

I want now to look at what lies behind this extraordinary plague of stealing.

Things, Theft and Idolatry

We have made idols of money and things. The tenth, ninth and eighth commandments with their prohibitions of coveting, lying and theft, are all linked. It is impossible to seriously want to steal something without breaking the tenth commandment, and it is practically impossible to carry out a theft without breaking the ninth commandment. As we have seen already, the commandments hang together and reinforce each other. When it comes to stealing, I want to suggest that yet another commandment is closely involved. This is the second commandment, which prohibits idolatry. For most of us idolatry isn't about carved wooden statues surrounded by incense sticks in the corner of a room, or gold images gleaming in a temple. It is far subtler than that. Idolatry is when things, often good in themselves, are worshipped as if they were God.

We might not see ourselves as an idolatrous nation, but imagine if some intelligent aliens were to arrive in the middle of one of our cities. As they surveyed the evidence of our civilisation, what might they conclude was the centre of our lives? The answer is simple. They would conclude from our monumental shopping malls, our advertisements and our bustling shops that we lived for possessions. And when not consumed with earning money, we are consumed with spending it. Consumerism has become a primitive passion, as in the catch phrase 'shop until you drop' or the one-line meditation on mortality: 'whoever dies with the most tags, wins'. The biggest, grandest and newest buildings are shops and malls, the most eye-catching posters are for sales and special offers, the greatest throngs are in the shops, the largest car parks are around superstores and the chief crowd-pulling ceremony of the year is the January sale. Increasingly, in a digital age, the shopping frenzy that we see on the surface is only part of the story. Online sales, whether through internet retailers or direct downloads of software, music and video, are growing rapidly.

The problem is that idolatry distorts values. It elevates to ultimate importance something that is not ultimately important. It can corrupt us, lead us astray and fill us with false hopes and aspirations. This is not, of course, a problem just of the modern West. The worship of material things has always been a temptation for human beings. Jesus talked bluntly about the worship of possessions. He said, 'No one can serve two masters. Either you will hate the one and love the other, or you will be devoted to the one and despise the other. You cannot serve both God and money' (Luke 16:13). In the original Greek of the gospels the word Jesus used for money was *Mammon*, a word that has passed into English almost as the personal name of the god of wealth and possessions. In fact this is a valid term because possessions are more than some abstract economic concept. They are god-like and they make god-like demands. People talk about 'retail therapy' almost in the same way that a previous generation would have talked about going to church. It is perceived to lift them up and make their life worthwhile. But, as we have seen, false gods are doubly false: they do not exist and they fail to deliver anything of what they promise.

The significance of idolatry is that by making Mammon our god we open the door to stealing. We recalibrate our lives around pursuing Mammon and acquiring more. *How* we acquire more simply doesn't matter. Just get it!

We are afflicted by an epidemic of stealing because we have turned to possessions and wealth for fulfilment rather than to the living God.

Idols are thieves and liars. They rob God of his glory, and they are liars, never delivering what they offer us. Paul, in his letter to the Romans, says that idolatry is a primal sin – the displacement of God for that which he made – leading to loss of glory and to death. The brilliant G.K. Chesterton described the consequence for those who follow idols: 'they became as wooden as the thing they worshipped'. In the late eighteenth century, travellers discovered Easter Island, where there are hundreds of giant stone statues, idols, objects of ancestor worship associated with the former Polynesian inhabitants. To manufacture and move these idols, the indigenous people had cut down the forests covering the island. However, in doing so it appears they destroyed the delicate ecosystem. By removing the trees they killed off all the birdlife and wildlife that depended on the trees for the balance of life. The idols consumed everything and gave nothing. After the birds had flown, eventually the inhabitants had to leave as life could no longer thrive. All that was left were the lifeless stone idols, commanders of a lifeless island. Worshipping God brings life; worshipping idols brings death.

Whose Things are They Anyway?

Another factor that has affected our attitude to stealing is our flawed understanding of possessions.

For many people, the world and everything in it is a product of chance. Any rules have arisen simply because we as human beings need some sort of code to live together. They are not absolute rules; in a godless world there can be no absolute rules. To follow evolution alone means that there can be no morality other than 'survive and breed'. Many other people believe that this world has come about through the divine activity of some cosmic creator God, but that the involvement of the creator stopped a long time ago. Now he is a long way away and doesn't watch purses or wallets. Help yourself!

The Christian view is different. The God who made the world and who gave us the commandments is still very much alive and active in the world today. This is still his world.

In the Old Testament we see that as David is about to reach the pinnacle of his achievements as king, he proclaims that everything he has is not his anyway – it is God's:

> Yours, LORD, is the greatness and the power and the glory and the majesty and the splendour, for everything in heaven and earth is yours. Yours, LORD, is the kingdom; you are exalted as head over all. Wealth and honour come from you; you are the ruler of all things. (1 Chronicles 29:11–12)

What the Bible says here, and in many other places, is stunningly simple and goes against the grain of our modern culture. Ultimately everything belongs to God and nothing to us. We have no rights over property or wealth. It is not ours; it is God's. A few verses later, David says, 'Everything comes from you, and we have given you only what comes from your hand' (1 Chronicles 29:14).

This does not mean that it is wrong to own things; after all, as king, David was himself a rich man. In the gospels we see that Jesus himself assumed that people would have private property. He was supported by wealthy people (Luke 8:3), enjoyed their food and hospitality and appreciated their gifts (Mark 14:3–9). Some of his disciples appear to have had houses and boats. There is no indication that this caused Jesus any problems. In the early church, rich and poor coexisted. It is clear in the Bible that God allows people – and indeed gives them – wealth and possessions. These gifts are always a blessing and sometimes, especially in the Old Testament, they are a divine reward to those who honour God. The reverse, however, is never true; nowhere does the Bible say that if you don't have wealth and material possessions then you have done something wrong.

The point is that everything we have comes from God and is on loan to us. I no more own my house than the books or films I have borrowed or rented on iTunes. They have all, in different ways, been issued to me. They remain the possession of someone else, and one day will be returned to them. The difference is that while the librarian or iTunes company may do no more than acknowledge the return of what I borrowed, God will want to know what I did with all that he lent me. We are accountable to him.

With regard to theft this has major implications. First, stealing is about increasing our possessions, yet from the Bible's perspective, 'our possessions' are not *ours* and we never *possess* them. We have them on temporary loan and we need to be reminded that they may be recalled to their rightful owner at any time.

Secondly, this issue of God's ownership of everything applies very strongly to stealing. When we steal, we do not wrongfully appropriate something from a company or another human being, bad as that might be. We steal from God himself as well. That ought to make us pause.

Generosity is built into God's character. God has graciously given us gifts in creation because he delights to bless us. In fact, he has given us everything that we need on this earth. If the Old Testament rejoices in God's love to us shown in the visible, physical blessings that we can touch and see, the New Testament talks about the invisible spiritual blessings that we are given: God's abundant, overwhelming kindness to us in Jesus. Paul writes, 'You know the grace of our Lord Jesus Christ, that though he was rich, yet for your sakes he became poor, so that you through his poverty might become rich' (2 Corinthians 8:9).

When we steal, we are denying God's goodness to us. By our actions we are effectively saying, 'God, what you have given me is not enough.' We are accusing God of being an inadequate heavenly Father. Furthermore, when we steal, we are telling God that we know better than he does. God is generous beyond our wildest dreams and he has trusted us with the world he lovingly made.

So how can we keep our consciences clean in this area?

In Paul's correspondence to the church in Ephesians, Paul teaches a theological model for all obedience (4:22–24). Then he gives illustrations of practical acts of obedience: in verse 25 he says, 'Don't lie; speak truth.' In verse 28 he says, 'Don't steal; work and give.'

There is a progression here from an inferior to superior way of life. First, you can steal in order to have. Second, you can work in order to have. Third, you can work in order to give. The first two ways of life describe an illegal and a legal way of satisfying the drive of covetousness and greed. You can be driven by greed to steal and you can be driven to work. One is illegal; the other is legal.

Stealing is part of the old self that we are to strip off (v. 22):

You were taught, with regard to your former way of life, to put off your old self, which is being corrupted by its deceitful desires.

Stealing is part of the corruption that comes from deceitful desires. Stealing comes from being deceived about what is truly desirable. Satan came to Jesus in the wilderness and tempted him to turn stones into bread and to short-circuit the way of the cross. 'Don't go the way of self-denial; use the powers at your disposal to get what you really want in the easiest way, not the painful way.' And so Satan comes to us and tempts us to steal from our employees with unjust wages, or from our employers with shoddy work and extended breaks, or from the store by shoplifting, or from the government on our tax returns. He tempts us to steal and short-circuit the way of justice. And he lies and says that the fleeting pleasure of possession is better than a hard day's work, a clear conscience and a respect for other people.

Jesus says in Matthew 15:19, 'Out of the heart come evil thoughts – murder, adultery, sexual immorality, theft . . .' Where does stealing come from? It comes from the heart that is corrupt with desires born out of deceit. Ephesians 4:28 says, 'Anyone who has been stealing must steal no longer.' Paul says there is hope for this thief. He can be forgiven. He can be changed and stop stealing and have a new future in righteousness. And if he thinks it is too late, what shall we say to him? We shall remind him of Luke 23:42–43 where the lifelong thief in the hour of his death cried out, 'Jesus, remember me when you come into your kingdom.' And Jesus said, 'Truly I tell you, today you will be with me in paradise.' So great is the power of the cross to forgive sinners.

That is the second thing we can say about stealing. It can be forgiven. It is not too late for anyone who is willing to repent and turn to Christ for cleansing and for power, love and self-control to steal no more. What truth does God use to free the thief from the compulsion to steal?

> *Keep your lives free from love of money, and be content with what you have, because God has said, 'Never will I leave you; never will I forsake you.' So we say with confidence, 'The LORD is my helper; I will not be afraid. What can mere mortals do to me?'* (Hebrews 13:5–6)

What this teaches is that the craving for things which drives us to steal is owing to unbelief in the promises of God. The Lord who owns all the cattle on a thousand hills, who has the wisdom to design DNA and the Milky Way and who did not spare his own Son – that Lord of lords and King of kings has promised his people, 'Never will I leave you; never will I forsake you'!

I ask, can you believe this and yet steal just to add a little to your security or your pleasure? In HIS presence is fullness of joy, at HIS right hand are pleasures for evermore (see Psalm 16:11). That is the third thing we can say about stealing: it must be overcome by faith.

STANDING UP TO STEALING

In offering advice I want to show how we can avoid theft. Then I want to show how, positively, we can adopt lifestyles and attitudes that are the opposite of what the eighth commandment condemns.

Be Honest About Theft

We need to be honest about what we are doing in this area. Very few people are prepared to look at themselves in the mirror and say, 'I have stolen; I am a thief.' The result is an ocean of words that obscure the reality of theft. Rather than admit they stole something, we hear people say that they 'borrowed' it, 'acquired' it or 'helped themselves'. Things mysteriously 'fall off the back of a lorry', objects are 'surplus to requirements', software 'accidentally gets loaded' onto my computer, items and equipment get 'creatively recycled'. People are 'less than totally transparent' about their income or engage in 'creative accounting' for tax officials. We need to stand firm here and point out that, however soothing the alternative words sound, all stealing is stealing.

We need to be scrupulous about ourselves. Some theft is so subtle that it may be both legal and perfectly acceptable to those around us, but it is still wrong. So we may delay paying bills in order to maximise the interest. We may upgrade the value of what we are selling while at the same time downgrading the value of what we want to buy. We may juggle accounts, operate our business from a different address or do all that we can to keep our wealth out of the hands of the taxman. Yet in doing all these things the result is that we can end up defrauding others: in other words, stealing.

Recent events have revealed the extraordinary lengths to which some large companies will go in order to avoid paying tax. In many cases, although their sales almost entirely occur in one country, they mysteriously manage to be registered in another, where taxation is minimal. Theft is still theft, even if it is wrapped up in the language of 'cost control'.

I acknowledge that this is a difficult area and the law distinguishes between tax avoidance and tax evasion. Tax avoidance (using all legal means to reduce your tax burden) is perfectly acceptable, but tax evasion (using illegal means to conceal income) is wrong. Nevertheless, the boundary between the two is sometimes not as clear as we might like, and we need both wisdom and honesty.

We also need to be honest about what are considered more 'respectable' types of theft. We all feel angry revulsion at a villain who makes away with a television from the children's ward of a hospital or a criminal who steals material from a highway construction site. Yet shouldn't we feel the same revulsion at the tax evader who, by cheating the state of its legitimate tax revenue, deprives it of the revenue to look after hospitals and roads?

Remember the Cost of Theft

All breaches of God's commandments have a cost and this one is no different. All this must be paid for by someone, whether in higher prices, elevated taxes or reduced social services.

There are other costs to society. Many people will not take their cars into town centres at night, while others become reluctant to leave their houses at all and are disinclined to open their doors after dark. Some are reluctant to use the internet for fear of being defrauded.

Theft in the form of corruption forces society to pay a particularly high price. Corruption erodes public confidence in government, penalises the weak and the poor, discourages investment, undermines justice and breeds discontent.

In a country where corruption is widespread there is probably no greater (and no harder) patriotic duty than to stand up against it. We all must be very careful in our dealings with the developing world, whether at governmental, organisational or personal level, that we do not encourage corruption.

Victims of individual theft also pay a very high price. I expect many of you reading this have been burgled. My wife and I have been burgled, we've had our car stolen and had my favourite winter coat taken zfrom a church meeting! You can probably still remember how, as you entered your house, the atmosphere seemed to have changed. Then, there were the feelings of panic, of being violated as you realised that an unwanted stranger had gone through your most private things. Such theft produces a far greater reaction than would be warranted simply by the things that have been stolen. Our safety and security, our control over our own private space, has been violated. The scars from theft can take a long time to heal.

Yet just as there are obvious costs to the victims, there are also costs to the perpetrators. Traditional wisdom has it that illegally gained goods provide little lasting satisfaction or pleasure to those that get them. Theft cannot satisfy. All sin is habit-forming and very soon those who engage in the act of thieving will end up becoming thieves by nature. A thief may strike once or twice out of perceived necessity but very soon it will be out of habit.

In committing a theft, a person demonstrates that they are a slave of Mammon, and you cannot belong to God and Mammon. Let me conclude this topic by giving you some words of warning – and hope – from the Bible. Paul, writing to a church of new Christians at Corinth, says:

> Don't you realise that those who do wrong will not inherit the Kingdom of God? Don't fool yourselves. Those who indulge in sexual sin, or who worship idols, or commit adultery, or are male prostitutes, or practise homosexuality, or are thieves, or greedy people, or drunkards, or are abusive, or cheat people – none of these will inherit the Kingdom of God. Some of you were once like that. But you were cleansed; you were made holy; you were made right with God by calling on the name of the LORD Jesus Christ and by the Spirit of our God. (1 Corinthians 6:9–11 NLT)

Notice that Paul includes thieves and greedy people in those who will never be in the Kingdom of God. That is the bad news. The good news is that, as in first-century Corinth, the work of Jesus and the Holy Spirit can transform even the worst of thieves.

Making Amends

One of the most extraordinary encounters that Jesus had was with a man called Zacchaeus, who was the chief tax collector for the occupying Romans in Jericho (see Luke 19:1–9). Small, wealthy, corrupt and loathed by the public, Zacchaeus was shown love and acceptance by Jesus, who invited himself to Zacchaeus' house for a meal. There, Zacchaeus stood up and announced he was going to give half his possessions to the poor and that he would give back to all whom he had cheated four times the amount they had lost. In doing this Zacchaeus was showing to everyone that he had wholehearted and genuine repentance and that he was truly and utterly sorry for what he had done. He now wanted to do all that he could to put things right.

A British tax inspector once received an anonymous letter. 'I am having trouble sleeping because of my conscience; please find enclosed £100. If this doesn't cure my insomnia, I will send you the rest.' The motive there certainly wasn't wholehearted repentance; it was merely an attempt to buy off a troublesome conscience at the lowest price. The generous and unstinting action of Zacchaeus shows us the pattern of true repentance.

When I speak about the subject of stealing, I encourage people to return stolen goods. If they can't return them to where they came from, I suggest they hand them over to a charity. When I ask people to do this, I know that it may be hard. When I became a Christian, I realised that I should do something about some books I had stolen from a bookshop in London. With a great deal of fear, I took them back. It was difficult and embarrassing. The first assistant I talked to nearly fainted and I quickly found myself taken to the manager's office where I explained that, as a result of becoming a Christian, I now felt I had to return the stolen books. The dumbfounded manager explained that he should either call the police or bill me for the books. However, he concluded that, as he had never encountered anything like this before, all he could do was thank me and send me on my way. You can imagine my relief, but also a great sense of freedom as if I was liberated from invisible chains that had bound me.

Where we can, we must make amends for thefts we have committed in the past.

SEEK INTEGRITY

Integrity is the state of being innocent, trustworthy, morally upright and free from dishonesty. It includes positive virtues rather than simply avoiding particular sins. The Bible makes it clear that there is more to being a follower of Jesus than simply avoiding sinful actions; rather, we are repeatedly told we are to become more like Christ. We are to seek to reflect his character of openness, honesty and justice in all that we are as individuals. The Christian life is not just about avoiding sin, it is about living out what is right.

A key element of integrity is the desire to seek justice. Justice is one of the biggest themes of the Bible – it is something that God demands of his people because he himself is just. The just nature of God's character is shown in many places in the Bible. In John 10:11 Jesus is called the good shepherd who watches over his sheep, protecting, nurturing and leading them. This is the perfect image both of what God is like and of what we should aim to be ourselves. In comparison,

Satan is described as the thief who comes only to steal and destroy the flock (John 10:10). It is a sobering thought that in every act of theft we align ourselves with Satan. Everything we do should be like Jesus, and to have integrity is to be like Jesus.

Integrity demands that every area of your life is treated with the same intensity. You have the same commitment to excellence in your marriage as you do in your career. You have the same commitment to excellence in ministry as you do in your parenting.

Let me give you five ways you can work to pursue integrity. You become a person of integrity by . . .

1. Keeping your promises

People of integrity keep their word. If they say they'll do it, they do it. If they say they'll be there, they show up. 'People who promise things that they never give are like clouds and wind that bring no rain' (Proverbs 25:14 GNB).

2. Paying your bills

You may not think this is a big deal, but it's a big deal to God. Do you spend more money than you make? That is a lack of integrity. Do you get yourself in debt for things that you can't pay off? That is a lack of integrity. 'The wicked borrow and never pay back' (Psalm 37:21 GNB).

3. Tithing faithfully

Wherever you put your money first is what's most important to you. 'Is it right for a person to cheat God? Of course not, yet you are cheating me. "How?" you ask. In the matter of tithes and offerings . . . Bring the full amount of your tithes to the Temple . . . Put me to the test and you will see that I will open the windows of heaven and pour out on you in abundance all kinds of good things' (Malachi 3:8–10 GNB).

4. Doing your best at work

'Work willingly at whatever you do, as though you were working for the Lord rather than for people' (Colossians 3:23 NLT). If you're a believer, your real boss is God and whether or not anybody else sees your work, God does.

5. Being real with others

A person of integrity doesn't act one way in church and another way at work. 'We refuse to wear masks and play games. We don't manoeuvre and manipulate behind the scenes. And we don't twist God's Word to suit ourselves. Rather, we keep everything we do and say out in the open' (2 Corinthians 4:2 MSG).

Seek Integrity in Personal Relationships

In the light of this we need to review all that we do as we seek to become people of integrity.

We can decide to be honest in the way that we treat other people's money. Have you ever borrowed money without having any intention of giving it back? Or have you conveniently had a memory lapse over some old debt? The Bible reminds us that it is the wicked who borrow and do not repay (Psalm 37:21). If you have done either, the advice I would give you here is simple: make amends. Practically, nothing sours friendships as much as unpaid debts and unreturned loans. Oh, and if you ever borrowed money for investment and made a good return on it, why not repay what you borrowed plus a share of the profits as well. Remember, if stealing is taking from people, integrity is giving to them.

This integrity does not just concern money but also applies to things. The French novelist Anatole France quipped, 'Never lend books, for no one ever returns them. The only books I have in my library are books other people lent me.' Can I suggest that it may be worth looking round your kitchen, garage or bookshelves for things that you have borrowed and failed to return? Such 'extended loans' are simply theft by another name. And when you find them, act! If they are in the condition they were in when you borrowed them, give them back. If they have been damaged or worn, then offer to replace them. As a good general guideline in such matters, adopt the so-called Golden Rule that Jesus said summed up all the commandments: 'In everything, do to others what you would have them do to you . . .' (Matthew 7:12).

Seek Integrity in Work

Just as we need to pursue integrity in personal relationships, we also need to pursue it at work. Firstly, I want us to be clear that God intends humans to work. That is not necessarily the same as having a job. I've always been of the opinion that the most hardworking people in this country don't get a wage. Bringing up children is the most demanding and crucial work of all. Any mother could perform the jobs of several air-traffic controllers with ease! Caring for elderly members of the family is also every bit as demanding and valuable.

We must all be wary of laziness. I'm reminded of the manager who said to someone seeking a job, 'I'm sorry I can't hire you, there isn't enough work to keep you busy,' and received the response, 'You'd be surprised how little it takes.' Not only is laziness wrong, it leads to other problems. As the old proverb wisely says, the devil finds work for idle hands.

Work is good and necessary and is meant to be fulfilling and beneficial. Even when it isn't the job we would like, we should still do our very best. Within the sphere of the work we do, this command speaks to us of the need to act responsibly and honestly. The Bible makes it clear that we are to do our work as if doing it for God himself (Ephesians 6:7). Here Paul is talking to slaves; how much more does it apply to salaried employees?

Integrity applies in every area of our work. The Bible tells us that 'honest scales and balances belong to the LORD' (Proverbs 16:11). There should be honesty with the tools and measures we use; there are to be no attempts to short-change people or to give them less than they require. If you are in a business in which you give quotations, make them realistic and fair. Don't rip people off. We should conduct our business transactions fairly and honestly. There are endless tricks in the workplace to boost either personal or corporate finances: fictitious sales, spurious claims, exaggerated costs and overlooked discounts. Avoid them all!

A particular area of concern is that of advertising. In a world that is increasingly image dominated, advertising shapes our thinking, but so much of it is misleading. Imagine if the advertising world was honest! It makes me smile just to think about it. Those who do work in that field must be careful to examine their morals and whether corporate greed is pushing them too far. There is legitimate concern that young girls in particular compare themselves with the Photoshop images of models in advertisements and become depressed because they fall short of these digitally manipulated pictures of perfection. In pursuit of improved sales, advertising ends up stealing innocence and satisfaction. Some people knowingly advertise dangerous products. The classic example – now, thankfully, banned in most western countries – is cigarette advertising. Yet we still advertise alcoholic drinks, which are definitely dangerous in excess. By encouraging consumption, advertising steals wealth. Not putting 'a stumbling-block in front of the blind' (Leviticus 19:14) means not deluding people into believing that they want and need certain things.

Do you handle expense accounts and travel allowances with integrity and complete accountability? Consider this true example of a government employee who decided that he needed to take a very firm line on stealing at work. He knew it was widespread; one employee's house was entirely decked out with fittings from work. He determined to set an example. He decided that instead of doing his own private photocopying on the office machine, he would walk to the nearby shop and do it during his lunch hour. Instead of using the phone on his desk for long private phone calls, he would use his own mobile. His expenses were always genuine. Slowly, though, everyone else around him started to act in a similar way, and within a short time the department became far more efficient and motivated. Being completely above board might not automatically make us friends, but it will gain us respect. It will certainly speak volumes about the different priorities on which we base our lives.

We can steal not only by what we take physically, but also by what we refuse to give. The Bible says of labourers, 'Pay them their wages each day before sunset because they are poor and are counting on it. If you don't, they might cry out to the LORD against you, and it would be counted against you as sin' (Deuteronomy 24:15 NLT). So much for 'the cheque is in the mail' or 'will pay within thirty days'. People are made in God's image. Therefore, we can't let them barter their dignity by pleading for what is due to them.

And in the context of the workplace where we work with others, if we don't pull our weight, everybody else is affected. We have stolen our labour from them. Consider, for example, the university lecturer who cannot be bothered to update her notes, the garage mechanic who claims that he has given a car a detailed service when he merely glanced under the bonnet, the cook who used cheap meat in a restaurant dish. It is worth every one of us asking ourselves whether we cheat or steal in this way in our own line of work.

This subtle form of stealing by 'giving short measure' does not just occur in the workplace, it can be found in families, classrooms and even churches. In the Bible Paul talks about this again and again. Everybody, he says, should contribute their gifts and talents with passion and commitment (1 Corinthians 12).

What about you? Are you holding back in any area, whether at work, home or church? If you are, you need to be honest with yourself. It is theft and you are stealing from those around you.

Seek Corporate and National Integrity

Stealing, unfortunately, is not confined to individual people but can also be carried out by institutions, governments and even nations.

The Bible is clear that we are not simply responsible for what happens in front of our noses but that our responsibility to be people of integrity extends to everything we are involved in. On this basis, we need to consider how our actions and investments affect the wider world. It is all too easy for us to buy trainers with little thought to the fact that the tiniest fraction of the price we pay may have gone to the person who made them. The same may be true of our clothes, coffee, chocolate or a host of other things we buy. Two hundred years ago Bible-believing Christians led the way against considerable economic pressure, to abolish slavery in the West. It is perhaps time for us, as their descendants, to push for the modern equivalent of slavery to be abolished worldwide. After all, what greater theft can there be than making someone work for an entire lifetime for a completely inadequate wage? In this area the work of the Fairtrade Foundation in the UK and Fairtrade International has been particularly helpful in campaigning for decent wages in the developing world.

The very least we can do is try to find out where our money is invested and how our products are produced. Thankfully, today's companies are very sensitive to allegations of unethical practices. A few awkward questions and requests for clarification of positions can work wonders.

One of the few benefits of a global recession is that companies are taking customers seriously. Ignorance and comfort aren't good enough excuses where the exploitation and stealing of another country's labour and resources are concerned.

Sadly, it is not just companies that are offenders here. The record of the developed nations in their dealings with the developing world is far from blameless. On average, an inhabitant of the US consumes around 90kg of resources (raw materials, energy supplies and food) each day. In Europe, consumption is around 45kg per day, while in Africa people consume only around 10kg per day. It is a sobering thought that 80 per cent of the world's population still live on less than $10 a day.[7] Global resource use is not just high, it is unequal.

The world's poorest countries still pay almost $23 million every day to the rich world. Good up-to-date details on global debt are to be found on the Jubilee Debt Campaign website. Every flood, earthquake or other natural disaster in these countries mean more borrowing at exorbitant rates and the financial crisis in the developing world has reduced the amount of aid available to them.

Finally, there is another area of international theft that we must look at: the environment. We saw earlier that we are only stewards, rather than owners, of our own personal wealth and possessions. They are merely lent to us. The same principle holds true for this world. Although we may see ourselves as lords of creation and free to do what we want with the earth, the reality is that we are responsible to God and one day we will be asked to account for what we allowed to happen to it. The devastation of the rainforests caused by reckless logging, the torn ozone layer produced by our CFCs, the reckless plundering of the oceans, the potential climate change caused by our senseless burning of fossil fuels, can all be seen as acts of theft.

One way of combating these environmental issues is through 'sustainable development', which is 'development that meets the needs of the present, without compromising the ability of future generations to meet their own needs'.[8] An unsustainable process is therefore one that *takes* from future generations, whether it be oil, woodland, species or fish stocks. Sustainable development is simply applying this eighth commandment to the environment; we mustn't steal the future from our children. On this basis alone, we need to reduce pollution, save resources and preserve species.

Of a global population of just over 7 billion, 3 billion people live in poverty.[9] These figures and others like them demonstrate that what we see in this grotesque inequality is a breaking of the eighth commandment on a global scale. The great danger of the economic crisis is that we only see what lies before *us*. However bad things are for us, they are even worse for many people across the world. We should do what we can to alleviate global injustice.

GET THE RIGHT ATTITUDES

What other measures can we take to avoid sliding into theft? Greed is not a financial issue; it's a heart issue. Today we will crush greed because we've been overwhelmed by amazing grace that moves us to reach out and give. Let me remind you of three helpful attitudes to try and acquire.

Hate Greed

Greed leads to theft. We want so much that we don't mind how we get it. One problem is that we always seem to assume that when Jesus warns about the dangers of possessions he is speaking to other people, not to us. Amazingly, however wealthy we become, we always manage to consider that 'the rich' are just above our level of wealth. *We* are merely 'comfortably off'. Yet by global standards – and the standards of Jesus' day – we are all rich and his words surely apply to us.

A bishop in South America, Dom Helder Camara, once said, 'I used to think, when I was a child, that Christ might have been exaggerating when he warned about the dangers of wealth. Today I know better. I know how very hard it is to be rich and still keep the milk of human kindness. Money has a dangerous way of putting scales on one's eyes, a dangerous way of freezing people's hands, eyes, lips and hearts.'

In the light of what we have seen, it might be worth taking time to examine whether wealth is pulling our lives off course. Ask yourself, what are you investing your time and energy in? What are you longing for?

Where is your treasure? For where our treasure is, Jesus said, there our heart will be (Matthew 6:21).

In Proverbs 3:5–6 Solomon writes, 'Trust in the LORD with all your heart and lean not on your own understanding. In all your ways submit to him, and he will make your paths straight.' Notice his focus is on God and a trust-based relationship with him. Solomon tells us that if we acknowledge God in everything we do – before we do it and as we do it – then he promises that God himself will direct our paths. It is impossible to acknowledge God in all your ways and walk down a highway of greed at the same time.

Love Giving

Generosity shows the world what God is like. Moreover, every act of giving is an act of rebellion against a life dominated by possessions or wealth, and if we have made a practice of regular giving then it is hard to be tempted to steal.

Let me encourage you to really think about your giving. Throughout the Old Testament we have references to the principle of tithing: giving a tenth of all that we have earned and received to God. Tithing is introduced in Genesis (14:18–20, 28:22) and detailed in Deuteronomy (14:22–29). In tithing, God's people regularly gave a tenth (and often more) of all they had earned to God. Practically, tithing was used to support the work of the temple and its priests as well as to help the poor. Yet tithing was more than fundraising; it was about something deeper and important. By giving God a tenth of your money and all your agricultural produce, you were showing your commitment to the Lord and, in effect, saying, 'God, I thank you and I trust you. You come first in my life.' To tithe was, quite literally, 'putting your money where your mouth is'.

In the New Testament there is every expectation that Christians will be regular and generous givers. Paul, for instance, states that believers should set aside a portion of their income in order to support the church (1 Corinthians 16:1–2).

Despite its value, the Bible reminds us that the tithing system could be (and often was) misused and such abuses still exist today. So although tithing was meant to be a joyful response to God's grace it sometimes became an attempt to bargain with God – something that never works. Jesus accused the Pharisees of being concerned about how to precisely tithe garden herbs while ignoring the far more important elements of the law: justice, mercy and faithfulness (Matthew 23:23). A more common abuse – and one that is more likely to tempt us today – was to cheat on the tithe. This is particularly condemned in the book of Malachi, where God accuses his people of robbing him.

> 'Will a mere mortal rob God? Yet you rob me. But you ask, "How do we rob you?" In tithes and offerings. You are under a curse – your whole nation – because you are robbing me. Bring the whole tithe into the storehouse, that there may be food in my house. Test me in this,' says the LORD Almighty, 'and see if I will not throw open the floodgates of heaven and pour out so much blessing there will not be room enough to store it. I will prevent pests from devouring your crops, and the vines in your fields will not drop their fruit before it is ripe,' says the LORD Almighty. 'Then all the nations will call you blessed, for yours will be a delightful land,' says the LORD Almighty. (Malachi 3:8–12)

This is a passage that is both troubling and encouraging. It is troubling because it says that to cheat God of his tithe is stealing. It is encouraging because it says that God will respond to our giving with yet more blessing. It has been said 'God is no man's debtor' and I am confident that if we tithe our income to God and his church, we will be repaid – with interest – either in the here and now or in the eternal future. If you have not acquired the habit of tithing then I urge you to start. In fact, it is well worthwhile getting into this habit as young as possible. My wife Killy and I encouraged our children to learn to give early; they had three tins for their pocket money labelled Save, Spend and Give. Such a threefold division of our wealth is no bad thing for adults either.

Let me encourage you to really think about your giving. Of course, our giving is not just about money; it can also be of time, hospitality and material things. I believe that we must give of ourselves as well. Let me suggest that you examine your hearts for the area (whether of money, possessions, time or something else) that you are most tempted to steal in and make a point, in that specific area, of giving away to the extent that it hurts. I believe that giving is the best antidote for becoming a slave to possessions.

We must remember that, however much we give away, God has always given far more. If we are to be like him, then we, too, should be generous. When we give away we are, in a little way, imitating God.

> As a result of your ministry, they will give glory to God. For your generosity to them and to all believers will prove that you are obedient to the Good News of Christ. (2 Corinthians 9:13 NLT)

When it comes to generosity, what encourages me is to remember the incredible generosity of God. Look at the world we get to live in. Look at the life he gave us. Look at the way he meets our needs. God is the perfect model of generosity. And when we are generous with others because of God's generosity towards us, it points others to God.

Trust God

Finally, we need to turn back to, and rely again on, the God who gives us all we need. There is a wonderful prayer recorded in the Old Testament book of Proverbs:

> Two things I ask of you, O LORD . . . Keep falsehood and lies far from me; give me neither poverty nor riches, but give me only my daily bread. Otherwise, I may have too much and disown you and say, 'Who is the LORD?' Or I may become poor and steal, and so dishonour the name of my God. (Proverbs 30:7–9)

We need to learn to live by relying on God rather than on possessions, investments or bank balances. We need to give God the space to be our provider. We can rely on God for everything we need; many times in my life I have known wonderful answers to prayer. If we do throw ourselves onto God then our praying takes on a new dimension. Again and again Jesus encourages us to bring all our needs to our Father God. He knows what we need and is ready and waiting to give.

Stealing is all around us. Whether open or subtle, personal or impersonal, private or corporate, it is increasingly part and parcel of the way that this world operates. Trying to live the way God wants us to in the area of possessions will make us stand out as very strange to those among whom we live and work. It seems impossible. Earlier I mentioned John Lennon's idealism in the area of possessions, yet I believe there is scope for a more biblical 'Imagine'. What if we simply took to heart these commands to neither covet nor steal? Imagine if there was no stealing. Imagine how it would change our working relationships and environment, our friendships, our fears, our communities, our economic policy.

We are not called by Jesus to imagine a perfect world. One day that world will come. In the meantime, he simply asks us to use whatever resources and gifts we have been entrusted with to make a difference.

So what are we waiting for?

1   https://www.weforum.org/content/global-agenda-council-anti-corruption-2012

2   https://www.wired.com/beyond-the-beyond/2017/07/global-cybercrime-costs-trillion-dollars-maybe-3/

3   https://www.bbc.co.uk/news/uk-17548260

4   https://news.gallup.com/poll/185759/widespread-government-corruption.aspx

5   https://news.gallup.com/poll/165476/government-corruption-viewed-pervasive-worldwide.aspx

6   https://aspe.hhs.gov/report/human-trafficking-and-within-united-states-review-literature/trafficking-united-states

7   https://cdn.friendsoftheearth.uk/sites/default/files/downloads/overconsumption.pdf

8   http://www.sd-commission.org.uk/pages/what-is-sustainable-development.html

9   https://www.dosomething.org/us/facts/11-facts-about-global-poverty

4

HOW TO AFFAIR-PROOF OUR RELATIONSHIPS

COMMANDMENT SEVEN: YOU SHALL NOT COMMIT ADULTERY

You shall not commit adultery. (Exodus 20:14)

SO, WHAT'S THE PROBLEM?

Sex is inescapable. If you've watched any TV, seen any advertisements, listened to the radio, flicked through a magazine, surfed the internet, or read a newspaper, it is there. There are now specific dating websites targeted at married people who want to have an affair. Thirty-three million people have signed up to an extra-marital dating site and cheat on their partners.[1]

As a society we are almost submerged by sex; the media flood us with talk about sex, innuendo about sex, images of sex, advice about sex, questionnaires about sex, assertions about sex and problems with sex. Sex is used to grab our attention for anything. Advertisers use sex to sell cars, ice-cream, toothpaste, deodorant, holidays, music and even pet food.

The constant barrage of sex attracts and entices us, yet at the same time we find ourselves repelled and even jaded by it. We have – it is claimed – better sex education than ever, yet both Britain and the US have extraordinarily high rates of teenage pregnancy[2] and depressingly high levels of abortion – which have increased since many states in the US have legalised abortion. From 1967 to the present in the US, 30,260,000 women had an abortion.[3]

We are told that sex is recreational and purely for pleasure, yet we are also told that it gives our lives meaning and purpose; can it really do both? The new openness about sex was supposed to be good for everyone and yet we have more sexual crime than ever, and women seem to feel less safe on our streets. This sexual 'freedom' was meant to get rid of backstreet shops that sold 'adult magazines'; instead we find a high-tech worldwide pornography business that makes around $100 billion a year.[4] We know more about the mechanics of the orgasm than ever before, yet we seem to know less than our parents about how to make a relationship last beyond a few years. Is it possible that what we took to be the gateway to freedom was, in fact, the door to slavery?

In the 1998 film *Pleasantville*, two teenagers from the 90s are transported back in time to a small US town during the 50s where everything is literally black and white. Into this stuffy, prim and proper town the modern teenagers bring liberation, signified by the characters coming into colour. The chief agent of liberation is, of course, sex and by the end of the film, the boring black-and-white United States has been brought into the multi-coloured vibrant world of the new millennium. The message is clear: sex is liberation.

The problem is not that we think too much about sex, but that we think about it so poorly. With sexual freedom still sold as the key to personal liberation, marriage as an institution is under attack. Today there is a lack of public confidence in marriage.

The number of church marriages in the UK has declined as couples opt for 'more social' ceremonies. Fewer than a quarter of all marriages in 2016 were religious ceremonies, according to data released by the Office for National Statistics. There were just 60,069 religious marriages, falling by 4.1 per cent from the previous year and by almost half from two decades ago.[5]

US trends are similar, with a steady decline in the number of people getting married despite the increasing population. In both countries, couples are increasingly cohabiting rather than marrying. There has never been a greater need for clear thinking about sexual matters The seventh commandment addresses exactly this subject. To understand what adultery is – and why it is a sin – we need to understand what marriage is. But to understand marriage we need to understand sex. And to understand sex we need to understand the body.

THE HEART OF THE MATTER

The Beauty of the Body

The first thing to say is that God is not opposed to either our bodies or sex. Actually, he cares about both more than we do. He made our physical bodies and in Jesus he inhabited one himself.

There is a widely believed lie that God is only concerned with 'spiritual' things: sacred thoughts, words and actions that are mysterious and a million miles away from the physical business of making love. This suggests that God is not interested in this area of our lives. Unfortunately, early in the history of Christianity, the church was influenced by the ancient Greek idea that bodies were bad and having sex was even worse. The result was that if you wanted to be a devoted Christian and become a priest, monk or nun, you gave up the whole idea of marriage. Presumably the rest of the population, while at least able to have marriage and sex, must have thought they were spiritually second-class. It was only five hundred years ago – with the rediscovery of the Bible during the period of the Reformation – that the equation 'sex always equals sin' was broken. Yet such ideas persist in popular culture. The same ideas occur in much religious music and much church imagery. They hardly encourage the idea that you can be holy and married.

The Bible, however, is refreshingly honest about our bodies. For example, when Jesus talked about heaven he frequently used pictures of feasting and parties. It is all very down-to-earth and very physical. God wants to be involved in every area of our lives, both the spiritual and the physical.

The Nature of Sex

God's concern about our bodies extends to sex. I want to plant the flag firmly in the ground of sexuality from the start and claim it for God. He made our sex organs and gave us hormones and far from being embarrassed by them, he decided which bits should go where, and how. We read in the first chapter of Genesis how, before sin had entered the world, God made people, male and female, in his image and that it was good. In the second chapter of Genesis, it is revealed that woman and man were designed to be mutual companions and helpers and to relate to each other. Humans are unique as a species in that relationship – not reproduction – lies at the heart of the sexual act. It is presumably no accident that our species has intercourse face to face.

We are, by God's design, sexual. Our sexuality, although twisted by our rebellion against God, is good and is one of his gifts. Rather than being, as it has sometimes been implied, a necessary act for the perpetuation of the human race, marriage (and therefore sex) is good. Jesus' first miracle was at a marriage feast (John 2:1–11), and wedding imagery is repeatedly used in the Bible about heaven and the Second Coming. In fact, there is even a whole book in the Old Testament (Song of Songs) which is a celebration of human love. God, the author of the Ten Commandments, is the foremost proponent of healthy sex. He is 'pro-sex'.

There is a very strong tendency in western society to declare sexuality off limits for God. The argument goes that he is only interested in our attitude towards him – our spirituality – and frankly does not mind what we get up to in the bedroom. On this logic, you can be involved in adultery but still be 'a good Christian'. All that matters is whether you are 'spiritual'. Such a view flies in the face of all the teaching of the Bible and also undermines the importance of sex. On this basis sex has no more importance than blowing your nose. Is it any wonder that so many people are in a mess over the subject?

Because of the confusing times we live in, I feel the need to make three clear points.

1. To say that God is 'pro-sex' is not the same as saying he is in favour of all sexual activity. There is only one approved context for sex: inside the secure framework of a married male-female partnership. The message of this commandment – and the whole of the Bible – is that sex is to be between one man and one woman within marriage. Here, as elsewhere, the Bible's standards are supported by research which shows that couples who cohabit before marriage have a higher rate of divorce and a lower quality of marriage than those who do not.[6]

2. The Bible is clear that men and women alone were made as counterparts to each other in physical, sexual and psychological

ways. I am well aware of the struggles of many men and women in the area of same-sex attraction, but the reading of Scripture leaves no room for argument on this matter. We must, of course, distinguish between having same sex desires, which I take to be morally neutral, and expressing those desires in sexual activity, which is sinful and contrary to God's word. God's rulings on sexuality are clear. There have also always been those who have felt incestuous desires, another area in which any physical expression is ruled out. The principle that men and women alone are each other's counterparts also rules out sexual relations with children and animals. I would also argue that it rules out sex with computer-synthesised systems, however lifelike or alluring they might be. And as this commandment makes clear, whatever the strength of your emotions for someone else's wife or husband, you cannot express them in a sexual manner. I suspect that the biblical teaching on sex challenges all. When I affirm marriage, what I am affirming is the biblical pattern of marriage between one man and one woman.

3.   While sex in marriage is good and God-given, I also want to point out that the Bible affirms singleness, too, as being good.

Sex is powerful and, if misused, can be destructive. Sex is often compared to being like fire. In the right place and handled in the right way sex, like fire, can be good; misused, it can destroy us. Another parallel with sex is creativity. Creativity is essentially good and is also a gift from God. But it has not just given us good things like language and art and science, it has also given us nuclear weapons and pornography. Sexuality, similarly, has the power for enormous destruction.

The Meaning of Marriage

Some of the most profound truths of the Bible are contained in the first few chapters of Genesis. There we see the blueprint of what it is to be fully human. In Genesis 1:27 we read that both men and women together are created in the image of God. In the next chapter we are given the basis of marriage: 'That is why a man leaves his father and mother and is united to his wife, and they become one flesh' (Genesis 2:24). From this we see that marriage corresponds to three things:

- *Leaving.* When a man and a woman leave their own families and marry, they start something new that is independent of their parents' lives. Marriage marks the beginning of a new legal and social unit in the community.

- *Uniting.* A marriage is the merging of a couple in every area of life. Marriage shows a commitment between a man and a woman that brings together every aspect of what they are, whether personal, emotional or social. There is to be no area where married people are to hold back from surrendering to each other.

- *Becoming one flesh.* A marriage involves creating personal unity at a very deep level. In the sexual act, there is something far more happening than just physical contact. There is total togetherness; a union to the extent that the two people concerned are, in a real sense, no longer individuals.

Anything less than this total relationship falls short of the definition of marriage. To underline this all-embracing and permanent bond, the Bible talks about a marriage relationship being a 'covenant'. The word covenant means agreement or promise and comes with the implication of a lifelong commitment between two parties with mutual obligations. Both parties freely enter a covenant and make promises to be faithful and true to each other. Marriage is similar and equally requires each party to make promises to be faithful and true. In fact, in many places God uses the imagery of marriage as an illustration of his covenant love for his people. Adultery is also used as an image, but as an illustration of what it means to turn away from God and reject his love.

If we think of marriage in covenant terms, this helps us to see the place of sex within it. Sex can be seen as the seal of the marriage relationship; the biological and spiritual equivalent of signing the wedding certificate. Marriage provides the only safe place for sex; only within the secure confines of a covenant relationship, where we are protected by security, love and commitment, can the power of sex be unleashed.

In our society, where freedom has been elevated to be the rule of life, it is no wonder that such a binding covenant basis to marriage is disliked. For a couple to decide that they will have a traditional marriage is for them to choose to go against the flow of our culture.

One of the criticisms of marriage is that because it is binding, it enslaves and oppresses those who are in it. I would argue that it is only by binding ourselves to each other with commitments that we find freedom. We can only be secure enough to open up to be the people that we really are when we know we can trust the person we are with. Far from marriage restricting freedom, it actually brings freedom. We have the freedom to love another without holding anything back. Only within the secure walls of a permanent marriage can we become psychologically and spiritually naked. To be loved unconditionally, without strings attached, and to love in return is true freedom.

In the last few paragraphs I have said almost nothing about feelings or emotions and *nothing whatsoever* about being 'in love'. The fact is that the key elements of marriage (leaving, uniting and becoming one flesh) do not require the emotional state that the modern media insists is the only basis for marriage. In fact, in an arranged marriage 'being in love' was either the icing on the cake or something that came later. The emphasis in marriage lay elsewhere. This may seem strange and even heartless to us, but it had its merits. The point is this: feeling 'in love' with someone is what it says – a feeling. And a feeling, even a strong one, on its own may fade. To hold a marriage together over many years, a better glue than emotions is needed. God knows this; that's why he wants marriage to be based and bound by promises. It is within the secure framework of marriage, that the emotion of love may thrive and grow.

What I have described as the biblical pattern of marriage is not an abstract dream. It has formed the basis for marriage in Britain for the last five hundred years. Indeed, I could have illustrated much of what I have said by quoting from the Marriage Service found in the 1662 *Book of Common Prayer* with whose words many, if not most, of our ancestors were wed. And, as our sobering contemporary statistics on divorce illustrate, we have nothing to teach our forebears about making marriages work.

AVOIDING SEXUAL IMMORALITY AND ADULTERY

As in previous chapters, first I want to address the sin of sexual immorality in general, and more specifically adultery, and show why it is so serious. Then I want to discuss how we can affirm and strengthen the institution of marriage. But before I can do either, I want to remind you that we need to think and talk straight about sexual matters.

Be Honest About Sex

There are lies about every area of our lives. But the lies about sex are bigger, more widespread and more seductive than in almost any other area. We need to be both honest and to think hard to challenge today's sexual myths.

First, let me warn you to beware of sex. Don't treat it lightly. Never ever say, as you see some scandal in the paper, 'It can't happen to me.' Our sexuality is such a powerful force that it is capable of tripping up presidents, politicians, princes and even preachers. Whether it wrecks more careers than greed or lying I don't know, but I do know that there is nothing the press likes more than to see a man or woman who aspires to morality, caught in the act of sexual immorality. Sex has an astonishing ability to make victims. Men, in particular, can labour for years with families and jobs, earning love, security and respect from many. Then, for a few moments of sexual gratification, they can throw it all away. A moment of pleasure and a lifetime of guilt. It is extraordinary what wreckage sex can produce. Take the actor Michael Douglas, who, when charged with adultery in his divorce proceedings, pleaded 'diminished responsibility'. 'Sex,' he claimed, 'is a wave which sweeps over me, the impulse that is, and when the urge comes I am helpless, every time.' Remember, this was not some adolescent struggling with his hormones on overdrive but a man who was over fifty! 'Sexual addiction' is a widely recognised disorder, in which people find a need for compulsive sexual activity. When sex goes wrong it can be astonishingly destructive.

Second, see through the lies. Don't be persuaded by the soft words. It may be termed by the media – or even your friends – as 'a fling', 'a bit of a romp', 'a harmless bit of fun', even 'a romance'. You should call it what it really is: immorality or adultery.

Third, remember that, as with other idols, sex promises what it cannot deliver. If you are a teenager, sex can offer maturity and fulfilment; if you are lonely, sex can offer closeness and companionship; if you are bored, sex offers excitement; if you are hurt, sex offers comfort; if you want to be close to someone, sex offers you intimacy. Yet outside the context of marriage, it actually delivers none of these things but instead gives only guilt, emptiness and yet deeper hurts and regrets, often experienced years later.

Fourth, sexual temptation is dangerous but not irresistible. To many people today, the sexual urge is unstoppable. No, you need to tell yourself that wrong desires can be fought and can be defeated. As an Oscar Wilde character quipped, 'I can resist anything except temptation.' It is a line rendered tragically painful by the fact that Wilde's own uncontrolled sexual desires led him to disaster. The battle is not easy and sometimes the victory is at a high cost. But the biggest lie is that there is no point in resisting.

Fifth, there is more to adultery than the physical act of sex. In the pattern of leaving, uniting and becoming one flesh, a marriage is based on more than physical relations. Technically, it might not appear to be adultery to have a deep, non-physical, emotionally tender relationship with someone other than your spouse. But it is still an action that strikes at the heart of a marriage and constitutes 'cheating on your wife' (or husband). We need to shun it and work to make sure that it does not happen.

Remember the Cost of Adultery

If marriage is an all-embracing covenant arrangement where both parties commit themselves to each other for life and give each other everything they are, then the horror of adultery becomes clear.

Marriage is a whole web of links of intimate giving and sharing between a man and a woman, and with the act of adultery all these bonds are severed. Adultery smashes the deepest and most intimate levels of trust, shatters the covenant promises and breaks down the walls of privacy and exclusivity that protect the heart of marriage.

Of course, it is not portrayed as this in the media where adultery is rarely if ever portrayed as what it really is: a shabby betrayal of the deepest and most intimate trust. At worst, 'an affair' ('adultery' has rather negative overtones) is portrayed as exciting and stimulating. Driven by the unstoppable and glorious emotion of falling in love, the hero or heroine slips into what is essentially a harmless and life-enhancing bit of sweaty, physical fun that brightens up their humdrum existence. At a more sophisticated level, adultery is portrayed as something that brings personal fulfilment. Through it, we can somehow 'move on' beyond our marriage and become 'what we ought to be' or 'achieve our own potential'. Adultery here is far more than lust: it is part of 'our deep quest for self-realisation'. Often the media will sweep under the carpet all the shame, the anger and the pain that adultery brings. Adultery hurts. It shatters trust and severs friendship. Please look out for the truth, not the illusion.

There are other costs. There are at least twenty-five sexually transmitted infections, including HIV, gonorrhoea, syphilis, genital herpes and chlamydia. They are widespread, difficult to diagnose, often hard to treat and frequently leave a legacy of infertility and other problems. Far from dying out, such infections are on the rise in both Britain and the US.

A report revealed that in England in 2018 gonorrhoea infections were up 26 per cent on the year before, with syphilis up 5 per cent. Gay and bisexual men accounted for 75 per cent of new syphilis cases. In 2018, 447,694 new sexually transmitted infections were reported in England.[7] Despite widespread awareness of AIDS, the number of people infected with HIV, both heterosexuals and homosexuals, continues to rise. Gonorrhoea among the over-65s is rising at nearly double the national average, with divorce and dating apps blamed for greater promiscuity.[8]

It is estimated that there are about 100,000 people living with HIV in the UK, of whom a quarter are unaware of the infection.[9] According to the Centers for Disease Control and Prevention (CDC) there are approximately 1.1 million people in the US living with HIV.[10]

In the US 25 per cent of the population are currently living with an incurable sexually transmitted disease.[11] More than 20 million people get sexually transmitted infections every year, costing the US economy $16 billion in medical costs.[12] Health professionals are pessimistic about the future because many of the infections are becoming untreatable as antibiotic resistance increases.

Although they vindicate the Bible's position on sex and marriage, I take no pleasure in these statistics at all. I would genuinely be delighted if a cure for HIV/AIDS was found. Yet the conclusion is surely obvious. For all the talk of condoms, safe sex and regular testing, the only guaranteed way never to catch a sexual disease is either not to have sex, or only to have it with someone who has only ever had sex with you. From the health point of view alone, it would be impossible to invent a better system than a lifelong exclusive marriage. God knew what he was doing.

Putting health concerns to one side, adultery also affects other people. Sexual sin is a social sin and the effects are staggering. The social cost of family breakdown in the UK is £47 billion a year.[13] On current trends 47 per cent of all children born today in the UK will see the breakdown of their parents' relationship.[14] US costs are well over a $100 billion a year.[15]

Clean Up Your Act

When I talked about theft in the last chapter, I asked you to make amends where you could. I want to be similarly practical here.

If you are involved in an adulterous relationship, end it *now*. Not tomorrow, not next week – *now*. Pick up the phone and do it. There is no easy way out and, yes, someone is always going to get hurt, but the only way to end it, is to *end* it. When Jesus talked about adultery, he said some strong things.

> If your right eye causes you to stumble, gouge it out and throw it away. It is better for you to lose one part of your body than for your whole body to be thrown into hell. And if your right hand causes you to sin, cut it off and throw it away. It is better for you to lose one part of your body than for your whole body to go into hell. (Matthew 5:29–30)

What Jesus is saying here, beneath the imagery, is simple: we need to take drastic action and do some radical spiritual surgery.

Where there has been adultery, you and your marriage partner will probably need to see a counsellor who is able to work through the issues of broken vows to regain trust. It is very delicate and painful and needs to be done with God's help in the context of repentance and forgiveness. But a marriage can be healed. Obviously, very few couples talk openly about how their marriage survived adultery but I know of several cases where God has enabled restoration to occur. In this context, I want to warn you against the peril of despair. The lie is that you cannot get out, or that you can't be forgiven and made clean: 'It is too late now, you are in too deep.' I believe that with a loving, caring God, the door for repentance stays open. But if we stay in a wrong relationship, then that commitment will make it harder to deal with. However painful it may be, *now* is the time to act.

As an encouragement to you, look at one of the most powerful stories in the gospels, where Jesus was directly confronted with adultery. In John 8:1–11 we read how the religious leaders dragged before him a woman 'caught in the act of adultery'. In fact, the text makes it clear that their real interest was to trap Jesus. Would he endorse the religious death penalty for adultery and in so doing break the Roman rule that only they could pass a death sentence? Or would he let her off and thus go against the Jewish law? So, they ask Jesus whether she should be stoned. 'What do you say?' they asked. In answer Jesus simply bent down and began writing with his finger in the dust. Incidentally, we do not know what he wrote but it is quite possible that it was the Ten Commandments. They kept badgering him for an answer until he said, 'Let any one of you who is without sin be the first to throw a stone.' Then, as he bent down again to write some more in the dirt, they slipped away one by one, leaving the woman alone. Jesus spoke to her. 'Woman, where are they? Has no one condemned you?'

'No one, sir.'

'Then neither do I condemn you,' said Jesus. 'Go now and leave your life of sin.'

In this, I see three things. First, sexual sin brings out the worst in bystanders; we need to be very careful about our own motives when we criticise in this area. Given that sexual desire generally fades with age it is sometimes all too easy for those of advanced years, who have forgotten how overpowering sexual desire can be, to thunder against the sins of youth.

Secondly, Jesus showed mercy to the woman. He, as the one without sin, could have thrown the first stone, but he chose not to. He offers her, in effect, a new start. But thirdly, I also see how he balances it with a requirement that she turn from her sin. I believe that he holds out the same offer of mercy to all who are in sexual sin today, matched with a call for repentance and a changed life.

One of the most notorious adulterers in the Bible was King David and I recounted in chapter one how his covetousness of Bathsheba led him into sin. The writer of many of the psalms, David was a wise and godly man but in this area of his life he was weak. The Bible recounts (in 2 Samuel 12:1–14) how, under the challenging rebuke of a man of God, David confessed and repented of his sin. Psalm 51 was written by David at this time and is a moving model for repentance in the circumstances of sexual sin. If you have committed adultery, spend some time reflecting on this psalm.

If you are caught in this net of sin, I urge you to let Jesus Christ free you. Admit to sin, confess it, repent of it and promise to do all you can, never to repeat it. Ask for his power to help you overcome it.

AFFIRM MARRIAGE

Having spent some time talking about adultery and sexual sin, let me turn to how you can positively affirm marriage.

Work at Being Married

Adultery happens because no marriage is perfect and all of us have something in our lives, whether it's a need for love, acceptance or intimacy, which can sometimes make adultery seem appealing. I believe that God wants our marriages to be satisfying and so let me recommend what I call 'The Five Rs' of a successful marriage.

Respect

Love is built on the foundation of mutual respect. Paul tells us, 'Each man must love his wife as he loves himself, and the wife must respect her husband' (Ephesians 5:33 NLT). One of the most unpleasant things to witness is people being rude to their partners in public – interrupting them, ignoring them, contradicting them or putting them down. As they say, you can bury a marriage with a lot of little digs. Husbands, don't criticise your wife's judgement – remember who she chose to marry!

A public lecture was once advertised under the title 'How to make your wife treat you like a king'. The lecture hall was packed out with men. Finally, the speaker stood up to address the expectant gathering. 'Gentlemen,' he said to them, 'the answer to the question being posed is very simple. If you want your wife to treat you like a king, there is one thing you must do: treat her like a queen.'

Respect is vital. The alternative is contempt and, frankly, where there is contempt it is almost inevitable that eventually you will be in one of those conversations where you find yourself looking longingly into someone else's eyes and saying, 'You know, I don't get this sort of respect at home.'

If you are not yet married, let me give you some advice. Never consider marrying anyone, however attractive or charming, whom you do not respect as a person and who doesn't respect you.

Responsibility

One of the ways you can help keep your marriage going is to take responsibility. This means fixing the problem, not fixing the blame. Couples having difficulties often spend much more time and energy attacking each other than attacking the problems. Marriage is a covenant and is about commitment rather than feelings. To make a marriage work takes an act of the will, so that both the heart and the mind act together. God encourages us to be honest about our weaknesses and failings, to own up and take responsibility when something is our fault. The trouble with the world is that so many people who stand up for their rights fall down miserably on their responsibilities.

Not only are we to take responsibility for our own actions but we should try to take responsibility for our partner. The apostle Paul wrote to one church, 'Look out for one another's interests, not just for your own. The attitude you should have is the one that Christ Jesus had' (Philippians 2:4–5 GNB). The same rule applies to marriages.

Relate

The figures on how little time couples spend together today are alarming. One survey concluded that one in four Britons speak to their loved one for less than ten minutes a day.[16] Surely the substantial amount of time we all spend on the internet or on social networks has weakened good face-to-face conversation. To develop your social relations with a stranger at the expense of your spouse opposite you is very foolish. I know these days we talk about quality time not quantity time, but it seems to me that nothing beats quantity-quality time. In a marriage we need to give time to nourish and cherish the relationship. We need to learn to talk and listen to each other.

Romance

I think if there was more courting in marriage there would be fewer marriages in court! I don't know whether you were surprised by what I said earlier on in this chapter about God being pro-sex, but I am convinced not only that it is true, but that marriage is the place to demonstrate it. God, the author of the Ten Commandments, is the foremost proponent of healthy sex. Don't hesitate to seek professional help if you encounter difficulties in this area.

Resolve

Decide to make it work! For a successful marriage you need to resolve to be committed to your wife or husband not only in the one-off wedding ceremony but on each day of your married life. Both partners must make a firm commitment to faithfulness, fidelity and honesty at all times. Tell yourself that you are going to make it work.

I'm not suggesting that marriages will never run into problems or endure storms. But I believe the kind of commitment God is talking about means that, when we hit a difficulty in our marriage, we decide to face it and carry on together. Trying times are not the times to stop trying. It might be that you are aware of problems in your marriage. If so, you need to be honest about those with your partner and also seek professional help. In all this, we need to treat the gift of our marriage with the highest respect and value.

A WORD TO THE MARRIED AND TO THE SINGLE

The roots of much marital breakdown go back to the mishandling of the whole issue of singleness. One reason, I believe, why there are so many difficult marriages is that people have been so misled by our culture that they feel that they *must* be married and they are so fearful of singleness that they flee from it at the earliest opportunity.

One of the biggest lies around is that sex is the same as sexuality, so if you are not sexually active you are not sexual. Freud said something similar, 'Those who are not sexually active are socially retarded, unbalanced and disturbed.' This, of course, is nonsense. A person may not be sexually active but this certainly doesn't mean that they are not sexual. Another lie is that if you live a single, celibate life you are unfulfilled and missing out. My response to this attitude is to point to Jesus. Here was a single man who was not sexually active, but would anyone dare to suggest that his life was unfulfilled or sad and boring? No, on the contrary, no one has ever lived as fulfilled a life as he had. In his many friendships, his love of fellowship, his risky relationships that cut across the rigid contemporary barriers of gender, race and even religion, he is the model for what a human life should be. We need to let Jesus be our pattern, not the magazines and TV programmes that scream out at us that we must be having sex in order to live a fully satisfying life.

It is clear from the Bible that God calls some people to be single. Singleness is not in any way an inferior or less godly way of life. In fact, it might be the opposite. However, we are all social people and single people will have relationship needs that for married people are met by their spouse. We need to find ways of integrating single people into families and communities and affirming their value as both single and sexual people. We need to build deep, strong and encouraging relationships with them, so that they do not feel alone and isolated. In particular, we need to remember that to be called to singleness is to be called to celibacy and, as St Augustine said, 'celibacy without community is impossible'.

While God may have called some of us to be single, he has called none of us to survive on our own. We are all made as relational beings who need each other. It is selfish to ignore those who are single and we need to do all we can to integrate singles into our lives. From my experience, I have no doubt that we will benefit as much from them as they will from us. My wife Killy and I have wonderful single friends who enrich our lives.

GET THE RIGHT ATTITUDES

Finally, I want to suggest that we arm ourselves with the right attitudes.

Guard Your Minds

Whether single or married you might be thinking, 'Well I've never actually committed adultery so how does this relate to me?' Listen to what Jesus does with this commandment in his teaching on how to live that we call 'the Sermon on the Mount'.

> You have heard that it was said, 'You shall not commit adultery.' But I tell you that anyone who looks at a woman lustfully has already committed adultery with her in his heart. (Matthew 5:27–28)

This is a fascinating and challenging passage. Notice, by the way, that Jesus considers men to be the problem, not women.

In terms of sexual sin, it is important to note here that Jesus shifts the emphasis back from the action to the desire. Clean hands are not enough; we need clean hearts. The look of lust or desire is, Jesus says, also adultery. He does not say that the look is as bad as the physical act, but he says that it does count as adultery. As we think about this, we realise that if our desires are to be judged then none of us can escape condemnation. We have all sinned. This is typical of Jesus, getting at the core of the issue: our thoughts, our desires and our hearts. There is a chain of things in our lives that can be summarised as follows: thoughts become words, words become actions, actions become habits and habits become character. We need to start at the root with thoughts. I remember hearing of a man who had just committed adultery. 'I don't know how it happened,' the man protested in bewilderment to his minister. The minister turned to him, 'I do. Had you ever committed the act in your mind with this woman?' Of course he had, and his actions had finally just followed his thoughts.

We are all prone to temptation and we are bombarded by images and ideas which try to divert us from God's way. Temptation isn't itself wrong. The question is: what do we do with it? The Bible encourages us to remember that 'the temptations in your life are no different from what others experience. And God is faithful. He will not allow the temptation to be more than you can stand. When you are tempted, he will show you a way out so that you can endure' (1 Corinthians 10:13 NLT). We can't stop being bombarded by sexual images, but we can stop them from taking root. It is better to shun the bait than to struggle on the hook.

We need to drag our wills and action into line. We need to choose purity. The stimulus of the erotic films, images and words that we inevitably encounter in this sex-obsessed world can play havoc with our thoughts and desires. They can act as fuel to a fire that is often already in danger of burning out of control. Many people who have everything else in their lives under control feel completely overwhelmed in this area. They feel enslaved and taken captive by thoughts they are ashamed of. If that describes you, then make a decision to choose God's way in this area. You don't need to live as a slave, under the domination of images that aren't pleasing to God. Allow Jesus to deliver you.

For some of you reading this, I need to issue a stronger warning. While others may have blundered into images that have aroused them, you have deliberately sought them out to feed your sexual appetites. By clicking on particular websites, reading certain magazines, letting your eyes roam over whatever you choose, you have relinquished control over your own life and are heading into slavery.

Over the last decade internet pornography has exploded. Pornography used to be something difficult to get hold of. Now, even the most extreme forms of video are just a couple of mouse clicks away from anybody at a computer. Some people have strayed onto pornographic sites, perhaps initially out of curiosity but then found themselves compelled to return. For some people it is addictive and even those for whom it isn't, it is unhelpful. It emphasises all the wrong aspects of sex and all too frequently portrays women as passive objects to be used simply for sexual gratification. Avoid!

A mind that persistently dreams and schemes is a mind that needs cleansing. If we don't confess and turn away from mental adultery and immorality it will eventually dominate our thought life. If we encourage it with sexually stimulating websites, books, magazines or social settings, our fantasy dreams will one day turn into nightmare realities.

The only solution is to deal uncompromisingly with the problem using the radical spiritual surgery that Jesus calls for. So in the case of internet pornography, take drastic action. You may want to let your browsing habits be accountable to someone, possibly by placing your computer somewhere in the house where it can always be seen by others. There are also various technological solutions. Set up a system on your computer which automatically informs friends whenever you enter any inappropriate adult sites.

If your temptation lies elsewhere, perhaps in a friendship where the potential for sexual immorality has emerged, make sure that you are never alone with that person. Far better to lose a friend than a marriage. Another piece of radical surgery is to find someone with integrity whom you can trust, to be accountable about your internal thought life. If struggles and pain can be shared with another, they often lose their power and hold, especially in this area of our sexuality.

If you choose God's way of living, far from missing out, you will become truly human.

Guard Your Behaviour

It is also important that our public behaviour is appropriate. In social situations, if you see someone who attracts you for whatever reason (and we know that it happens whether we are single or married), then don't take a second look. In the Bible, one man of God says, 'I made a covenant with my eyes not to look lustfully at a young woman' (Job 31:1).

We need to be aware of how our actions come over to those of the opposite sex. God wants us to have right relationships. Do you know that most affairs start with friends? If you are married, never flirt. If you are single, never flirt unless you have a serious intent and the object of your attentions is both unattached and suitable. Keep your boundaries with members of the opposite sex clear and firm and never give any ground for misunderstanding or ambiguity.

Choose purity today; choose God's way. I cannot encourage you enough to make up your mind to be sexually pure. Whatever you have done in the past, from this day forward you can choose purity.

A FINAL WORD

I believe that for all of us as individuals – and for our society as a whole – our sexuality is the most damaged and broken part of our humanity. Yet with God there is wholeness through healing and right relationships, through his Holy Spirit.

In the *Guinness Book of Records* 'Marriage' is under the category of 'Human Achievement'. But frankly, if we are honest, here we need more than human achievement; we need God's help. The wonderful thing, though, is that God does want to help us. After all, he is the great lover, the faithful partner, the one who is utterly committed to his covenant people. He doesn't show his love by sending us a romantic poem or dropping a bunch of red roses onto our doorstep. 'But God showed his great love for us by sending Christ to die for us while we were still sinners' (Romans 5:8 NLT).

He shows he cares through cries of agony and excruciating pain. It's not champagne he drinks, but bitter wine. He doesn't bear roses in his arms, but a crown of thorns wedged on his head. He doesn't bathe us in fine-smelling perfume, but saves us through sweat and blood. God's proposal was nailed to a cross. And he did it for us – that's true love.

The only way to resist the temptation to infidelity is to root our single life or our marriage in the rich soil of God's confirming love. Let go of your regrets about the past and experience God's forgiveness and healing for previous poor choices. It is when we allow ourselves to be loved by Jesus that we are free to love like Jesus. Faithfully, unconditionally, purely and selflessly, not for what's in it for ourselves but for what the other person's worth.

We can't alter our past, but we can bring our past to the altar of God, so bring it all to Christ at the cross and leave it there, asking for his healing and Holy Spirit to fill you with his love, power and self-control.

1   https://www.telegraph.co.uk/women/womens-life/11901598/I-dont-regret-joining-acheating-website.-The-sex-was-exhilarating.html

2   https://www.fpa.org.uk/news/uk-has-highest-teenage-birth-rates-western-europe

    https://www.hhs.gov/ash/oah/adolescent-development/reproductive-health-and-teen-pregnancy/teen-pregnancy-and-childbearing/trends/index.html

3   https://www.johnstonsarchive.net/policy/abortion/uslifetimeab.html

4   https://concernedwomen.org/porn-is-the-new-sex-trade/

5   https://www.independent.co.uk/life-style/marriage-religious-civil-ceremony-lgbt-humanist-ons-a8844916.html

6   https://www.psychologytoday.com/gb/blog/fulfillment-any-age/201208/take-it-slow-if-you-want-your-relationship-last

7   https://www.tht.org.uk/news/new-sti-stats-show-action-urgently-needed-tackle-soaring-rates

8   https://www.telegraph.co.uk/science/2019/06/04/gonorrhea-over-65s-rising-nearly-double-national-average-divorce/

9   https://www.tht.org.uk/hiv-and-sexual-health/about-hiv/hiv-statistics

10 https://www.cdc.gov/hiv/basics/statistics.html

11 https://www.hivplusmag.com/prevention/2015/09/25/shocking-stats-stds-america

12 https://www.cdc.gov/nchhstp/newsroom/2016/std-surveillance-report-2015-press-release.html

13 https://www.centreforsocialjustice.org.uk/policy/breakthrough-britain/family-breakdown

14 https://www.centreforsocialjustice.org.uk/core/wp-content/uploads/2017/11/The-forgotten-role-of-families-why-its-time-to-find-our-voice-on-families-1.pdf

15 http://www.americanvalues.org/pdfs/coff-executive_summary.pdf

16 https://www.dailymail.co.uk/news/article-2085995/Too-busy-talk-One-Britons-speaks-loved-10-minutes-day.html

5

HOW TO MANAGE OUR ANGER

COMMANDMENT SIX: YOU SHALL NOT MURDER

You shall not murder. (Exodus 20:13)

SO, WHAT'S THE PROBLEM?

The sixth commandment prohibits unlawful killing or, more precisely, the intentional killing of an innocent human being. It seems a straightforward rule but as we look at it more closely, we will find ourselves forced to cover some unfamiliar ground. Most importantly, we must look at anger.

To begin with, though, we need to think about death. There are fashions in attitudes as well as clothes. In the Victorian age, everyone talked about death, and sex was a taboo subject. In our generation, we are preoccupied with sex but don't talk about death. The whole business of dying is hidden behind a screen of words: 'passing away', 'the departed', 'at rest' and 'no longer with us'. The change is fascinating because we face the same risk of death as our Victorian ancestors did: 100 per cent of us will die. Yet unless we work in hospitals or funeral parlours, most of us will rarely see dead people.

Bizarrely, though, we are more familiar with death and killing than any previous generation. On our television and cinema screens we have seen fictional death in a thousand ways. Violence is continually pumped into our culture. We have spawned a generation of movie heroes – from James Bond to Jason Bourne – who are not exactly walking models of 'anger management'. Over our popcorn, we have watched men and women getting shot, drowning, exploding and being burnt alive, crushed by cars, eaten by sharks, swallowed by snakes, consumed by aliens and even dying quietly in bed. What was once an X-rated film suitable only for adults is now branded on re-release as suitable for fifteen-year-olds. Death – like money – is suffering from inflation.

Nightly, our children stalk around their computer worlds armed to the teeth and generating body counts worthy of a respectable war. Battlefield simulations allow teenagers to inflict realistic bullet wounds with every conceivable weapon on vast numbers of people. For serious mayhem and extreme gore, watch any zombie computer game. It's hardly killing, is it? They're already dead.

On news programmes and documentaries, we gawp at the bloodied dead of wars, shudder at earthquake-crushed bodies and wince at malnourished infants. Then we switch channels. Worryingly, as we stare at the screen, the worlds of reality and illusion increasingly merge. Was that film of a bomb explosion or was it a clip from a computer game? Are those really burned bodies or is it Hollywood computer-generated imagery (CGI)?

There are strange parallels between our modern views of sex and death. We know more about the mechanics of both sex and death than ever before, yet we seem to know less than ever about the reality and significance of either.

Our confusion is unfortunate because there is a lot of death about. In the twentieth century it seems probable that there were 187 million war-related deaths.[1] The past hundred years have seen truly horrific acts of evil against humanity: Hitler's extermination of six million Jews, the tens of millions who perished under Stalin, the millions killed in Cambodia, Uganda and Rwanda. Famine and disease, most of it either caused or made worse by human beings, have killed hundreds of millions more. And there is no sign that the present century will be much better.

The sixth commandment raises other issues. How unique and valuable is a human life? How should we treat each other? How do we cope with difference and disagreement?

The principles behind these four words, 'You shall not murder', are far-reaching and go beyond simply putting a law on the statute book.

Anger confounds many people in our world today.

We simply don't know how to handle our anger like we have in the past. One of the Bible's simplest yet most profound answers for our anger comes in Proverbs 29:11: 'Stupid people express their anger openly, but sensible people are patient and hold it back' (GNB).

Think before you speak. Delay is a tremendous remedy for anger. If you've got an issue you need to deal with, you need to do so. Anger delayed indefinitely can become bitterness. That's worse than anger. Anger isn't always a sin. Bitterness is.

If you respond impulsively, you tend to respond in anger. If you wait to talk about whatever conflict you're dealing with, you'll be more rational and reasonable when you do. The longer you hold your temper, the better your response will be. But before we do this, we have to get to the heart of the matter.

THE HEART OF THE MATTER

The Value of Life

Life is from God. The first chapters of the Bible declare that God made heaven and earth and created men and women. Speaking of Adam, the first human, we read, 'The LORD God formed a man from the dust of the ground and breathed into his nostrils the breath of life, and the man became a living being' (Genesis 2:7). Life comes from God.

Abortion, Euthanasia, Surrogacy, Cloning

Some of the most contentious and disputed issues of our day are matters of bioethics: an interdisciplinary field that addresses what we should and should not pursue in matters of life and health. These issues touch on the very core of our humanity: dignity and worth, sickness and health, life and death.

Yet the harsh reality is that while bioethical concerns are increasingly confronting us in the media, in the public square and in our personal lives, few people grasp the science involved in the 'bio' or the moral dilemmas involved in the 'ethics' of bioethics. We need to reflect on these advances, changes and controversies and to know how they are changing the way we live.

Recently, there have been multiple scientific advances in the area of genetic manipulation and artificial intelligence and there is much talk about 'making life in the laboratory'. The three main branches are based around: making life (IVF), taking life (euthanasia) and faking life (genetic manipulation). The reality is that we cannot create life. All we can do is copy God's original template and tweak it. God created life first and he remains the origin of all life, whether formed in the womb or the test tube. In fact, the origin of life remains one of the great mysteries of science. This is important. Life is not something that we automatically have or some sort of natural right. It is a gift from God: he alone gives life and he alone takes it away. The pivotal point around which the sixth commandment hangs is *God*. He is the God who freely, generously, wonderfully gives life to each one of us. To murder is to take away someone's life. That, simply, is beyond our authority.

What is more, human life is special. *Homo sapiens* are not just the top of the evolutionary tree or the dominant ecological species; we have been given unique honour and dignity, as we alone are the ones whom God made in his image. The Bible says, 'So God created human beings in his own image; In the image of God he created them; male and female he created them' (Genesis 1:27 NLT). And Jesus confirms our status. In Christ we see the ultimate illustration of a human being in God's image.

People are valuable. This idea underpins the sixth commandment. A few chapters after the story of the creation of the world we read one of God's first warnings to people: to kill a person is to kill a living being made in God's image (see Genesis 9:6).

Another way in which human beings are made in the image of God is that we are social beings who inter-relate with each other. The Bible reveals that God, though one being, is Father, Son and Spirit. Between these three persons of the Trinity there is a deep relationship. We reflect this aspect of God's character most when we are with other people, whether in a marriage, a family or at work. God gives us each other; it is his plan for us to be interdependent, living in a society where each person is valued and able to make their unique contribution. The poet John Donne well expressed the significance of death in such an interlocked society:

> No man is an island, entire of itself; every man is a piece of the continent, a part of the main . . . Any man's death diminishes me, because I am involved in mankind. And therefore never send to know for whom the bell tolls; it tolls for thee.

Wisdom demands that we be prepared, that we develop a carefully reasoned, biblically based approach to why human life is sacred. We see three reasons why human life is sacred.

First, God alone has the power to give life and therefore is the only one authorised to take life away.

Second, as we are made in the image of God, to take the life of another human is to destroy someone patterned after God.

Third, God made us to live together, each contributing what we have and are to others. Murder is the most brutal breach possible of that interlocked social life.

Think of the most valuable object you can imagine. Perhaps it is a painting, a piece of jewellery. Imagine that its value is so high that it cannot be insured. Now think of a human being, any human being, perhaps your wife, your brother, your friend. Now ask yourself this: which is more valuable? The answer is easy: it is the human life. To say otherwise, even to hesitate, is to insult the very God in whose image we are all made.

We need to value all human life. We live in a society of disposable razors, disposable contact lenses and disposable nappies. We need to protest loudly that the one thing that is not disposable is human life. To regard human beings as expendable, as if they were merely pawns in a chess game, is wrong. To treat death as if it was of little consequence ignores the intrinsic value of humanity. It is a crime against the God whose image we bear.

In the light of this, I want to look at some important issues of life and death that this commandment addresses.

ISSUES OF LIFE AND DEATH

Two issues emerge here. Is killing in the name of the law or the state ever right? How are we to respond to the issues of abortion and euthanasia?

Killing Under Authority

Is it ever right for the state to take a life? What about war or capital punishment? After all, in the time of Moses, the Israelites had both.

Killing in war

Apart from some appalling aberrations, of which the Crusades are the most notorious, almost all Christians have agreed that war is only to be undertaken as the very last resort. Every other option must be tried first. There are no Christian holy wars. Some Christians have gone so far as to say that all fighting is wrong and have taken the pacifist position. Others have said that limited and restrained wars may, at times, be justified as the lesser of a number of evils. The classic example is the defeat of Nazi Germany, which spared yet more millions from the gas chambers.

The issues over justified war are complex and need more space than I have here. All Christians today would, I think, agree that because of the value of human life even a war that is justified should be restricted in its scope and care should be taken to avoid civilian casualties. But, as the bombings of Dresden, Hiroshima and Nagasaki show, even justified wars have a way of getting out of control. And all too frequently, as in the liberation of Iraq, the body count rises.

Let me give you some brief guidelines expressed as cautions.

Beware of any simplistic glamorisation or glorification of war, whether by the cinema, software makers or the military industry. Even where (and if) war is justified, it is never more than an appalling necessity.

Beware of military euphemisms. Remember the human cost behind such phrases as 'mopping up', 'taking out' and 'degrading of enemy capabilities'.

Beware of hate, the language of revenge or retaliation or the lowering of the enemy to the subhuman level ('rats', 'animals', 'scum'). War kills men, women and children; all are made in the image of God. Wars may be the lesser of a number of evils, but they can brutalise all involved and under wartime conditions 'decent people' end up being capable of doing things that are not at all decent.

Beware, too, the creeping 'digitalisation' of warfare; weapons technology is evolving rapidly. Take the use of robotic aircraft armed with missiles – 'drones'. This is of concern because drones are controlled at a distance by men and women who identify and eliminate 'targets' on computer screens. It is 'killing by remote control'. Digital technology distances us from brutal, bloody reality.

The goal for us as individuals is always to pursue peace and righteousness across all barriers of race, language and culture.

Killing in punishment

Generally speaking, capital punishment is not a major issue in Britain; you would have to be well into your sixties to remember the last hanging. It is more of an issue in the United States. Nevertheless, even in Britain, after every brutal mass slaughter, act of terrorism or murder of a young child someone suggests the return of the gallows.

All Christians today would, I imagine, accept that capital punishment, if employed at all, must be reserved exclusively for those who murder.

Christians who support capital punishment for murder would argue that it is *precisely* the value of human life that justifies the death penalty. Nothing less, they say, will show our high assessment of the victim's life. Those opposed to the death penalty would say that capital punishment is barbaric and dehumanises society. And, since all legal systems make mistakes, we should not impose sentences that are so irreversible. A compromise position is to propose that while the death sentence for murder should be passed (to show society's high view of life) it should always be converted to life imprisonment (to avoid the problems of enacting capital punishment). The debate will continue.

Killing at the beginning and end of life

Abortion

Medicine and common sense tell us that a child in a womb experiences consciousness and pain; Christianity teaches that life is valuable from the moment of conception and that the foetus is fully human. Since the legalisation of abortion in 1967, over 6 million pregnancies have been terminated in the UK.[2] Despite the widespread availability of many different kinds of contraception, abortion rates stay high.

As of 31st December 2018, there have been some 41.9 million abortions performed in the course of the year.[3] By contrast, 8.2 million people died from cancer in 2018, 5 million from smoking-related illnesses, and 1.7 million died of HIV/AIDS. In 2016, according to Department of Health statistics, the total number of abortions performed on residents of England and Wales was 185,596.

This number excludes the 4,810 abortions performed on non-residents in the UK. Therefore, the total number of abortions performed in England and Wales was 190,406.[4] Alarmingly, the Royal College of Obstetricians and Gynaecologists states that at least one third of British women will have had an abortion by the time they reach the age of forty-five.[5]

The responsibility for an unwanted pregnancy must be shared by a man and a woman together, yet all too often the guilt and pain are born only by the woman. I am well aware that there will be women who read this who have had abortions, often because they were pressured into them. Abortion can cause crippling guilt and regret, and I believe that God doesn't want to increase those feelings but to heal them. If you have had a pregnancy terminated, I urge you not only to seek God's healing but also the help of a wise counsellor who can work through some of the emotional issues. There are organisations that are able to help anyone in any position of pain. You need to know and experience the living, forgiving God who wants to heal you.

I believe that the current rate of abortion in both Britain and the United States is horrific. In Britain the most frequent justification given for abortion is the 'risk of injury to the physical or mental health of the mother or her existing children'. In reality, the abortion occurs because contraception either failed or was not used and that the pregnancy is inconvenient or unwanted.

The national rape-related pregnancy rate is 5 per cent per rape among victims of reproductive age (aged twelve to forty-five); among adult women an estimated 32,101 pregnancies result from rape each year. Among 34 cases of rape-related pregnancy, the majority occurred among adolescents and resulted from assault by a known, often-related perpetrator. Only 11.7 per cent of these victims received immediate medical attention after the assault, and 47.1 per cent received no medical attention related to the rape. A total 32.4 per cent of these victims did not discover they were pregnant until they had already entered the second trimester; 32.2 per cent opted to keep the infant whereas 50 per cent underwent abortion and 5.9 per cent placed the infant for adoption; an additional 11.8 per cent had spontaneous abortion.[6]

Rape is cited in fewer than 1 per cent of all abortions. Barely 1 per cent of abortions occur because there is a likelihood of foetal handicap and only a tiny fraction of 1 per cent occur because the mother's life is at risk. In short, most abortions appear to be for convenience or as 'retro-active contraception'. The US position is much the same. I think it must break God's heart to see how this disposable society will even dispose of its unborn children. I cannot understand how a mother's 'right to choose' can be exercised without any regard for an unborn child's 'right to life'. There is a tragic irony because there are very large numbers of childless couples who would love to have a baby to adopt. Every baby *is* a wanted baby!

In an increasing number of cases, the foetus is aborted because prenatal scanning has revealed some sort of abnormality. Yet in many cases, the abnormalities are relatively trivial and, as in the case of cleft palate or club foot, can fairly easily be resolved by surgery.[7]

In the face of such figures I believe that we must stand up for the voiceless and question the values of a society that allows such actions on such a scale. But we cannot just proclaim our opinion and retreat. We must offer care and practical and financial aid to those who have chosen not to terminate their pregnancy.

With genetic testing it is now possible to determine the sex of a baby early in development. Given the high value that many cultures place on boys over girls, it is not surprising that preferential abortion of girls is becoming widespread. This practice has been given the appropriately ugly phrase 'gendercide'. Sex-selective abortion is now so common in countries such as India that it shows up in population statistics on the gender ratios of infants.[8] Sadly, there is evidence that in certain ethnic communities, within both the United States and Britain, a higher number of boys are being born, suggesting that illegal sex-selective abortion is actually occurring here.[9]

A great concern of high levels of abortion and its acceptance among large numbers of the public is that it will lead to the logical next step: infanticide. When Christians and others have made this suggestion they have often been ridiculed. Nevertheless, there does appear to be a growing mood in some sectors of the scientific community towards the idea that the killing of 'defective' newborns should be allowed. The

Princeton ethicist Peter Singer has led the way here,[10] but others are following with the idea of what is euphemistically called 'after-birth abortion', a troubling term that could actually be used for any type of murder.[11]

Abortion presents itself as an easy solution but it is one that we need to resist. Some medical students were attending a seminar on abortion where the lecturer presented them with a case study. 'The father of the family has syphilis and the mother, tuberculosis. They have had four children already. The first is blind, the second died, the third is deaf and dumb and the fourth has tuberculosis. The mother is now pregnant with her fifth child and is willing to have an abortion if that is what you suggest. What would your advice be?' The students overwhelmingly voted to terminate the pregnancy. 'Congratulations,' the lecturer responded. 'You have just murdered Beethoven.'

Euthanasia

The literal meaning of the word euthanasia is 'dying well', but the term has come to mean the intentional medical termination of a person's life. It is important to distinguish euthanasia from two other practices. The first is that of allowing patients suffering from fatal diseases to die in peace without being subjected to painful treatments that cannot restore them to health. The second is the use of pain-killing drugs to control severe pain even at the risk of shortening life. The intention in both practices is to allow patients to end their days in as peaceful, dignified and pain-free way possible. Such methods, although not without medical issues, are widely practised and raise no significant moral problems.

In theory, euthanasia sounds harmless. The terminally ill decide voluntarily that 'enough is enough' and, at the time of their choosing, are given such drugs as will cause a speedy and painless death. Supporters of euthanasia are careful to avoid any phrases that might suggest that the doctors 'kill' the patient and, as with abortion, the language of 'choice' and 'rights' and 'freedom' is widely used.

There are, however, many problems with euthanasia, particularly in providing safeguards. Medical science is not always as exact and precise as we might like. Many of us know people who have either recovered from an illness that was presumed to be fatal or long outlived predictions of their death. There are also real concerns that euthanasia might be encouraged for other reasons than the well-being of the patient. In some cases, particularly where the patient is young, there may be organs that can be harvested for transplant. In the case of the elderly, there are issues of cost to the health service; when there is pressure on hospital beds, the temptation to free up a few by speeding up death is actually quite strong. Proposed candidates for euthanasia are generally elderly and are almost always those who need a lot of looking after. Although it is claimed that safeguards would be put in place to prevent relatives and other potential beneficiaries of the person's will from influencing a doctor's decision, the reality could easily be otherwise.

Euthanasia also sets worrying precedents. Doctor Leo Alexander, a psychiatrist who worked with the Nuremberg Tribunal, described the process that led to the horrors of Auschwitz, Belsen and Treblinka. He wrote:

> The beginnings at first were merely a subtle shift in emphasis in the basic attitude of the physicians. It started with the attitude, basic in the euthanasia movement, that there is such a thing as a life not worthy to be lived. This attitude in its early stages concerned itself merely with the severely and chronically sick. Gradually the sphere of those to be included in this category was enlarged to encompass the socially unproductive, the ideologically unwanted, the racially unwanted and finally all non-Germans.[12]

Both of these medical issues raise similar questions about what life is. Abortion and euthanasia allow us to become judges of what is a valid life and what isn't. The view that *all* human life is valuable is unpopular today as its basis is the existence of God. Here we can be grateful for the controversial Princeton professor of ethics Peter Singer's blunt expression of the issues at stake. 'Once the religious mumbo-jumbo surrounding the term "human" has been stripped away . . . we will not regard as sacrosanct the life of every member of our species, no matter how limited its capacity for intelligent or even conscious life may be.'[13] In Singer's view you have to reach some biological or mental level before you are to be allowed to live. The mentally handicapped, the brain-injured, the unborn and even newborns have no right to life; indeed, killing them may be morally acceptable. What those standards are, who sets them, and whether you and I – and our children – will always reach them, are alarming and disturbing questions.

Influential bioethicist Nigel Cameron has proposed a useful framework for thinking of the three main categories of bioethics: taking life, making life and faking life.

1. Taking life

The first category of bioethics addresses the issues that were once common in the pagan days: abortion, infanticide (partial-birth abortion), euthanasia (both voluntary and involuntary) and physician-assisted suicide.

The taking life stage progressed as individuals began to expect complete autonomy and control over their bodies.

- When disease has progressed to the point where we can no longer control our health we choose euthanasia – 'good death'.
- When we want to regain control over our bodies after becoming pregnant we choose abortion.
- When we lose control over our will to live we expect physicians to assist in our suicide.
- We are willing to kill our children or ourselves in a desperate attempt to regain one last measure of control.
- Eighty per cent of the world's countries have abortion legalised. There are 43 million abortions a year worldwide – an astonishingly big number as the causes of all other deaths is around 57 million – meaning that almost 1 in every 2 human beings will die an unborn child. That's: 1 child aborted for every 1 born.
- Sex selection abortion. Common in African and Asian nations, females are aborted creating an imbalance of males and females in the population.
- Countries are trying to legalise Euthanasia.

2. Making life

Until the 1970s, all but one child ever born was the result of sexual intercourse; today, there are at least *38 ways* to make a baby.

In an attempt to conquer infertility we've developed dozens of methods, a veritable alphabet soup of acronyms, to create a child: IVF, IUI, ICSI, DI, AI, ET to name but a few.

The growing number of reproductive technologies has undoubtedly been a blessing to thousands of infertile couples. Yet the methods raise an equal number of ethical concerns.

A number of the reproductive methods and technologies violate God's ideal for the family by involving a third party (i.e. egg or sperm donation, surrogacy).

Other problems arise from the creation of 'spare' embryos that will either be discarded or donated for 'research'.

The technology has also paved the way for human cloning, the creation of 'designer' babies and the individualistic eugenics of pre-implantation genetic diagnosis.

3. Faking life

Think of this third category as the third act of a story. However, instead of resolving the story, like a postmodern tale, this third act of bioethics only complicates the situation further by, as Nigel Cameron claims, faking life: 'dis-integrating' the biological human and melding him with other species or machines.

- Genetic engineering (the creation of designer humans).
- Neuro ethics (such as the use of 'enhancement' drugs or implantable brain chips).
- Transhumanism (merging of man and machine to create a new form of existence).

All of these concerns seem bizarre – yet they are all being considered, debated and pursued by biotechnologists.

The controversies in each of these categories – taking life, making life and faking life – raise serious challenges. It's a muddy global canvas – a reflection of different worldviews and the battlefield that goes on.

So, why is ethical decision-making so difficult? What is giving it extra complexity? Many of our worldview changes have fed into these issues.

- Decline of Judeo-Christian values, Christian theism (reformation/ puritan movement, evangelical revival and awakening in America which led to reforms) slowly gave way to the New Atheism movement and now secular humanism, moral relativism. We no longer have a moral consensus about what's right and what's wrong.

- Doctrines have been discredited. Post enlightenment, the idea that humans aren't made in the image of God (or made for relationship with him), has meant that rather than looking forward to redemption, judgement and life after death, humans are seen as 'clever monkeys', a product of matter and time. Death is the end, and morality is what we decide it to be, ultimately bringing it down to personal choice.

- When you get more and more people embracing an atheistic worldview and secular post-enlightenment values, it's not surprising that they get into the corridors of power or the mountains of culture. For example: parliament, the courts, the arts, media, entertainment, universities and schools, business and institutions. Once people with atheist worldviews and secular humanist values get into these positions they will impact the trajectory of the culture.

How Should We Respond?

We have got to go right back to first principles in terms of coming to our opinions on these bioethical issues.

Are we guided by gut-feeling, or by conscience?

What makes us feel guilty or doesn't?

We are guided by authorities. What are people saying? What is the consensus of opinion?

Two bioethicists who have explored that question in detail are John Kilner and Ben Mitchell. They offer a model for addressing bioethics from a Christian perspective that is God-centred, reality-bounded and love-impelled.

1. God-centred

Our radical dependence on God must be our primary point of reference. Because of our fallen-ness, our human reasoning is inadequate.

A God-centred model, however, acknowledges that inadequacy and recognises that God is more than adequate for the task.

2. Reality-bounded

To be realistic is to understand reality – the way things really are – and to live accordingly. Because God alone sees all of the reality that exists, we must put our trust in him and what he has revealed, both in creation and in Scripture. Indicators of God's intentions serve as guides or principles for moral living. Past and present realities include that God is the author of all creation, including humans who are made in the image of God yet are fallen and sinful. The most important future reality is that Christ will return (1 Thessalonians 4:13 – 5:11) and will restore all of creation (Revelation 21:1).

By reflecting on these realities we can gain a better understanding of the legitimate boundaries. We will gain a better grasp of the forms, freedoms and limits of autonomy, control and technology.

3. Love-impelled

All of life is to be directed by love for God and love for our neighbour. We are to seek the greatest possible well-being of all people. Love considers the consequences of our decisions and the motives for our actions. Jesus shows us what love looks like in the face of suffering, whether from infertility or from impending death, and calls us to live in the same way.

Armed with these categories – **taking life, making life, faking life** – and this model – **God-centred, reality-bounded and love-impelled** – you'll be able to inform yourself, educate others, and work towards bringing a Christian perspective to bear on issues of bioethics.

Now let's consider some ways we can bring a Christian perspective to bear on issues of bioethics in our own circles of influence.

Raise Awareness

We often find that people are unaware of the challenges that arise, particularly from the emerging field of biotechnology. Consider, for example, the issue of the creation of chimeras: hybrid creatures that are part human, part animal. Many people assume that we are talking about futuristic scenarios of science fiction, rather than experiments that are taking place in university laboratories today. They are often shocked to learn that Chinese researchers fused human cells with rabbit eggs or that a professor at the University of Nevada created the world's first human-sheep chimera – a creature that has 15 per cent human cells and 85 per cent animal cells. They are usually even more surprised to find those events occurred in 2003 and 2007.[14] This is an example of an issue that has been around for over a decade.

Even when the mainstream media covers the stories, they often pass from the public's attention before the underlying questions can even be examined. By helping to draw attention to such articles, we can provide the invaluable awareness that is needed to provide an adequate response.

Shape the Language

The preservation of human dignity requires us to fight for the hearts and souls of our fellow man. One of the key ways in which Christians can aid in this struggle is to reclaim the linguistic high ground. Language not only shapes the thought processes of individuals but moulds the public discourse about bioethical issues.

When you stop to consider the differences between such phrases as 'methods of procreation' and 'reproductive technology' it begins to become clear why we are losing ground in the fight to preserve the concept of human dignity. Any attempt to argue that embryonic human life is deserving of a particular moral status is undercut when we are using such phrases like 'blastocysts produced by the technological advances of in vitro fertilisation'. The language of the factory and of human dignity is as incompatible as would be the interchangeability of machine and life. Such degradation of language only leads to linguistic confusion and muddy thinking.

Engage Popular Culture

On almost every issue in bioethics, our initial introduction comes not through medical journals, scholarly essays, or even articles on websites. They come from stories and narrative forms. Most of us first learn about infertility and surrogacy through the story of the biblical patriarch Abraham, his wife Sarah, and their servant Hagar. We are exposed to the themes of reproductive technology and genetic engineering through high school book reports on Aldous Huxley's *Brave New World*. And many of our fellow citizens gained their initial exposure to voluntary euthanasia from watching Clint Eastwood's Oscar-winning film *Million Dollar Baby*.

In fact, movies are one of the primary mediums in which bioethical issues are most commonly presented. Most people will react emotionally to such narratives – as the authors and directors intended – but few will examine their intellectual content. We can help illuminate these issues by discussing such films, books, plays and stories from a Christian worldview. This can help guide your friends and family in thinking as a Christian about these issues.

William Wilberforce said his second greatest achievement after seeing the bill passed for the abolition of the slave trade was what he called 'a reformation of morals'. Not in a legalistic sense, but he felt that when an individual accepts the peculiar/fundamental doctrines of the faith – justification by faith, Jesus' death and resurrection, coming judgement – it will lead to moral change and transformation in an individual which will lead to political reformation. That is people who have met Christians in their world, who believe the life-changing doctrines that have been passed on to them, whose hearts have been changed and morally transformed, get into positions of influence, in the corridors of power, whether it's parliament, the judiciary, or the institutions, the arts, media or entertainment, and be salt and light in all these areas, and it'll begin to shape and change society.

Of course, there are boundaries we don't cross. We never compromise our Christian beliefs, but in a democratic society we should collaborate and incorporate with other people who share our objectives. Perhaps even for different reasons with specific public policy goals. I think of people in biblical history – Joseph, Nehemiah, Mordecai, Esther, Daniel – who were able to shape societies which were in many ways quite hostile to their faith and values by, on the one hand, engaging with them, but on the other hand, not becoming personally compromised.

The Value of All of Us

Clearly, the command not to murder plays a vital role in providing healthy limits to society. Yet this commandment isn't just about the negative concept that God is against murder, it is also about affirming a wonderful positive truth. That truth is that we all have value. We are to see each other as made in the image of God.

Now this truth relates not just to such difficult areas as war and euthanasia, but also to everyday life. It applies whenever we meet and deal with other people. It also applies whenever we look in the mirror. We need to assert – and reassert – that all human beings are special. This is important because the media gives the impression that only the beautiful people we see on television and at the cinema, with their perfect teeth, hair and figures, really count. Let me say again, we are all made in the image of God. That applies whether we are world-class athletes or bedridden paraplegics, whether we are models or scarred burn victims, whether we are academic geniuses or struggling to pass the most basic school exam.

When we look at any other human being, whether a tramp or a superstar, we need to remind ourselves that in them we see reflected something of God. Because he made us in his image, we all have a priceless dignity and value.

I want to also remind you that we can break this commandment by simply doing nothing. There have been frequent and disturbing accounts of people being attacked in public while onlookers did nothing, and of people abducted at knifepoint with crowds watching passively. Of course, we are aware of the dangers of interfering in an often-brutal society, but by not intervening we are allowing wrong to happen. Sometimes we need to act in defence of others. Such actions are not just required on the streets of our towns; they may be required at an international level. For instance, I do not believe that we as a nation should stand passively by while genocide is committed. I believe that we are in danger of committing sin by doing nothing when we ignore people in rags whom we could clothe or people who are hungry whom we could feed.

THE ROOTS OF MURDER

The Bible suggests that breaking the sixth commandment is not as far from each of us as we might like to think. The classic example is in the fourth chapter of Genesis. Here the first story of family life soon becomes the story of the first murder as Cain kills his brother Abel.

Anger and Murder: Episode One

I believe the Bible tells us about Cain and Abel not to illustrate how bad some people can get, but rather to emphasise that every one of us could end up like Cain. Cain and Abel were the sons of Adam and Eve, a family line that we all belong to. The two brothers, who could have been both equal and unique, grow up differently. This may reflect a different treatment by their parents. Cain, the firstborn and heir, is given a significant name and becomes a landowning farmer. Abel's name is rather belittling (meaning 'breath' or 'temporary') and he becomes only a shepherd. The two brothers come to bring their offerings to God. Wealthy Cain brings some of the fruit of the ground but Abel brings the best portions of his best animals. We are told that God looked with favour on Abel's offering and not on Cain's. What matters, it seems, is not so much the offering but the attitude of heart behind it. Only Abel's motivation and attitude were acceptable to God. This annoyed Cain and his pride was hurt.

> Cain was very angry, and his face was downcast. Then the LORD said to Cain, 'Why are you angry? Why is your face downcast? If you do what is right, will you not be accepted? But if you do not do what is right, sin is crouching at your door; it desires to have you, but you must rule over it.' (Genesis 4:5–7)

Notice here that God both offered Cain the possibility of change and warned him of the peril that his anger was leading him into. Yet, instead of Cain looking to God in repentance, he ignored the caution, took his brother into a field and killed him. God then asked Cain where his brother was. Cain pretended ignorance and denied any responsibility for his brother. God revealed that he knew of the murder and pronounced judgement on Cain.

Envy, anger, deceit, lack of responsibility, lies, refusing to heed a warning and, ultimately, murder, are all ingredients that can be found in many real-life tragedies today.

Anger and Murder: Jesus Makes the Link

When Jesus taught on the sixth commandment, he broadened the scope.

> You have heard that it was said to the people long ago, 'You shall not murder, and anyone who murders will be subject to judgment.' But I tell you that anyone who is angry with a brother or sister will be subject to judgment. Again, anyone who says to a brother or sister, 'Raca,' is answerable to the court. And anyone who says, 'You fool!' will be in danger of the fire of hell. (Matthew 5:21–22)

Now I am aware that 'Raca' isn't one of the top insults we hear today. It is actually a harsh Aramaic insult, a very strong term for the time that literally means 'empty-head' or 'fool' and implies that the person doesn't actually deserve to be alive. The nearest modern equivalent is probably something along the lines of 'I wish you'd never been born!' or 'drop dead!'

What Jesus is teaching us here is that murder is simply the ultimate and most destructive form of anger. It is where anger, if unchecked, will ultimately end up. God wants not only to stop the action of murder; he wants to go further and stop those thoughts that act as the seeds of murder. In the previous chapter you will remember that Jesus did exactly the same thing with the seventh commandment. There he pointed out that adultery was not simply the outward physical action; it was also the inward action of the heart in lust. Here he makes it clear that the crime of murder is not just the shedding of blood; it is about the hatred that leads up to it.

We see the progression in the story of Cain where uncontrolled anger led to a murderous rage. Jesus, focusing on the seriousness of anger, should make us think. There is no shortage of rage in today's society. We have long used the term 'road rage' to describe aggressive driving. It has since acquired such ill-tempered siblings as 'air rage', 'bike rage' and 'computer rage'.

There is a lot of anger about today, not just on roads but also in offices, shops and, worst of all, homes. While domestic violence isn't a modern phenomenon, what does seem new is the level of violence against women and children. According to the BBC, in the UK more than 10 per cent of women aged between sixteen and nineteen in England and Wales say they have experienced domestic abuse in the past year. The Office for National Statistics' annual report on domestic abuse says they are the group most likely to be victims of it, and women in their twenties and early forties are also vulnerable.

According to the data, about 7 per cent of men who are still in their teens have also experienced domestic abuse. This includes non-physical abuse, threats, force, sexual assault or stalking by a family member or partner, the most common of which is abuse by the latter.[15] The report pulls together data from the police, the government and victim support groups.

The Crime Survey for England and Wales for the year ending March 2017 shows about 1.2 million women and 713,000 men reported being victims of some form of domestic abuse.[16] However, a large proportion would not have gone to the police.

The situation is no better across the Atlantic. 'More than 1 in 3 women and more than 1 in 4 men in the United States have experienced rape, physical violence, and/or stalking by a partner in their lifetime.'[17] It's pretty depressing, isn't it?

If you have been subjected to domestic violence – or if you fear it – take whatever steps necessary for your own safety and seek professional help either from a specialist organisation or from the local social services. If you yourself are the abuser in this situation, then I urge you as strongly as possible to get professional help before you do more damage. Abusive violence is never an appropriate way to show anger.

HOW TO HANDLE ANGER

I now want to spend some time talking about how we can handle anger.

Right Anger

Not all anger is wrong. Anger is a God-given emotion. The root of anger is often the fear of losing something we really care about, whether it's a physical item like a car, or an emotional one like pride.

Saint Augustine said, 'Hope has two beautiful daughters: anger and courage.' Anger at the way the present situation is and courage to believe it doesn't have to stay that way. Given some of the injustices in the world today, it is *good* to feel anger.

Interestingly, the word 'anger' appears 455 times in the Bible and in 375 cases it refers to God. God gets angry. Let's face it, if he didn't get angry, what kind of God would he be? God becomes angry at injustice, hypocrisy and lies and at people who inflict pain on each other. Jesus himself became angry in the temple at the way the money changers and sellers had got in the way of people meeting with God.

However, there is a difference between God's righteous anger and ours. God is perfect and all-knowing and is always justified, both in the way he is angry and the way that he expresses it. We, on the other hand, need to know how to manage our anger.

Types of Human Anger

When it comes to dealing with anger, at least four types of reaction can be identified.

- The *maniac* is a pressure cooker, just waiting to explode. These people have a short fuse and can blow up at any time and in any place. Their anger spills out and is obvious. When they are angry, you know about it. These people can get angry at the slightest thing. If this is you, remember your temper is the one thing you don't get rid of by losing it.

- The *mute* doesn't blow up, they clam up. They are people who cannot or will not show their anger in public or in a relationship. Instead, they just bottle it up. The problem is, when we don't express our anger, our bodies keep the score. Anger eats us up, sometimes literally, and does us no good. Many of those who mute their anger end up with ulcers, depression or other symptoms as a direct result of their bottled-up anger. Sometimes people think this kind of attitude is Christian, but I cannot see how. It is more like the Roman Stoics who tried never to show any emotion. Be assured that if you try to bottle up anger it will still find other ways to come out.

- The *martyr* never gets angry because everything is always their fault. They act like guilt magnets, always blaming themselves for what has happened. These are the people who throw a pity party and invite only themselves.

- The *manipulator* is someone who expresses their anger by getting even. The situation that has annoyed them may never be mentioned again, but they make sure by their actions that they inflict revenge on the person who angered them.

Now if you are anything like me, you have probably seen yourself in all four of those categories. Apart from the manipulator, there are healthy things about the other three responses to anger. The positive side of the maniac is that at least they let their anger out, and you know where you are with them. The negative side is that it can be quite tense either living or working with them. The positive side of the mute is the high level of self-control.

Negatively, they ignore the fact that God wants us to be honest and genuine about our feelings of anger. If problems are not brought into the open, it is hard to see how they can be sorted out. Martyrs don't ever consider themselves to be in the right and therefore have a humble attitude, but allowing yourself to be treated like a doormat is neither wise nor honest.

The ancient philosopher Aristotle said, 'Anyone can be angry – that is easy. But to be angry with the right person, to the right degree, at the right time for the right purpose and in the right way – that is not easy.' Let's face it; most of us do not do very well in managing our anger.

Reflect

So how should we handle our anger? The book of Proverbs isolates at least three causes of anger: injustice, humiliation and frustration. We can see here some of the things that led Cain to be angry. Cain felt aggrieved because he expected that his offering would be accepted. He certainly wasn't humble enough to learn a lesson and admit he had been wrong. Whenever we get angry, it is good advice to try and analyse the reasons for our anger and to be honest about them. Unfortunately, being angry is quite the wrong frame of mind in which to try and analyse anything!

President Lincoln's secretary of war, Edwin Stanton, had some trouble with a Major General who accused him, in very abusive terms, of favouritism. Stanton complained to the President, who suggested that he write the officer a sharp letter. Stanton did so and showed the strongly worded note to the President who applauded its powerful language. 'What are you going to do with it now?' he asked. Surprised at the question, Stanton said, 'Send it off, of course.' Lincoln shook his head. 'You don't want to send that letter. Put it on the fire. That's what

I do when I have written a letter while I am angry. It is a good letter and you had a good time writing it and feel better. Now burn it and write another one.'

Speak when you are angry and you will make the best speech you will ever regret. As we saw in chapter two, the Bible warns us of the danger of the tongue: 'Everyone should be quick to listen, slow to speak and slow to become angry' (James 1:19). Words have power. Can there be any more untrue playground rhyme than 'Sticks and stones may break my bones but words will never harm me'? That is not a nursery rhyme, it is a nursery crime. Many of us can still remember unkind words that were said to us in anger. To understand our anger, we need to take time and, in certain situations at least, keep a hold of our tongue until we are sure we know what we should say, rather than what we want to say.

Have Self-respect and Humility

One of the things that made Cain's anger burn was he couldn't handle the fact that his younger brother was preferred over him. His previously superior position as the firstborn was overturned and he could not cope. His self-worth seems to have been based entirely on his status.

A proper self-respect is the key to managing our anger properly. Self-respect means that we are secure enough in ourselves to know when we are in the wrong and humble enough to admit it. Some people think so little of themselves that they think they are always in the wrong; others are so proud because they think they are always right. We need a correct view of ourselves. On the one hand, because God made us in his image and loves us, we are of very great worth. On the other, as weak, fallible and sinful human beings, our assessment of ourselves may be flawed. We need to have both humility and self-respect.

Deal With the Anger You Feel

The Bible teaches that when we feel there is a problem between us and another person we should go to them and sort it out. In Matthew 5:23–24 Jesus taught that dealing with disagreements was of such a high priority, if someone was worshipping and there was something between them and someone else, they should go and sort it out immediately. The Bible also says that we shouldn't go to sleep angry but should sort it out first. There is great value in this because if we go to bed angry, it will start eating into us. We may have to stay up pretty late to deal with it, but the right thing to do is to sort out our anger in order to clear the air.

This, of course, doesn't give us the excuse to vent our spleen on anyone who crosses our path. Neither does it give us the right to give people a good talking to, just because they have made us unhappy. We need to do everything in humility, love and respect and be prepared to listen to the other person's point of view. Situations that could otherwise escalate into big rows can often be prevented from doing so by the right attitude.

Forgive – Don't Bear Grudges

'Do not take revenge, my dear friends, but leave room for God's wrath, for it is written: "It is mine to avenge; I will repay," says the Lord' (Romans 12:19). The Bible works on the principle that in all our disputes, God is a just judge and he is in charge of handing out punishment in due time. Our job is to forgive, and not to be eaten up by our desire for revenge. It takes more inner strength to forgive than it does to inflict revenge. There are times when the most disarming thing to do in a situation of conflict is to offer appropriate apologies and forgiveness.

Forgiving others doesn't just happen because we feel like it; it happens because we make a decision of our will. Clara Barton, the founder of the American Red Cross, never bore grudges. She was reminded by a friend of a wrong done to her some years earlier. 'Don't you remember?' asked her friend. 'No,' replied Clara firmly, 'I distinctly remember forgetting that.'

Where there is forgiveness and the decision to move on, anger can be constructive and actually good for a relationship or situation. This is how God deals with us.

The LORD is compassionate and merciful, slow to get angry and filled with unfailing love. He will not constantly accuse us, nor remain angry forever. He does not punish us for all our sins, he does not deal harshly with us, as we deserve. (Psalm 103:8–10 NLT)

At the start of this chapter we talked about the dignity that each one of us has because we are made in the image of God. Are we like God in the way we deal with others? In the Bible, Paul encourages Christians to show the fruit of God's presence in their lives: love, joy, peace, patience, kindness, goodness, faithfulness, gentleness and self-control (Galatians 5:22–23).

When you squeeze a tube of toothpaste, what comes out is what is in there. So it is with us. What comes out is what's inside. If we are full of God, there will be evidence of that when we are squeezed. In order to be able to live God's way, we don't need a self-help manual; we need to be changed from the inside out. Jesus does that by transforming us by his Holy Spirit. We all need this transformation because we have all broken Jesus' interpretation of the sixth commandment by our angry words and by our angry attitudes.

All anger is hard to fight. It's a selfish, hot-blooded passion our flesh enjoys indulging. But I find it particularly difficult to fight the sinful anger that I feel I have a right to feel.

This kind of anger is different from irritation or short-term mad flares. We usually know those are wrong because they are usually manifestly wrong. But anger we want to justify typically results when we feel disillusioned, disappointed, discouraged or hurt. It might be because:

- A relational conflict keeps recurring despite countless attempts at resolution.

- An intractable, exasperating personal weakness keeps dogging us despite countless attempts to change.

- We feel trapped in a difficult, painful or apparently dead-end situation.

- A betrayal has left us suffering and our betrayer prospering.

- We are seeking God's guidance on an important decision and he just seems quiet.

- In spite of all our labours and prayers, a reviving, regenerating move of the Holy Spirit in our family, church or community just doesn't come.

We can feel that it's our right to be angry over such things because from our perspective they appear unjust and therefore we feel more a victim than a sinner.

Angry Over Ambiguity

Or perhaps we're angry over the ambiguities such situations raise for us. They leave us with questions. At a high level we know that God promises to work all things together for our good (Romans 8:28) but closer to the ground, where we live, things look more ambiguous and we're confused.

Is it possible things are as they are because we aren't working out our own faith like we should (Philippians 2:12–13)? Are we, like the disciples, not seeing the results we desire because our faith is defective (Matthew 17:19–20)? Are we not praying correctly or praying enough (Luke 18:1–8)? Like the twelve Christians in Ephesus, are we ignorant about something important (Acts 19:1–7)? Do we feel stuck because God isn't acting or because we aren't?

When we look at our situation, we aren't exactly sure. We can think of biblical examples that point in different directions. What does God want from us? Why doesn't he make it clearer?

Frustration builds. Perceived injustice and ambiguity can tempt us to anger. And the anger can feel seductively justifiable.

However, this kind of anger is not righteous anger. A tree is known by its fruit (Luke 6:43–45). We can tell if anger is sinful because we feel its defiling effect of impurity on us.

Righteous anger bears redemptive fruit. In righteous anger, we join God in anger over evil. It is an anger we feel *with* God, not *at* God. This kind of anger moves us towards acts of faith and love and true justice. Righteous anger feels grief (Mark 3:5), and because it is actually an expression of love, a deep displeasure over the way evil defames God and destroys people, it is not arrogant or rude or stubborn or resentful (1 Corinthians 13:4–5). It does not, in reality or fantasy, want revenge (Romans 12:19–20). And since we join God in this love-induced displeasure, it moves towards prayer.

But sinful anger does not bear redemptive fruit. Rather, it leaves us with a grey, burned-over barrenness of exasperated frustration. It produces a sour feeling in the pit of our gut. Sinful anger alienates us from God. It does not move us towards acts of faith and love and true justice, but rather towards acts of selfishness like sullen withdrawal, irritability, rudeness, obstinacy and bitterness. Sinful anger is characterised by the self-oriented grief of self-pity, not godly grief over evil. And it produces cynicism that eats away at faith, eroding our desire to pray.

We all know that sinful anger needs to be dealt with, but this kind is hard to eradicate because its objection is so emotionally compelling: 'But I have a right to be angry!' That's how it feels; how we *want* it to feel. It speaks self-flattering words to us that feed our pride and, like sexual sin, there is a selfish pleasure in indulging it and the sinful part of us doesn't want to stop.

There is only one way to deal with sinful anger: self-humbling. Sinful anger is fuelled by pride, so we have to cut the fuel supply. And most of our anger is diffused in two simple, self-humbling ways.

We must pray. We know that, but the problem is that when sinful anger is roused we don't feel like praying. And that's what we need to remember: expect to not want to pray. Prayer itself is an act of self-humbling faith. Despising our initial emotional resistance, praying from the heart really does begin to diffuse anger. God wants us to be very honest in our prayers. Regardless of perceived injustice, we don't have a legitimate reason to be angry with God. Anger at God is unbelief. But we most definitely need to honestly confess our anger with him, repent as best we can, plead for his help to understand what we can and to trust him with what we can't. He promises to respond to our humility with grace (James 4:6).

We must talk about it. Pride hates confessing sin to other people. If we feel resistance to doing it, it's an indicator that pride is likely at the root. Talking to someone about it wages war on sinful anger. It has a head-clearing effect on us. And objective input helps correct our perspective and honestly address the question, 'Why do I have a right to be angry?' Answering this question out loud often exposes our errant presumptions and pride.

FIND THE WAY OF LOVE

Finally, the good news is that God works with people like us. Think about some of the main figures of the Bible: Moses, David, Paul. What do they all have in common? Yes, they were all followers of God and they are credited with writing large sections of the Bible but, astonishingly enough, they were all people who had committed murder. Yet we do not remember them for this; we remember them for what God did in and through them. And if he can do it in them, he can do it in us.

Two thousand years ago God gave his Son to be murdered, so we could be given life. That death allows us to be transformed from those who hate and who desire to take life, to those who are loving peacemakers and want to give life. We are to be witnesses to a different way of living.

Never in the last two thousand years has that witness been more needed.

1   https://www.theguardian.com/education/2002/feb/23/artsandhumanities.highereducation

2   http://www.lifenews.com/2012/08/10/six-million-abortions-in-the-uk-since-abortion-legalized/

3   https://catholiccitizens.org/uncategorized/82783/abortion-leading-cause-of-death-in-2018-with-41-million-killed/

4   https://assets.publishing.service.gov.uk/government/uploads/system/uploads/attachment_data/file/ 679028/Abortions_stats_England_Wales_2016.pdf

5   https://www.rcog.org.uk/globalassets/documents/guidelines/abortion-guideline_web_1.pdf

6   https://www.ncbi.nlm.nih.gov/pubmed/8765248

7   https://www.telegraph.co.uk/news/health/news/9845780/Cleft-lip-abortions-10-times-as-common-as-reported.html

8   https://en.wikipedia.org/wiki/Sex-selective_abortion

9   https://www.telegraph.co.uk/news/uknews/crime/9794577/The-abortion-of-unwanted-girls-taking-place-in-the-UK.html

10 https://www.utilitarian.net/singer/by/1993----.htm

11 https://www.telegraph.co.uk/news/health/news/9113394/Killing-babies-no-different-from-abortion-experts-say.html

12 http://www.chninternational.com/leo_alexander_.htm

13 Peter Singer, 'Sanctity of Life or Quality of Life?' in *Pediatrics* (July 1983 volume 72, issue 1), https://pediatrics.aappublications.org/content/72/1/128

14 https://www.guinnessworldrecords.com/world-records/first-human-sheep-chimera

15 https://www.bbc.co.uk/news/uk-42093346

16 https://www.ons.gov.uk/peoplepopulationandcommunity/crimeandjustice/articles/domesticabusefindingsfromthecrimesurveyforenglandandwales/yearendingmarch2017

17 https://www.ncjrs.gov/spotlight/family_violence/summary.html

6

HOW TO KEEP THE PEACE WITH OUR PARENTS

COMMANDMENT FIVE: HONOUR YOUR PARENTS

'Honour your father and your mother, so that you may live long in the land the LORD your God is giving you.' (Exodus 20:12)

SO, WHAT'S THE PROBLEM?

Once upon a time, or so it seemed, families were simple. There was a mum, there was a dad and there were kids. Associated with them, and close at hand, were grandmothers and grandfathers, aunts and uncles. The family was a tight, precisely defined unit made up of people who played a well-defined role. The result was enduring; its fixed arrangement of people was only modified by births, deaths and marriages, events so major as to be marked by official ceremonies and certificates. Wars, epidemics and economic depressions came and went but the family continued, scarred but always stable.

The world has changed, and what makes up a family is now difficult to define. Partners get changed with the seasons, people come and people go, there are few if any ceremonies. Most schools no longer have 'Parents' Evenings'– to call them that is to presume too much. Instead they are more cautiously termed 'Progress Evenings'.

It is easy to be nostalgic about the 'good old days' of the nuclear family with a mum, a dad and 2.4 children. The family then was a part of a whole society that has vanished and, however deep our wishes, is not going to return. Another reason against 'forward to the past' solutions is simply that we are called to live in the present, not the past. Besides, memory can easily be over-romantic and selective, and behind the golden glow painted by nostalgia there were problems.

All too often the smiles of the cosy family concealed troubled relationships. In fact, there are some current social patterns that have much to commend them: parents taking joint responsibility in the raising of children; the possibility of victims being able to get out of abusive family situations; society's recognition of the empowerment and dignity of women.

Yet just as we don't want to return to the past, neither can we be complacent about the pain and brokenness of so many people's family life today.

According to recent divorce statistics, 42 per cent of marriages in England and Wales end in divorce. There were 101,077 divorces in 2015 (the most recent year for which official statistics are currently available). This was a 9.1 per cent decrease from 2014 and a 34 per cent decline from the most recent peak in 2003.[1] In fact, figures show that in Britain just 68.9 per cent of children live with both parents – that puts the UK twenty-seventh down the list of thirty countries in the western world.[2] The United States is only slightly better: there, 70.7 per cent of children are living with both parents. It is worth pointing out that children are probably better off in a secure, single-parent family than in a troubled and violent two-parent family. But when families explode, children get caught in the fallout.

Behind these statistics lies great suffering of individuals involved. Figures for the UK demonstrate that the impact of divorce on children is largely negative. Children affected by family breakdown are:

- 75% more likely to fail at school
- 70% more likely to become addicted to drugs
- 50% more likely to have alcohol abuse problems
- 40% more likely to have serious debt problems[3]

These statistics, of course, represent only the families that have failed enough that they have emerged on the statistical radar; they do not show the far greater number of families that are under strain and suffer silently.

The breakdown of families is having an enormous effect in all sorts of other areas. There is undoubtedly increased stress within a single-parent family, with increased demand for smaller housing and increased costs for all concerned.

The problem can be gauged by the fact that we have a whole new vocabulary of 'maintenance agreements', 'access or visitation rights', 'current partners' and 'pre-nuptial agreements'. We must remember that behind all these statistics and words lie real people, real lives and real hurt. The truth is that we don't need figures to prove any of this to us – the statistics only confirm what we have seen happen to friends, neighbours, relations and even ourselves.

So why are families failing? The causes are no doubt complex but, put simply, families are breaking up under pressure. The pressures on the family today have never been greater and come from many areas. In the area of *work*, changing labour patterns have wreaked havoc on family life. The days when it was the full-time (if unwaged and unpraised) responsibility of the mother to mind the family have gone. Indeed, in most cases the recession has made things worse by forcing both parents to go out to work. And having more than a sole breadwinner means the entire family has to negotiate complex timetables in order that, just occasionally, they might all eat and dialogue together. The fact that few jobs now are for life has also combined to put strain on families. Do you move for Mum's job or for Dad's?

In the area of *lifestyle*, there are new pressures. Families might live under the same roof but this might be all they have in common. Whether it's down to different timetables, microwave meals, the tyranny of television, or homework calls being made easier with video chat, I suspect that the average household only sits down to eat together about once each week. Technology has contributed to this rapid cultural change. After all, we no longer have to watch the same programmes on the television; we can always catch up on the internet. Parents used to be concerned about the amount of time their children spent watching television. Now the concern is the amount of time they spend texting, accessing social networking sites and browsing the internet, increasingly accessed through smartphones. In fact, the rise of the smartphone has drastically changed family life.

In 2016, an online survey revealed that half of all teens admit they are addicted to their smartphones and other mobile devices, and nearly 6 per cent of parents say they think their teens are too tech-addled.[4] A 2012 survey of teenagers in the United States aged between thirteen and seventeen showed a dramatic increase in smartphone adoption, with a majority (58 per cent) of teens owning a smartphone, up from 36 per cent the year before.[5] Another recent survey in the US suggests that 68 per cent of smartphone owners claim they 'cannot live without' their device.[6] Although it is too early to be sure of the effects of smartphones and social networking sites on relationships, it does seem that together they are having a major impact in at least two areas. The first is that smartphone users spend a lot of time staring at the little screen. Recent British figures suggest that the average smartphone owner spends more than two hours each day using the device. Of that time, an average of 25 minutes is spent using the phone to browse the internet, 17 minutes on social networking, 13 minutes playing games and 16 minutes listening to music. Those two hours have to come from somewhere, and much of it must come from time that used to be spent in traditional social interaction: talking and listening to others.[7] Certainly one major area of impact is on the family. Why bother to talk to your family in the next room when you can talk to your friend on your phone?

New technology takes away as much as it gives. If you have ever spent time next to someone who is staring at a screen while simultaneously listening to headphones, you will know that while they may be physically present with you, they are in all other respects utterly absent. This new technology communicates with those at a distance while alienating those nearby.

The second effect is that social networking sites and smartphones have changed the pattern of our relationships: from having a small number of strong relationships we now have many weaker and more distant relationships. We connect virtually with the many, rather than connect physically with the few. With digital technology, more is less.

Another major change has been in personal development. Children mature faster and face life-determining decisions at an ever earlier age. Most teenagers have to deal with sexual issues only faced by adults in previous generations. Again, through the internet most teenagers will have been exposed to pornographic images that most previous generations would not dare to imagine. In our age of instant information – of Google and Wikipedia – children struggle to read through books for information. Some people claim that young people are so used to constant on-screen action (in primary colours and with loud sound) they struggle to process the low-key, silent, black-and-white information of books. Perhaps. What is less debatable is the fact that children have become cynically targeted as consumers and customers by fashion firms, phone companies, the music industry and even banks. Some social commentators talk about the 'erosion of childhood as we know it'.

Perhaps the most worrying trend is the way that failure in parenting has become infectious. Let me explain. No one is born a naturally good parent: parenting skills have to be learned. And, as always, we learn more from subconscious imitation than we do from acquisition of knowledge. So, sadly, a child growing up in a failing family unit is likely to pick up bad habits rather than good ones. The bitter result is that the chances of their own marriage failing are heightened. Unless there is a dramatic change, one dysfunctional family is likely to breed others.

How can the family be saved? With the pressures on the family being so great, no amount of government intervention or state-sponsored 'Initiatives for the Family' is likely to do much good. Something more drastic is needed. It is against this background that we come to this fifth commandment to 'honour your father and mother'. What does it mean for us to 'honour' our parents in families that are so fragmented? What can this commandment, based on a culture so different from ours, have to say to us, in a world where the dysfunctional family seems to be normal?

To begin with, it is easy to over-estimate the differences between twenty-first-century-AD Britain and the fifteenth-century-BC Near East. Moses' day was hardly the golden age of the family either. In those days, families didn't consist of a mother, a father and 2.4 children, but were huge, extended and intermingled groups of everybody related by blood or marriage. There were also problems. Frequent wars, famines or epidemics gave rise to many vulnerable widows and orphans (a fact widely recognised in the Old Testament). And with some men practising polygamy, with several wives or concubines (essentially second-class wives with lesser legal rights), there was obvious potential for conflict. The Bible tells of families just as dysfunctional as any we see today. These people knew about the complexities and difficulties of family life.

In these extended families, it was the links between parents and children that held everything together. It was the way that parents brought up, disciplined and taught their children and the way that the adults looked after their own ageing parents that tied these extended families together. In Hebrew society, as in many cultures today, the most important relationships were those between different generations of a family. That is why the Bible lists genealogies. The bonds between parents and their children were the cement that held families – and indeed the whole structure of society – together. The rebellious child, particularly the son, who failed to look after his parents was an outrage. In explaining why the disaster of the exile had come upon the people of Israel, the prophet Ezekiel says that, among other abuses, 'Fathers and mothers are treated with contempt' (Ezekiel 22:7 NLT).

So, what does it mean to 'honour' parents? It means to give them value and respect. It means esteeming them of worth, even if we disagree with them. It rules out any attitude where we reject our parents as worthless. It does not mean automatically obeying them. If it did, we would have the awkward case of Jesus – who went against his mother's wishes – breaking a commandment. I also want us to avoid seeing this commandment as exclusively to do with the relations of parents and children. The fifth commandment addresses the whole concept of the family.

THE HEART OF THE MATTER

The Family is a Gift of God

The good news is that the Bible is positive about families; the family was God's idea. If we return to the earliest chapters of the Christian and Jewish Scriptures, we are struck by the fact that the family is an integral part of being human. God has made us and shaped us for relationships – with each other and with him. Families are the God-designed structures where we can grow and learn to understand ourselves and to relate to others. It is clear that God intended children to be raised by their natural parents and for a monogamous, lifelong, male-female relationship to provide the intimate, secure and supportive environment for a child's nurture until maturity. When in adulthood a child leaves their father and mother to start, by marriage, a new family unit, the old family links are not severed but transformed. The new family acquires a distinct individuality of its own, but the parents are not neglected. God affirms families. There are biblical standards for family living, norms for parental care and the nurturing of children, for unconditional love, respect and honouring of parents by offspring, and a commitment to the welfare of the whole family. We may find these standards hard to keep, we may fall short of them, but they exist.

The Family is Always Under Threat

Even though the Bible sets forward the family as God's ideal, it is under no illusions that making a good family is easy. The fact that there are so many rules and guidelines about families in the Bible suggests that there were always problems to be addressed. Making a family work is hard, and the Bible records many examples of failures, even by the best of men and women. Neither Jacob nor David or Solomon can be held up as models of good fathers. In fact, in the first family history ever recorded, that of Adam and Eve, relations broke down to the extent that one of their children killed another.

The honest portrayal of these calamitous families demonstrates a simple but wise saying: 'the abuse of the best is the worst'. God intended families to be something powerful for good, to be places of belonging and trust, of learning and loving. Yet when family relationships go wrong, their very power can make them places of long-lasting bitterness and hurt.

But that isn't God's fault, it's ours.

God Wants to Help the Family

Faced with these threats to the family, the encouraging news is that God does more than simply lay down a commandment and then frown at us when we mess up. Time and time again we are told in the Bible that God isn't distant or remote. He cherishes us and grieves over us. We are even told that he knows the number of hairs on our heads, a task that, with some of us, gets easier every day!

God sets us an example by being the model parent who cares for and nurtures us. He endorses parenting to the point that he is happy to be considered a parent himself. This idea is there in the Old Testament and, most of all, in the language of Jesus. Jesus talked of God as his

Father and encouraged his disciples to use similar language. In fact, the word he used, *Abba*, is respectfully intimate and corresponds to our word 'Dad'.

I am aware that the idea that God is a father is problematic for some people. Some object to the concept of 'Father God' as 'sexist language' reflecting an offensive patriarchal culture. I can only briefly touch on some of the issues here. First, there are problems with describing God as any gender: male, female or neuter. Secondly, there is a gentle but progressive thrust throughout biblical history that is subversive of the patriarchal culture and seems to quietly undermine it. We even see it in this commandment, which encourages the honouring of not just the father, but both mother and father. But it is seen most clearly in the ministry of Jesus, who risked scandal by treating women as equals. He also – again risking scandal – used the image of himself (and by extension, God) as a mother hen (Luke 13:34).

Others have problems with the idea of a Father God because they have had difficult relationships with their own fathers. The idea that God is like their earthly father, but only larger and in heaven, is enough to send them running. After all, why on earth would we want, trust or feel safe with a God like *that*? I can sympathise. It is, however, worth getting to the root of what the Bible (and Jesus) is really saying when using 'father' language of God. When Jesus talks of God as his Father, he is *not* saying, 'You know your dad? Well, God's like that.' What he *is* saying is that God is everything that a father should be. He is the perfect father; the true ideal. God is like no father anyone has ever known. He is perfectly good, faithful, true and trustworthy. He can always be relied upon. He is the ultimate parent, like the closest, most caring guardian or gentlest mother, and he particularly cares for those who are broken by their upbringing. He is a 'father to the fatherless' (Psalm 68:5). If you find that the image of a good father is hard to grasp because of your own experience, let me offer an illustration. Imagine that the first time you are given a large banknote it turned out to be counterfeit. 'Never again!' you promise and refuse to accept such notes ever after. Of course, that would be foolish because the genuine version of your banknote *does* exist. The same goes for fathers. If you have been disappointed by a 'counterfeit' earthly father, don't let that put you off a relationship with your real, heavenly one.

I have spent some time on this idea of God as a loving and perfect father because it helps us to understand how we are to behave in a family context. We are to model our heavenly Father. The way that he loves us is the way that we should love each other, both within our families and more widely.

God does more than provide an example. He provides the power for healing in families through the Holy Spirit that he gives to all who have come to him through Jesus. You may feel the idea of God as our role model for family relationships is impossible, and that all I am doing is setting you up for a guilt trip. Yet the wonderful truth is that, not only does God command us to be like him, through the power of the Holy Spirit he also *enables* us to be more like him. Some of the deepest teaching on families is to be found in Ephesians 5:21 – 6:4 where Paul talks about the duties and responsibilities of wives and husbands, children and parents. But he prefaces his remarks by commanding the Ephesian Christians to let the Holy Spirit fill and control them (Ephesians 5:18). The Holy Spirit is God's power for the healing of our lives with others. Only with his power can we hope to live out God's pattern for families.

CREATING FAMILIES THAT WORK

I want to talk about some general principles for families, based on a biblical example, then I want to apply these to how we relate to our parents and then to how we relate to our children. Finally, I want to end on a note of encouragement.

Learning from Failure: A Biblical Case Study

The best way to be part of healthy families is to get into healthy patterns of behaviour, not just to deal with the fall-out, but to stop the hurtful behaviour at the root. To illustrate some principles on which to build family life we're going to consider a case study – learning from a family history over three thousand years ago.

At the end of the book of Genesis is the story of Joseph, of *Technicolor Dreamcoat* fame. This saga is a classic example of how families can get into bad patterns. Joseph was the son of Jacob, a man with a complex family.

When Joseph was seventeen years old he often tended his father's flocks with his half-brothers, the sons of his father's wives Bilhah and Zilpah. But Joseph reported to his father some of the bad things his brothers were doing. Now Jacob loved Joseph more than any of his other children because Joseph had been born to him in his old age. So, one day he gave Joseph a special gift – a beautiful robe. But his brothers despised Joseph because of their father's partiality. They couldn't say a kind word to him (Genesis 37:2–4).

Incidentally, the one thing everyone knows about Joseph – his coat – may be incorrect. We really don't know the exact meaning of the word that the older versions translated as 'multicoloured'; it may be 'long-sleeved', but that wouldn't make such a good title for a musical. What we do know is that it was an ostentatious and rather posh coat that clearly indicated to everyone that Joseph was special and that his favoured position carried unique rewards. Joseph was given this coat, we are told, because 'Jacob loved Joseph more than any of his other children'.

As a result of his father's favouritism, Joseph was despised by his brothers. This is hardly surprising. Often, when one child is preferred over another it causes jealousy and feelings of inferiority and of being overlooked. The fact that Jacob had twelve sons by four different mothers (some wives, some concubines) would hardly have produced a stable and secure family setting. Instead, it must have bred insecurity and competitiveness.

This family background clearly had an effect on Joseph who comes over, at this point in his life, as an arrogant and unpleasant young man. Whether his telling tales on his brothers was a result of his brothers' hatred or a contributory factor to it, we do not know. Matters got worse when Joseph revealed some dreams to his brothers and father, the obvious interpretation of which was that they would one day bow down to him.

Irritated beyond their limits, the brothers decided that enough was enough and planned to murder Joseph and blame it on an attack by a wild animal. However, Reuben, the eldest of the twelve brothers, intervened and persuaded them not to kill him. Finally, a compromise was agreed and Joseph was thrown down a pit. Reuben left, intending to come back later to recover his brother and take him home. When he returned it was too late; Joseph had been sold into slavery.

I find it interesting that Reuben, despite being the eldest brother, lacked the authority to stop the whole saga. Previously, Reuben had slept with one of his father's wives. This act of immorality and flagrant breach of the fifth commandment probably undermined any authority he had. There is no evidence that Reuben's father had disciplined him over the matter, and it therefore requires no great stretch of the imagination to see that the children probably despised Jacob as a father. They certainly had no qualms about lying to him.

After many twists, God works it all out for good (see Genesis 50:20). But even in this brief introduction to the story, we see a classic dysfunctional family with fractures developing between parents and children and amongst the children themselves. I think we can draw a number of general lessons from this situation about principles for family life.

Lesson 1: learn to learn

One of the most important things we can ever do is be part of a family. Yet most of us drift through, muddling along and only really considering how we are doing when we hit a family crisis. I want you to think about how you are doing in your family situation, and to seek to learn how to do it better.

Jacob is a man who needed to learn. He himself had been at the rough end of some poor parenting (Genesis 26 – 28) involving favouritism, sibling rivalry and a split between his parents. Yet he seems to have learned nothing from it. The really bad news about bad parenting is that it can get passed down to the next generation. Indeed, I wonder if the Bible is giving us a nudge in that direction when we read at the start of the Joseph story the strange words, 'This is the account of Jacob' (Genesis 37:2 NLT). Hold on, we say, Jacob is hardly the main figure in the story. Surely it ought to be 'This is the account of *Joseph*'? But as the story unfolds, we see that the events are an almost inevitable outworking of Jacob's bad family management.

Jacob seems to automatically pass on his bad habits to his children. This pattern has been repeated throughout history. For example,

King George V was a remote and distant man, always abrupt and cold with his children. Once, when a member of the royal court gently suggested to the King that he might be a little more relaxed with them, he chillingly replied, 'My father was frightened of his father, I was frightened of my father and I'm damned well going to see to it that my children are frightened of me.' This expresses with painful clarity the way failure in families can, if unchecked, echo on for generations. Yet it doesn't have to be that way. Can I urge you, particularly if you are from a family that did not function well, to 'learn to learn'? Look for opportunities to see 'working' families and model your behaviour on them, not on your own past. Over everything you do, say to yourself, 'Is this good?' or 'Can I do it better?' Don't let the past ruin your future. I highly recommend The Parenting Course (www.relationshipcentral.org).

Lesson 2: learn to be fair

A major problem in Jacob's family was his blatant favouritism towards Joseph. While we may not display it quite as openly as Jacob did, a thousand generations later favouritism is alive and well in twenty-first-century Britain.

We need to avoid favouritism and being unfair in our treatment of others in the family. We cannot, of course, make everyone the same, nor should we try to. Some members of our family are more like us and we relate to them more easily. An introverted, musical mother will probably have a closer relationship with a shy, artistic daughter than with her extrovert rugby-playing son. That is not favouritism. Favouritism is when she treats the daughter with more affection than she does the son and gives her preferential treatment. The problem with favouritism is that it hurts the child who is not favoured and fuels the fires of sibling rivalry.

It is easy to slip into being unfair. When, say, a son gets mediocre results compared to his brilliant sister, it is tempting to make hurtful comparisons. We need to learn to stand back, put aside our natural emotions and learn to be absolutely and completely fair.

Incidentally, favouritism is not confined to parents with children. It is also possible for children to takes sides with one parent against another. The same principles of fairness hold true there.

Lesson 3: learn to communicate

Another problem in Jacob's family seems to be that individual members did not communicate with each other. When I read the story, I get the feeling that here are people from the same family who do not know each other. There is no doubt that they *talked* to each other but whether they *communicated* is another matter. There seems little evidence that the brothers really talked things through, either with Joseph or their father. Their hatred seems to have simmered quietly until it manifested in nearly lethal anger.

This problem has not gone away. A lot of talking in families today is simply making words, not engaging in communication. We have all been part of a dialogue like the following:

> A sixteen-year-old daughter went into the front room and asked the assembled family members, 'Has anyone seen my new jumper?'
>
> Her dad replied, 'You mean the one that cost as much as a meal in a restaurant?'
>
> Her grandmother replied, 'You mean the one with the low neckline?'
>
> Her mother replied, 'You mean the one that has to be hand washed?'
>
> Her brother replied, 'The stupid one that makes you look fat?'
>
> Her sister replied, 'The one that you won't let me borrow?'
>
> Everyone was talking about the same jumper, but no one answered her question. There were many words said, but no communication took place.

Good communication has to have both quantity and quality. All too often we find ourselves saying that 'we haven't got time'. What with working late, staggered meals, updating social media, and the TV programmes we have to catch up on, children can easily get squeezed out. There is increasing evidence that today's children are not as good as those of previous generations at engaging in conversation. Making time to talk to our children must take priority over everything else.

The problem is that our work and lifestyles demand more time, and we are left franticly trying to keep all the plates spinning in the air. As a result, the gap between us and our children grows. Shared times become increasingly marked by stilted conversation, criticism or silence. Not spending time with children sends out the message that they are less important than work or other people who might ask for Mummy's or Daddy's time.

In 2015 the BBC produced a report concluding that children growing up in the UK were the unhappiest in the industrialised world, and that part of the problem is a failure of communication and safety in their environment.[8] Parents in more than half the economically advanced countries surveyed, spent more time 'just talking' to their children than those in the UK.[9]

You don't have to be a sociologist to take a reasonable guess at what is going on here. The recognition that there has been a failure to spend time with the children leads to an attempt to compensate by giving gifts. This, of course, leads to a vicious circle where parents work longer hours to earn the money to buy goods for their children, and so spend even less time with them. More talking and fewer toys seems to be a better idea! Our children need our presence more than our presents.

Just as we need quantity in our conversation, we also need quality. It is not enough to set aside time to talk; we need to use it wisely. We have reached a dreadful state of affairs if, whenever a child hears a parent say, 'I want to talk with you,' they think that it is about something they have done wrong. An internet search on 'talking to children' shows that almost all the articles are about confronting difficult issues: death, sex, keeping safe, terrorism attacks and so on. This is all well and good and there are times when we have to have conversations about painful or awkward topics. We also need to be able to honestly express irritation, hurts and even anger. Yet the secret is to spend time talking to children about the normal topics of life, to build up our relationship with them so that when we do have to deal with difficult issues, we have a good basis to build upon.

Where there is intense love, there is also the possibility of intense anger. If we keep brushing things under the carpet, we will only trip over them later. The family ought to be the best forum to honestly discuss problems, feelings and hurts, because it should be a place of security and acceptance. Every family must work out for themselves how this works in practice, but I cannot stress enough how healthy it is to talk things through. Even if things get heated, it saves them growing and mushrooming into bitterness and resentment.

I want to make a particular plea here for fathers to be more involved in talking to their children, particularly their sons. For a number of years now, people have been talking about the 'Dad Deficit', where some fathers have had little or no involvement with their sons.[10] Bringing up boys cannot be 'left to Mum'. All the evidence suggests that if fathers take an interest in their sons, it helps to encourage self-confidence. Susan Faludi, a social commentator who has researched and written on the 'American Man', was surprised to find how many men really wanted to talk about their fathers. She wrote: '"My father never taught me how to be a man" was the refrain I heard over and over again.'[11] It is curious that thoughtful parents will concern themselves with their child's educational and financial welfare but somehow feel it possible to ignore their social and psychological needs.

Incidentally, this does not just apply to *young* children. Research in the United States suggests that shared time between parents and teenagers is important for their well-being. According to Professor Susan McHale of Penn State University, 'research shows that, well into the adolescent years, teens continue to spend time with their parents and that this shared time, especially shared time with fathers, has important implications for adolescents' psychological and social adjustment'.[12]

We need to learn to talk with each other now, or we will shout at each other later.

Lesson 4: learn to forgive

The most basic attitude we need to have is to be givers (and receivers) of grace, kindness and forgiveness. If we are not then not only will we carry hurts and wounds around with us, but we will pass them on to others.

Even in the best families, large doses of forgiveness are often needed. In every family there will inevitably be different temperaments and personalities. This creates the potential for tension, disagreements and clashes. The problem with dealing with disagreements within families is that unlike, say, work, the people concerned are not simply going to go away. While you can choose your friends, you have to live with your family.

The key ingredient to resolving disagreements and clashes within a family is our willingness to forgive and to be forgiven. Forgiveness, of course, is never easy and this is particularly true when the other party is not sorry. Nevertheless, for our own good if nothing else, we must forgive unconditionally. Only in that way can we release the pain that we feel from being let down and hurt by members of our family, and move on. One very respected doctor wrote: 'The psychological truth is that holding on to our past resentments towards parents robs us of our current peace of mind and our ability to experience satisfaction in the here-and-now relationships.'[13]

Now I know that asking anyone to forgive unconditionally is difficult. If you have been significantly hurt by your family, it can often be of great benefit to receive professional help. If you carry huge burdens and resentment because of family problems, I urge you not to hide or ignore them, but to begin to deal with them.

To help you here I want to attack two commonly heard statements that I believe are very harmful. The first is *to forgive is to forget*. I think this is rather patronising and belittles the horrendous experiences that some children and spouses have gone through. Many people hold back from forgiving because they incorrectly assume that if they forgive they will have to minimise (or even forget) painful things that happened to them. I can forgive my parents without minimising the pain they caused me. Forgiveness allows us to build something positive in the present while making sure we don't repeat what happened in the past. While forgetting is not the automatic result of forgiving, the act of forgiveness means a start to healing and, from that, forgetting *may* in time come.

The second cliché is that *time is a great healer*. It may be, but without forgiveness it is all too possible that hurt is simply driven into the subconscious where it festers away. It is important to deal with grievances as soon as we can. Again, God helps us here. We have a God who is forgiving and gracious and knows all about unconditional forgiveness and what it can cost. What do you think the cross was all about?

Even with the power of the Holy Spirit working in your life, I cannot in all honesty guarantee you a quick fix or pain-free solution. But I am certain that God has all the resources you need to enable you, if you are truly willing, to forgive the one who has hurt you and leave that resentment behind.

RELATING TO OUR PARENTS: GIVING HONOUR

We've looked at good qualities to have in our families, but what does it mean to really honour our fathers and mothers?

Accept Them

The first thing we need to do is to accept our parents. The Bible gives us some helpful advice here about what that means in practice: 'Listen to your father, who gave you life, and do not despise your mother when she is old' (Proverbs 23:22). We are to respect our parents and not despise them.

Now, God isn't asking us to pretend that they are perfect when they are not, or that they are always right. We are instructed to honour our parents despite their faults and failings. In court, we address the judge as 'Your Honour'. That has nothing to do with our attitude to their personality; it simply shows our respect for a judge's position and authority. 'Honouring', likewise, is an act of duty that applies to our parents.

For good or ill, we must remind ourselves that they are *our* parents. Nothing we do can change that fact. We must learn to accept them.

Appreciate Them

Even if we find our parents difficult, we can appreciate them for their effort in bringing us up. Parenting is a difficult, time-consuming and demanding responsibility. It is easy to criticise parents when we are young but, interestingly, criticisms tend to wane when children become responsible for parenting themselves. In fact, we have probably learned far more than we think from our parents. Many of the skills, abilities, attitudes and interests we pride ourselves on have been passed on to us by our parents.

One of the greatest things our parents pass onto us is their wisdom, a fact repeatedly recognised by the Bible. 'My son, obey your father's commands, and don't neglect your mother's instruction' (Proverbs 6:20 NLT). Often, children think they know best and there is nothing their parents could possibly say about the situations they find themselves in. Actually, one real way in which parents can be honoured is by their children asking, listening and even heeding their advice and wisdom.

It does not hurt to find practical ways to express our appreciation too: a card and gift on Mother's or Father's Day, a regular phone call, a diversion from a trip to pass by and see them. Simple appreciation and gratitude can make all the difference in family relationships.

Affirm Them

We honour our parents by affirming them. To affirm someone means to strengthen and support them. One way is by voicing our praise to them. Praise, of course, is not the same as flattery. We all know flatterers whose smooth tongues will say anything to get on someone's right side. Praise is different; it is affirming something about someone that we know and have experienced to be true. Have you ever told your parents how grateful you are for all they gave you, for all they taught you? If not, why not do it now? A letter is perhaps the best way. Even hearing simple words of thanks means a great deal to all parents – I can vouch for it.

Another way to affirm our parents is by involving them in our lives; discussing work and home issues with them. This is especially true if we have left home. It might be that in the end we do not take their advice, but for them to feel they have been consulted is a good way of honouring them.

We can also affirm our parents in how we speak to them. We need to be more respectful in the way we talk to the 'older generation'. After all, one day we will be part of it.

Avoid Abandoning Them

As parents get older, the way we honour them is not to abandon them. The question of how to deal with the needs of ageing parents, without compromising our responsibilities to our own immediate families, is a complex issue.

The New Testament lays down the general principle that there is a duty to care for the elderly and vulnerable within our families. 'If a widow has children or grandchildren, these should learn first of all to put their religion into practice by caring for their own family and so repaying their parents and grandparents, for this is pleasing to God' (1 Timothy 5:4). Each family will need to weigh up the particular situations their parents face as they get older. There is no doubt that at times we may feel put out, inconvenienced and frustrated. However, honouring our parents is a duty that should continue whether it is easy or hard.

Act Now

There are two distinctive features about the fifth commandment: it is the only command with a promise attached and it is the only one that doesn't last a lifetime. A day will come when at a hospital bedside or in the funeral parlour we will realise that death has removed the opportunity for us to carry out this commandment. This, then, is an urgent ·command; when our parents die, it is too late and our opportunity has gone. A friend of mine is a minister who officiates at many funeral services. He finds that when he visits the families, he only hears praise for the dead parent. He says it seems that they only bury saints! However, he knows that in reality the families often didn't get on, that there was a huge amount of pain, remorse and anger, and much left unsaid and unforgiven at death. No amount of expense on a fine funeral is equal to a thank you, a visit, a letter or a phone call while we still have the opportunity.

We must not wait for a crisis in which death threatens either us or them to make peace with our mother and father. We must start right now.

To honour our parents means to obey them in our younger years, to support them in their older years and to respect them through all the years.

Let me add a personal and hard-earned footnote to this advice on honouring parents. This is a hard commandment. I have struggled with what it means for me to honour my father and mother. To say that my relations with my parents have been strained is an understatement. They both refused to come to my wedding. It is hard to honour your parents when what they do seems to be so dishonouring to you. Yet my wife Killy and I have endeavoured to fulfil our side of this commandment. It has not been easy.

RELATING TO OUR CHILDREN: EARNING HONOUR

This commandment works both ways. Yes, it says children have a duty to honour their parents. But I believe it also implies that parents need to earn the right to be honoured.

Work at Parenting

As we have seen, parenting ability is not an automatic skill. Unfortunately, no manual comes attached to a baby. In fact, it appears to be an extraordinary inconsistency that in order to adopt a child in Britain you have to pass stringent tests and meet all sorts of criteria, but anyone can have a child the good old-fashioned way without having to pass any test at all.

Earlier I encouraged you to 'learn to learn' about parenting. I would, though, advise caution about using rigid methods. Parenting involves the careful use of a series of flexible skills, not the rigid, unyielding application of an exact science. Children do not come off some digital production line in manufactured perfection; instead, parents have to work with living and developing creatures with very individual (and often wayward) temperaments and wills. Flexibility is a great virtue: what may work with one child may not work with another. I sometimes think that by the time we get the hang of parenting, our children have left home. The Earl of Rochester wrote in the seventeenth century, 'Before I got married I had six theories about bringing up children; now I have six children and no theories.' In the three hundred years since, all that has happened is the number of theories has multiplied while the success rate has stayed the same.

In the sad story of Joseph's upbringing he was singled out for preferential treatment, partly because he was born to Jacob in his old age, but also because he was born to Rachel, the wife whom Jacob loved above the others (Genesis 29:30). The stability of the parental relationship is pivotal to family life. Part of the problem with Jacob's children undoubtedly came from the unstable relationships between him and the four women who bore him children. The nature and quality of the parents' relationship has lifelong consequences for the children. As we have seen elsewhere, one commandment reinforces another; keeping the 'no adultery' rule is a good basis for this fifth commandment.

A stable marriage is the best possible foundation for a solid family and the greatest gift any parent can give a child is to love their spouse.

The number of lone mothers with dependent children in the United Kingdom in 2017 was 1.6 million.[14] According to 'Custodial Mothers and Fathers and Their Child Support: 2009', a report released by the US Census Bureau, there are approximately 13.7 million single parents in the United States, and those parents are responsible for raising 22 million children.[15]

On both sides of the Atlantic we have a lot of single parents, and I feel it is important to say something to any of you who are in such a situation, whether it results from a failed relationship, a divorce, a separation or death. You belong to a group of people whom I especially want to affirm. Remember that God knows you; he knows your situation and he knows all the circumstances you face. I can only guess at how tough it is, bringing up children on your own. My wife Killy and I have found it hard enough bringing up three children *together*. That single parents manage at all (and many manage very well) fills me with awe and respect.

What I do know is there are stories in the Bible where God supports a lone parent – comforting, healing, providing, taking away any shame and blessing them.

Helping Parenting

Here I want to address not parents or children, but the church. Although the Bible affirms parenthood from beginning to end, there is also something else going on. Jesus, in fact, offers a number of cautions about families. One of the sternest passages is to be found in Matthew 10:34–37:

Do not suppose that I have come to bring peace to the earth. I did not come to bring peace, but a sword. For I have come to turn 'a man against his father, a daughter against her mother, a daughter-in-law against her mother-in-law – a man's enemies will be the members of his own household.' Anyone who loves their father or mother more than me is not worthy of me; anyone who loves their son or daughter more than me is not worthy of me.

This is not an isolated passage; see, for instance, Matthew 12:46–50, Luke 12:51–53 or 14:26–27. Jesus seems to be warning that although they are good, family relationships should not be allowed to take priority over the most important relationship of all: following Christ. There is a profound saying that 'the good is the enemy of the best' and this applies very clearly in the area of following Jesus.

Jesus goes even further than simply expressing caution about the family. In Mark 3:31–35 we read:

> Then Jesus' mother and brothers arrived. Standing outside, they sent someone in to call him. A crowd was sitting around him, and they told him, 'Your mother and brothers are outside looking for you.'
>
> 'Who are my mother and my brothers?' he asked.
>
> Then he looked at those seated in a circle around him and said, 'Here are my mother and my brothers! Whoever does God's will is my brother and sister and mother.'

Here we see Jesus not just putting limits on the role of a biological family but setting out the pattern of a replacement family based around himself. Similar views can be found in Mark 10:29–30, Luke 18:29–30 and Matthew 19:29. The rest of the New Testament develops the idea that Jesus' followers can become an alternative family. When we become believers in Christ, we become the sons and daughters of God (John 1:12–13). As such, we enter into a new relationship with God in heaven and can now see him as our heavenly Father. Because we are now in what you might call a right *vertical* family relationship with God, we express this in a right *horizontal* relationship between those who are called to be children of God. There is a great deal in the letters of the New Testament about how people from very different backgrounds are now united together into the household of God (see Acts 2:42; Ephesians 2:11–22; Colossians 3:11–15).

This has two implications. First, those of us who are believers in Christ but who have happy and satisfying families should realise that we also have a responsibility to a second family: the church. We should willingly give our time, our talents and our treasure to build up this community and we should welcome into it all who have come to faith in Christ.

The second implication is for those who have come to faith in Christ but do not have good human families. Whether this is due to geographical separation or because coming to faith has cost you your family, whatever the cause, you should find new brothers and sisters in the church. Some religions impose penalties on those who 'break faith' and so the price of following Christ is often separation from the family. The Christian church needs to be able to provide an alternative family for these people, as well as for single people and single parents.

In fact, we all need church to be a family and at times we will all need to lean on this God-given family. It may be in comfort, support, advice and prayer; it may be in practical ways like babysitters or meals; or even in bigger practical ways like shelter, finance and holidays. Please do not think that if you do have such wants or needs, it is because you have failed. It is because God allows us to need each other. In fact, you will often find that the most generous and helpful people in a church are those who, at some earlier point in their life, were blessed by the church being a family for them. We receive when we are in need and we give out when we have plenty: that's what families are all about.

To be an alternative family means doing far more than saying polite words to someone over a cup of coffee after the church service. To become an alternative, supportive family will require costly sacrificial action on our part. But unless we do this we are hardly modelling authentically biblical Christianity. It was always important for the church to provide a family for those without families. As our societies become more introspective and individualistic, it is more important than ever that the church models an alternative to the biological family.

So, I want to ask a hard question of those of you who are involved in leading churches. *Is your church a place where the single parent – or even the single person – can find a home?* Can you read that paragraph above and say, 'Yes, thank God, that is true of our church; we are a family for those without family'? I'm sorry to ask such an impertinent question but I feel it may be easier if it comes from me now, rather than Jesus later.

Enforce Discipline

Let me say something about the unpopular subject of discipline within families. Discipline is urgently needed these days. Some families can trace their ancestry back three hundred years but can't tell you where their children were last night.

No parent enjoys practising discipline and I'm sure all of us wish for families in which it is never needed. Yet the principle of discipline is good, and indeed the Bible tells us that God 'disciplines the one he loves' (Hebrews 12:6). God disciplines us because he does not want to see us hurt. That pattern should be the model for our discipline. The purpose of discipline is never to inflict pain or shame; it is to help teach a child so they will learn and not harm themselves in the future. A failure to discipline is a failure to love, a point made by the book of Proverbs: 'Those who love their children care enough to discipline them' (Proverbs 13:24 NLT). Jacob, it seems, refused to discipline Reuben for his immorality. This caused them both harm, making the father seem ineffectual and stripping the son of respect.

A detailed discussion on the practice of discipline is beyond the scope of this book, but one suggestion of imposing discipline may be the removal of privileges (phone or computer is a good start). However, when any punishment is imposed a number of rules must be obeyed:

- It should be strictly limited and there should be no risk of physical harm.
- It should not be psychologically hurtful. It is worth noting that some non-physical punishments, such as humiliation, can be very damaging.
- It should never be carried out in rage.
- It should be agreed between both parents.
- It should be appropriate to the offence.
- It should not be carried out unless there was a clear and wilful breach of some previously defined limit.
- It should be explained.
- It should not be cruel.
- It should be followed immediately by an affirmation of love.

Once punishment is carried out, the matter should be closed; the price has been paid.

We parents must be careful. The Bible says, 'Fathers, do not embitter your children, or they will become discouraged' (Colossians 3:21). Centuries ago Martin Luther said, 'To spare the rod and spoil the child is true. But beside the rod keep an apple to give him when he has done well.'

And on that note let me move on to the positive counterpart to discipline – praise.

Praise Them

An atmosphere of praise is the best environment for children and parents to grow. Giving praise is not easy in a culture where it is cool to use sarcasm and cynicism, so parents must set an example. One of the saddest things is to see a parent who grinds down their children. The result is children who have become crushed and lack self-confidence. Yet if parents can learn to create an atmosphere of praise by being quick to compliment and credit and slow to criticise and condemn, their children will thrive and grow. Not only that, but through this they will teach them how to relate to others. This will be of great blessing in the future.

Learn to Let Go

Parents can nurture an atmosphere of acceptance by giving space to their children. Tempting as close control is, we can be too protective. After one couple had just had a child, there were complications and the baby girl had to be taken away from her mother to the intensive care ward. The new mother was distraught; her baby was just hours old and already she had been taken away from her. Later on that day, her own mother came to visit her and said, 'Today – the day you gave birth, my daughter – you have had to learn the most difficult but the most important lesson of parenting: to let them go.'

Letting go doesn't mean letting children do anything they want, but it does mean freeing them to be themselves, letting them make their own mistakes and letting them learn the hard way. However much we might want to, we parents cannot live our children's lives for them.

Accepting love frees, protects and ultimately releases. One of the wisest sayings about raising children is that it is a parent's responsibility to give their children 'roots and wings'.

BE ENCOURAGED

Even if our experience of family has been a positive one, we would all agree that it is hard work. Both parenting and relating to parents is tough. Two mothers were talking: the first said, 'My daughter doesn't tell me anything. I'm a nervous wreck.' Puzzled, the second mother looked at her, 'My daughter tells me everything and I'm a nervous wreck.'

If You are Struggling with Parenting

If you are struggling with parenting, then let me remind you that God is for you and what you are doing. He understands. Indeed, it may help you to realise that Jesus probably understands far more than you think about having a family. You see, the last we hear of Mary's husband, Joseph, is when Jesus is twelve. Afterwards there is no mention of him and it seems probable that he died some time before Jesus started his ministry. If this is so then Jesus, as the eldest son, would have taken on the responsibility of being head of a household that included a number of younger children. He knows what it is like.

Not only does God sympathise but he longs to help. He has provided us with resources in Jesus, the Holy Spirit and the church to enable us to parent faithfully.

If You are Struggling with Parents

One of the most fascinating incidents in the gospels comes when Jesus' mother, together with his brothers and sisters, came to take him away from the crowd (Mark 3:31–35). They had heard rumours of what he was doing and were worried that he was going out of his mind, so they thought they were doing it for his sake and for the sake of the family. Jesus is forced to defend his own ministry against their well-meaning attempts to intervene. Often the cry of children caught up in family difficulties is, 'But no one understands.' Jesus does. His family misunderstood him. If you feel everyone else is against you, make sure you remember that God knows what you are going through.

Yet at the same time, Jesus was actually the model son. Some of his last words on the cross were to arrange for the apostle John to look after his mother.

Again, we see that not only does God sympathise with us, but he desires to help, and the resources of Jesus, the Holy Spirit and the church are available to us.

Have Hope

Above all, I want you to remember that God can transform things. It is easy to be discouraged; families are an area where we all make mistakes. There are casualties of 'family' everywhere – not just openly broken families, but the ones which appear secure but have tensions below the surface. Your experiences and regrets over your own family may have cast a shadow that you feel powerless to break free from. Yet God can forgive and can change things, even the worst things.

The good news is that God wants to help us make families work. Jesus came, died and rose again so the gap between people and God might be restored. He also came so that our relationships with each other might be healed.

1   https://www.crispandco.com/site/divorce-statistics/
2   https://www.bbc.co.uk/news/uk-20863917
3   https://www.eauk.org/culture/statistics/family-life-in-the-uk.cfm
4   https://www.nbcnews.com/health/kids-health/half-all-teenagers-are-addicted-their-smartphones-survey-finds-n566811
5   https://fortune.com/2012/09/10/nielsen-58-of-american-teens-13-17-now-own-smartphones/
6   https://digitalcontentnext.org/blog/press/todays-smartphone-user/
7   https://www.telegraph.co.uk/technology/mobile-phones/9365085/Smartphones-hardly-used-for-calls.html
8   https://www.bbc.co.uk/newsround/33977706
9   https://www.theguardian.com/society/shortcuts/2012/jun/27/why-british-children-so-unhappy
10 http://www.fatherhoodinstitute.org/2008/the-dad-deficit-the-missing-piece-of-the-maternity-jigsaw/
11 Susan Faludi, *Stiffed: The Betrayal of Modern Man* (William Morrow & Company, reprint edition 2019)
12 https://news.psu.edu/story/147370/2012/08/21/research/time-parents-important-teens-well-being
13 Harold H. Bloomfield and Leonard Felder, *Making Peace with Your Parents* (3rd edition, Ballantine Books, 1990)
14 https://www.statista.com/statistics/281640/lone-parent-families-in-the-united-kingdom-uk-by-gender/
15 https://www.verywellfamily.com/single-parent-census-data-2997668

7

HOW TO PREVENT BURNOUT

COMMANDMENT FOUR: REMEMBER GOD'S DAY OF REST

For in six days the LORD made the heavens, the earth, the sea, and everything in them; but on the seventh day he rested. That is why the LORD blessed the Sabbath day and set it apart as holy. (Exodus 20:8–11 NLT)

SO, WHAT'S THE PROBLEM?

Time is relative. Albert Einstein remarked, 'There certainly seems less of it about than there used to be.' I wonder how often you have heard yourself say:

'I'm too busy.'
'It's been all go.'
'There aren't enough hours in the day.'
'I don't know where all the time goes.'
'The week's simply flown.'

Technology has achieved wonders in almost every area. Entire shelves of books and DVDs have been shrunk onto fingernail-sized chips on smartphones, and sports matches can now be streamed and watched live from the other side of the world. Yet no one has been able to multiply time. The best that technology has done is to allow us to measure ever more accurately how fast time flies. Our ancestors, listening to the steady ticking of clocks, were reminded that their time was slipping away. We stare at spinning digits on screens, much more accurate, but the feeling is the same. Time is fixed and unalterable and, whatever we do, it slips away from us.

It is because time is so fundamental and unchangeable that it is the most precious commodity we have. We are masters of so much but, whatever our wealth, we still cannot create more time. Time cannot be bought, sold or stored. Time passes at the same rate for the rich as it does for the poor. In fact, attempts to create more time are often counterproductive. Consider the following story:

A business executive, talking into his smartphone, is walking across a beautiful sun-drenched beach. Over his phone conversation he can hear the sound of the waves and the seagulls crying. Ahead of him, a man in simple clothes is dozing in the shade of a fishing boat that has been pulled up onto the beach. As he passes, the fisherman wakes up and the executive, now waiting for a call to be returned, decides to make conversation.

'The weather is great; there are plenty of fish; why are you lying around instead of going out and catching more?'

The fisherman replies gently, 'Because I caught enough this morning.'

'But just imagine,' the executive says, 'if you went out three times a day and brought home three times as much fish. You know what could happen?'

Puzzled, the fisherman shakes his head.

'Why,' says the executive, becoming enthusiastic, 'you could buy yourself a motorboat. Then, after perhaps three years, you could have a larger boat – or two. And just think, one day you might be able to build a freezing plant – you might eventually even get your own helicopter for tracing shoals of fish and guiding your fleet of boats. You could even acquire your own trucks to ship your fish to the capital, and then . . .'

'And then?' asks the fisherman.

'And then,' the executive concludes triumphantly, 'you could be calmly sitting at the beach side, dozing in the sun and looking at the beautiful ocean!'

The fisherman replied, 'What do you think I'm doing now?'

In our pursuit of time we sometimes lose more than we gain.

'Time is money' we say, but we mislead ourselves – time is more than money. Money can be replaced; time cannot. Actually, 'time is priceless'. If we knew this, we might treat our hours and days with more respect. Because time cannot be traded, how we use it is vital. And, as in so many other areas of life, when it comes to our use of time we are in an utter mess.

One of the most played pieces of classical music is Beethoven's Symphony No. 5 in C Minor. It's immediately recognisable because of its iconic opening, a four-note motif that is among the most famous in western music. But did you know that it actually begins with silence? Beethoven inserted an eighth rest before the first note.

Beethoven's Fifth is so familiar to us that it's difficult to recreate the full effect it had when it debuted at Vienna's Theater an der Wien on 22nd December 1808. And although it's difficult to discern Beethoven's original intent, that eighth rest served as a sonic buffer. At the beginning of a concert there is ambient noise: conversations between concertgoers, a few stragglers finding their seats, the rustling of programmes. A bit of silence at the beginning of a symphony is ear cleansing, even if it's only an eighth rest. It was silence that set up that symphony and the same is true in our lives.

We need more eighth rests, don't we? Especially if we want our lives to be symphonies of God's grace. I would recommend an eighth rest at the beginning and end of the day. A few moments to collect our thoughts, count our blessings, and pray our prayers. We also need a day of rest one day a week.

God's message is clear: 'If creation didn't crash when I rested, it won't crash when you do.' It is not our job to run the world. We must maintain our inner balance and REST:

Routine, to maintain it

Emotions, to manage them

Sabbath, to remember it

Thoughts, to conquer them

Our modern lifestyles are ruthless. We never leave the office without our inbox constantly accessible from our pockets. We no longer have office hours; we carry our office wherever we go. Statistics and experience show that while we now work harder and earn more, we have less time or energy to enjoy the money we've made.

More Americans than ever before suffer from stress, depression and anxiety, with those affected often too poor to afford general medical treatment. Based on analysis of federal government figures from 2006 to 2014, a study found that around 8.3 million people suffer from some form of serious psychological distress (SPD), which is defined as a mental health problem serious enough to require medical treatment. This makes up 3.4 per cent of adult Americans, an increase on the 3 per cent recorded as having mental illnesses in a survey almost a decade ago, according to the research published in the journal *Psychiatric Services*.[1]

Pressure is enormous. It has been claimed that during any twenty-four-hour period we receive over three thousand messages seeking to persuade us that we need something we do not have. I can well believe it. Far too much of our time is spent working to pay for things that we can't afford and don't need.

And on top of earning a living, there is so much more to do. If we were to list everything that we had to do today, then for most of us it would run onto several sides of paper. There are friends to phone or text, exercise to take, appointments to make, computer software to upgrade, shopping lists to write, books to read, films to watch, emails to answer, web pages to browse, social media to update, hobbies to pursue. We know that our time is finite, but the demands on our time seem infinite. The responsibilities and requirements we face day by day seem overwhelming. The chances are that if I asked you to tell me how you are, the word 'busy' would come up in the first few sentences. We end up with so many irons in the fire that we put the fire out.

Any moments of time we save in one area of our life seem to be snatched away from us. Technology promised to make our lives easier but computers, smartphones and email have increased the pace and demands of work rather than diminished them. We were delighted when the boss gave us a shiny new notebook computer; we are less impressed when we realise it means we no longer leave work, we just take it home with us. From transport to communications, from industry to entertainment, time saved is constantly eroded, whether by greater travelling distances, more appointments or 'enhanced productivity requirements'. In fact, so bizarrely twisted is human nature that if we are not rushed off our feet we begin to fret. 'What's wrong with me?' we say, as we look up from our novel and realise that everyone else on the train or plane is working. In the twenty-first-century West, people seem to feel guilty about relaxing!

All this ceaseless rushing around inevitably has a physical effect on us. If your body could talk, what would it say to you at this moment? I expect it would say 'slow down' or 'take a break'. When we refuse to co-operate with God's laws for our body's proper maintenance, we run the risk of malfunction. Our modern lifestyle of hustle and bustle places us in the grip of what psychologist Paul Tournier called 'universal fatigue'. We constantly complain about how tired we feel. We wake up in the morning and look at the clock in disbelief: 'It can't be morning already – I'm still tired!'

How many times have you said, 'I wish I had just a few more hours in the day?' The assumption is that – given more hours – you would accomplish everything you need to, with less stress. But there is just as much chance that, given this wish, it would only mean a few more hectic hours to live through. Perhaps we should actually be wishing for a shorter day in which the crazy pace of our lives is limited to fewer hours. We have bought into the idea that the busier we are, the more important our life is.

In the middle of such overwhelming pressures, one of the things we need to do is to evaluate our priorities. If we don't live by priorities, we will live by pressures.

In the fourth commandment, God speaks directly about how we order our time. One day in seven, we are told, we need to have a holy day in which we do not work. It is my strong belief, based on the Bible and supported by my own experience, that we need to revive the biblical practice of setting aside one day a week to rest. For the sake of our health, our sanity, our families, our relationships, our spirituality and our society, we all need a Sabbath.

I realise that this is harder than it has ever been. Only twenty-five years ago, if you walked down any road on a Sunday, the only shop open would have been the newsagent, and your town centre would have been eerily silent. Many people are not old enough to remember those Sundays: our world has changed. Now our town centres and shopping malls echo with the sounds of people and traffic, and there is professional sport almost everywhere.[2] And many of us have grown used to having things open. The idea of going back to silent Sabbaths is hardly going to be popular. Besides, people protest, we don't have time to take a day off.

We profoundly misunderstand this commandment if we think it is God making another burden for us. On the contrary, the Sabbath is God's gift to us. If human beings were not so distorted by sin, God could have dealt with this topic as a gentle 'Maker's Recommendation' along the lines of 'Your creator advises that you will function better if you take one day off in seven'. The fact is that because God knows taking a day off is so contrary to our desires, he has made it a rule. In this commandment, God is ordering us to take a break.

THE HEART OF THE MATTER

Taking this commandment seriously doesn't mean simply putting the clock back and trying to get everything shut down on Sundays. In fact, as you have probably found out by now, all the commandments require serious thought as to how we apply them today. What we need to do first is to delve a bit deeper into why this commandment was given.

This command is the longest one in the Ten Commandments. That is not only because God wants to make it clear that it applies to everyone (sons, daughters, workers, visitors and animals!) but also because God sets out the reasons for it being given. It is linked with how God himself works. Since we are made in his image, and are patterned after him, we must listen carefully.

The Rhythm of Life

God bases his ruling of a Sabbath rest on the way that he created the universe. Now I know that there are different theories on how the first couple of chapters of the Bible are to be interpreted. Personally, I think to have an argument about whether God took six twenty-four-hour time spans to make the universe misses the point. The point of the Genesis account is not to tell us scientifically how God created the universe; if nothing else that would spoil the challenge of science. No, it is to answer those really important questions that science cannot answer: who made the world and why. Everything, Genesis says, was brought into being from nothing by the will of the one supreme God. The universe isn't the product of a random and impersonal nature (as modern atheists see it). It is the deliberate creation of a personal, all-powerful, perfect and loving God.

Into this vast universe God himself has imprinted an order and rhythm that can be seen at every level. Whether in the cells of our body, in the flow of our blood or in the vast carbon and oxygen cycles of the atmosphere, there are regular pulses and beats as energy and elements are interchanged. The most prominent and unmistakable examples of rhythm occur in the heavens: the earth rotates on its axis, giving night and day; its path around the sun gives seasons; the moon's orbit produces monthly cycles and tides. These rhythms come from God who ordered, 'Let lights appear in the sky to separate the day from the night. Let them be signs to mark the seasons, days, and years' (Genesis 1:14 NLT). As human beings, a response to these daily, monthly and yearly rhythms occurs at a very deep level. We sleep and wake, eat and drink, grow and develop in similar rhythmic patterns. Attempts to modify or ignore the frequency of these cycles can produce negative results – as I can frequently testify when I have jet lag!

As if to emphasise that he is a God of rhythm, God tells us that he worked in creating the universe on a daily basis and that he himself rested at the end of his efforts. The principle of regular work followed by rest has the highest endorsement possible: it comes from our creator himself. Not only that, but as human beings made in his image, this rhythm of labour followed by leisure is inherited from our heavenly Father. It's in our blood.

WHAT IS GOD'S DAY OF REST?

Before we consider all the practical implications of this commandment, I need to discuss briefly what God's day of rest means for us today.

A Brief History of God's Day of Rest

The commandment, as it was originally given, refers to the seventh day of the week – our Saturday. Keeping the Sabbath by refraining from all work was one of the great distinguishing marks of the Jewish people in the Bible, a tradition that modern Judaism continues. In the Old Testament there are various other Sabbath laws that strictly limited the extent to which, for example, you could travel or prepare food. By Jesus' day, however, the religious authorities had added a number of restrictive and often petty rules to the God-given Old Testament laws. Jesus came into conflict with these, and had a number of disputes with the religious leaders over the true purpose of the Sabbath.

After the resurrection of Jesus, something remarkable happened: Christians started worshipping on the Sunday, the first day of the week. The fact that the resurrection had occurred on a Sunday must have been the key factor in making the switch. That the Holy Spirit had been given on a Sunday was probably also an important factor. Interestingly, when the Ten Commandments are restated in the book of Deuteronomy, the purpose of this commandment is that the people should 'Remember that you were slaves in Egypt and that the LORD your God brought you out of there with a mighty hand and an outstretched arm. Therefore the LORD God has commanded you to observe the Sabbath day' (Deuteronomy 5:15). In other words, the Sabbath was to be a celebration, not just of creation but also of deliverance. On that basis, it is hardly surprising that Christians felt at liberty to shift the day to commemorate the greater deliverance achieved by the cross and resurrection of Christ.

There may also have been a practical element in switching the day from Saturday to Sunday. If some of the Christians from a Jewish background were observing the Sabbath, the only time they would have been able to meet for worship would have been either before the start of the working day on a Sunday morning or in the evening (as in Acts 20:7). There is no evidence of early Christians applying the old Sabbath rules on work to a Sunday. In fact, for several centuries, the first day of the week must have been a normal working day, marked only by fellowship meetings outside work hours. As the church grew and spread, so did the importance of meeting together. Soon churches all around the Mediterranean started to meet on Sundays. In AD 321, the first Christian Roman Emperor, Constantine, decreed that Sundays were to be an official public holiday, on which most work was forbidden. Since then, Sunday has been the normal Christian day of rest and worship.

The Jewish Sabbath and Christian Sunday

There are differing views on how Sunday relates to the old Jewish Sabbath. Some Christians have felt that at least some of the Old

Testament rules on the Sabbath should be transferred to Sunday. For them, Sundays are solemn days of rest and devotion; reading, kicking a football or playing computer games would definitely be out. To support their position, they would point out that nowhere in the New Testament does it say that the Sabbath is abolished. Other Christians consider that the new era that Christ brought in rendered this part of the Old Testament law obsolete, as it did the laws on diet. They would point to the fact that although Jesus tightened up the commandments on murder and adultery, he said nothing about keeping the Sabbath. For such Christians, Sunday is very different to the Jewish Sabbath and they don't see a problem with watching a film or having a kick around in the park. Opponents of the first view say that with it you run the risk of legalism, of trying to please God by doing things, rather than by just accepting his grace in Jesus. Opponents of the second view say that you run the risk of using grace as an excuse for moral sloppiness and that soon Sunday will blur into any other working day.

There is something to be said for both sides. While I do not believe that all the Sabbath laws can be brought over to Sunday, I am concerned that under the relentless pressure of modern society we may end up throwing away one of the Ten Commandments that we really need to keep. Our need for a one-in-seven day of rest is unalterably built into the human frame. At the same time, I am unhappy about adding rules and restrictions to what should be a joyful day of liberation from work. I would say that for Christians, the Sabbath principles rather than the rules remain. So when I talk about 'observing a Sabbath', it does not mean that I am suggesting keeping all the Old Testament laws. I mean keeping the Sabbath principle of enjoying God's day of rest.

When Do We Keep God's Day of Rest?

Does this mean that God's day of rest for us must always be Sunday? No, not necessarily. In most Islamic countries Sunday is a normal working day and Christian believers often have Friday as a Sabbath day. Even here in Britain, many people cannot avoid working on a Sunday: those in medical professions, in the emergency services, in charge of the public utilities and, last but not least, church staff! (If you hadn't realised that for most Christian leaders Sunday is the most demanding day of the week then think again!) If this applies to you or your spouse and Sunday is a working day, then it is vital that you make sure you get another day off during the week. If it can be the same day every week, that is wise. If that is not possible, I encourage you to arrange for a full twenty-four-hours off, plan it out and guard it. If you are married, it is essential that your 'Sabbaths' coincide.

However, because of traditional working patterns, Sundays still make the best Sabbaths for most people in Britain and the United States. It is because of this that I supported the Keep Sunday Special campaign in 1993, which attempted to stop the large-scale lifting of restrictions on Sunday shopping.[3] I did this not because I was under any illusion that, if shops were closed, people would go to church. Rather, because I believed – and still do – that there is great value in keeping a common day of rest. After all, if everyone in a family has a different day off, much of the value of a Sabbath rest day for family and society will be lost.

This is hardly a minority opinion: nearly 90 per cent of the British population remain opposed to any further relaxation of Sunday trading laws.[4]

The important thing is that we all need a regular weekly break, whether on Sunday or a replacement day. But before I look at how we are to use that day, it is important to look at the whole issue of work. This commandment says something about that too.

THE BLESSINGS OF WORK AND REST

I want to make two suggestions here with regard to work and rest. The first is that we thank God for work. The second is that we take God's designated day of rest seriously.

Thank God for Work

This commandment upholds the goodness and privilege of work. Yes, we are told to take one day of rest a week, but the clear assumption is that we will spend the other six days in productive work. Doing nothing is the most tiresome job in the world because you can't stop and rest.

There is a distinction between work and employment. Employment implies a paid position while work is something you can have and not be paid for it. Many people – most of them women – work very long and antisocial hours to care for children or families. Yet these jobs (surely the most valuable of all) are unpaid. Beware of the widespread tendency to estimate the value of a job on the basis of the salary. Some of the most valuable jobs are actually the lowest paid or unpaid.

I believe work is good. We read that Adam was given work to do in Eden (Genesis 2:15). Work was part of God's good design for humanity. Only after the calamity of the fall do we find that work becomes burdensome (Genesis 3:17–19). Human beings were designed to work.

Each of us has a part to play in maintaining and developing our society. Each of us has different skills and talents, and because God gives these to us we glorify him by using them. A tragic element of being unemployed is that it results in this inbuilt God-given desire to work lying fallow and frustrated. That is one of the reasons we should support policies to enable the long-term unemployed to get back to work. There are, of course, those who are unavoidably unemployed because of disability or illness. For such people, we need to implement what the Bible says about 'the strong supporting the weak' and make sure that financial provision is made for them. We should also try to find something for them to do that is rewarding and which fulfils their innate desire to work.

Those of us who are in employment need to thank God for it. I know that for some, the idea of thanking God for our job can, at best, raise a grim smile, but I am not being flippant – I urge you to count your blessings. Employment always is a blessing but in these days of widespread economic downturn it is even more so. Unemployment is a depressing situation. It is also important to know that the nature of your employment or whether you are employed at all does not alter your value before God.

I believe, too, that not only should we be working, but that our work should be positive and good for us. Does that describe your current attitude to your work? Do you enjoy your work? Are you fulfilled by what you do? You may find it helpful to remember that whatever your work, you are doing it for God. Writing to the Colossian church, Paul gives the following instructions to – of all people – slaves: 'Work willingly at whatever you do, as though you were working for the Lord rather than for people. Remember that the Lord will give you an inheritance as your reward, and that the Master you are serving is Christ' (Colossians 3:23–24 NLT).

Taking such an attitude is actually possible. Brother Lawrence, a seventeenth-century cook in a French monastery, had that attitude. He learned to bring a devotional attitude into virtually every action of his day. This enabled him to find not only meaning but also purpose in all his work. In his book *The Practice of the Presence of God*, he wrote:

> *I turn my little omelette in the pan for the love of God. When it is finished, if I have nothing to do, I prostrate myself on the ground and worship my God, who gave me this grace to make it, after which I arise happier than a king. When I can do nothing else, it is enough to have picked up straw for the love of God. People look for ways of learning how to love God. They hope to attain it, I know not from how many different practices. They take much trouble to abide in his presence by varied means. Is it not a shorter and more direct way to do everything for the love of God, to make use of all the tasks one's lot in life demands to show him that love, and to maintain his presence within by the communion of our heart with his? There is nothing complicated about it. One has only to turn to it honestly and simply.*

We all need to have some of that attitude to our own work.

I have been eager to defend work in general. That does not mean that I am saying every job is fine and all you need to do is thank God for it. There are some jobs that are wrong, perhaps because they involve dubious practices or because they are producing things or services that the world doesn't need. Equally, there are some jobs that are right but which may be wrong for you. All I can say is this: give your job its best and pray for those you work with. Thank God for whatever you can about your job and seek guidance from wise and godly people about a way forward.

I believe it is God's will that we all have jobs that are fulfilling. But I should warn you, his idea of a fulfilling job may not be quite what *we* had in mind.

Taking Rest Seriously

If this commandment shows us something of the value of work, it also allows us to see the value of rest. The problem is that we tend to consider work as being important and rest as being trivial. We can think of rest as merely being 'not-working'. It is far more than that.

At the most basic level, a day off every week is good for us physically and mentally. It gives us the opportunity to relax the pace at which our body's machinery is working. We can rest eyes strained by computer screens, ease backs stressed by office chairs or give a break to metabolisms sustained by caffeine. Although many people insist their workload is such that they cannot take a day off, the fact is that keeping going without a break is often detrimental for overall productivity. A day off may help to re-energise us to the point that we work at a higher level of efficiency on subsequent days. In contrast, continuously working may result in a low level of efficiency and competence. A vicious circle forms: we refuse to take time off because we have so much to do. We then become so tired that we aren't able to do what we have to properly, so it takes more time to do our tasks. This leaves us with even less time, and reduces further the opportunity of taking time off. There is an illustration from Stephen Covey that is very relevant to the topic of the Sabbath:

Suppose you were to come upon someone in the woods working feverishly to saw down a tree. 'What are you doing?' you ask.

'Can't you see?' comes the impatient reply. 'I'm sawing down this tree.'

'You look exhausted!' you exclaim. 'How long have you been at it?'

'Over five hours,' he returns, 'and I'm beat! This is hard work.'

'Well, why don't you take a break for a few minutes and sharpen that saw?' you enquire. 'I'm sure it would go a lot faster.'

'I don't have time to sharpen the saw,' the man says emphatically. 'I'm too busy sawing!'[5]

Taking a day off a week to renew yourself is not a luxury, it is the way we were made to exist.

A day of rest is also important because it enables us to assess what we are doing. The problem with working continuously is that there is no opportunity to stand back, get things into perspective and see the big picture. Deadline after deadline force us to focus on immediate crises rather than on the overall design of our lives. Many people today have a work style like racing cyclists: head down and pedalling furiously along the road. A day of rest allows us to stop pedalling, look around, pick up the map and work out where our efforts are taking us. I have often found that it is when I am recharging, away from the place of my restless 'doing', I discover what exactly it is that has to be done.

William Wilberforce (1759–1833) is well known in British history as the MP who brought forward legislation to ban slavery. Wilberforce was a Christian and never felt it right to work on a Sunday. Within a few years as a politician, he had made a great impression and was tipped for a high position in the Cabinet. Wilberforce felt flattered that his hard work was at the point of being rewarded. However, after spending a Sunday resting, his view of his possible promotion changed and he wrote the following in his diary: 'these earthly things assume their true size'. His day of rest had given him a sense of perspective. Incidentally, Wilberforce was also well aware of the physical and mental value of a Sunday's rest. Later in life, he wrote sadly of his contemporaries who had broken under the pressure of politics, 'with peaceful Sundays, the strings would never have snapped as they did from over tension'.

Taking a day of rest also makes a statement about who we are and who runs our lives. It deliberately dethrones work from being central to our existence. In the passage in Genesis to which this commandment refers, we read how, when God made everything, he stopped and stood back and saw 'that it was good'. Even on the ultimate job of making the entire cosmos, God does not become work-obsessed. We who are made in his image would do well to learn the same principle. We need to remember that who we are isn't defined by what we do. We are human *beings* not human *do*ings. If all we do is *do*, then we will stop being. It is no coincidence that many people who have worked intensely in jobs find retirement or unemployment profoundly stressful. They have let their jobs take over their lives and when their jobs end it is a savage blow to who they are.

In Leo Tolstoy's short story *How Much Land Does a Man Need?* the main character travels to a tribe in the Russian hinterland. They offer to give him as much land as he can cover in one day. Anxious to cover as much ground as he can, the man makes a frantic journey. As the sun sets, he collapses with exhaustion and dies. Ultimately, the amount of land he actually gets is the six-foot plot that is his final resting place.

In grasping for the material benefits of our society, we are no different from Tolstoy's character. If we judge ourselves only by what we produce, then we become slaves to what we do. Work becomes an end in itself. We eventually conclude that to *be* more, we must *do* more.

This is a lie. Instead of liberating us, work enslaves us and owns us – we become 'workaholics'. As Diane Fassel wrote, 'work is god for the compulsive worker, and nothing gets in the way of this god'.[6]

With workaholism, work becomes a way to escape family, the inner life and the world. Like other addictions, workaholism consumes the addict's time, energy and thoughts. It can be literally fatal. Its toxic fruits are heart disease, hypertension, depression and more. In Japan, *karoshi* or 'death from overwork' is a major killer. In 2016 the Japanese government said one in five employees were at risk of death from overwork.[7]

Forcing ourselves to take a break is also helpful because it reminds us of our limitations. We tend to think that we are indispensable. This is an illusion. We love to be busy and to be needed and there is no greater boost to our egos than to think that we personally hold everything together. However, making ourselves step away from the action can give a healthy sense of proportion. Very often, when we do stop we find that not everything stops with us. To act as if the world – or worse still, God – cannot get along without our work for one day in seven is to demonstrate a pride that denies the sufficiency of our generous creator.

Sometimes it is difficult to say 'no' to people. Yet a forced break is good and guards us from becoming slaves to other people's demands.

Besides, if we get into a regular pattern of taking time off, then people come to respect that and learn to work around it. If it is known that we are always available, we not only create an unhealthy reliance on us, but we can end up becoming the property of other people. Taking a day off is actually a really good test of our freedom; as Dorothy Bass said, 'slaves cannot take a day off; free people can'.[8] Which are you?

For many people a day of rest seems too risky. 'How would I survive?' they ask. We can trust God to provide if we keep his commands. This is one of the lessons that the people of God learned just before Moses was given the Ten Commandments. After the Israelites crossed the Red Sea, they journeyed through the desert of Sinai. Faced with insufficient food, they made their needs known to God. In response, he miraculously provided manna for them, a substance which appeared like dew in the morning and which was 'white like coriander seed and tasted like wafers made with honey' (Exodus 16:31). With the manna came strict instructions: for five days they were to collect only what they needed for that day and if they tried to collect more it would rot and be full of maggots by the next morning. On the sixth day – the day before the Sabbath – they were told to collect twice as much, because on the Sabbath itself none would be given. The manna of the sixth day stayed fresh and did not rot, and on the Sabbath they were able to eat what they had stored. The lesson they learned was that God would provide for his people in every way and that they were not going to suffer for keeping his day of rest. We need to learn a similar lesson.

MAKING GOD'S DAY OF REST SPECIAL

In this section, I want to give some guidelines on how we can get the most benefit from God's day of rest.

Guard Your Rest

Paradoxically, you may need to work hard to keep God's day of rest special. A day of rest does not just happen; the phone will not suddenly stop ringing or the emails piling up just because you have decided to take a day off. You need to make a definite effort to guard your day of rest. This is particularly a problem if your day of rest is not on a Sunday;

everybody will assume that you are working. You will need to take positive and proactive action to make sure that your much-needed Sabbath rest is not disturbed by interruptions.

Even Jesus, in the midst of a busy ministry, was proactive in taking rest. We often read in the accounts of his life how he went to a solitary place in order to escape the crowds. Sometimes he took his closest friends to be with him and at other times he went alone. We, too, must make firm resolutions to ensure that we rest.

If you can, divert phone calls somewhere else and refuse to check your email. Make the rules for your day of rest widely known to others and if you have responsibilities then get someone else to deputise for you. Getting out of the house also makes it harder for people to find you and removes the temptation to finish off that report or write that email. Just leave the mobile at home or turn it off, rest from the things you do during the week, and create a day of distinction.

If you are a news addict, then give the radio, TV and internet a break. Why not give your computer a Sabbath too? Don't try to tackle household tasks that will leave you drained. Resolve to guard your rest. Unless you do, pressures will inevitably erode it. The time to relax is when you don't have time to relax!

Be Refreshed in Your Rest

The Sabbath is to be a day of physical non-productivity, a day to rest and recharge our bodies. Resting is about recovering from the week that has been; recharging is about getting ready for the week to come. One doctor said, 'The periods of rest I prescribe for my patients are often Sabbaths in arrears.'

Force yourself to do things that are not stressful. If you don't have young children you might want to sleep in a bit longer. Find out what makes you relax and do it. In our household we often relax with family, friends, food or a film, or all of them together! Other people like to listen to music or read a book. Many people feel refreshed by the beauty of God's creation and are especially aware of God by lakes, coasts or rivers and in woods or gardens. The Sabbath should be a time when we step back to admire nature, rather than figure out how to change it. I believe that God gives us his creation as a gift and through it he can refresh us and rebuild us. If, on the other six days of the week, rushing is your norm, walk slowly and calmly on the Sabbath. In the most famous of the psalms we read that God 'makes me lie down in green pastures, he leads me beside quiet waters, he restores my soul' (Psalm 23:2–3). While this might be symbolic language, many have found it to be literally true.

Monitor your Sabbath over a period of time to make sure you are getting the most from it. Do you feel better as a result? Are there ways that you could make it of greater benefit for yourself? Are there things that you do on your day of rest that are stressful? Some people who are very committed to working hard can carry the same dedication over into their hobbies and sports. The result is a new area of stress. If this is you, ask yourself some hard questions. Does it really matter if you don't break your personal record for the marathon? Do you need to remodel the *whole* garden? Is it really relaxing to learn Chinese? Otherwise, the real truth might be 'work hard, play hard, die soon'.

You need to be blessed by your rest; make sure that you are.

Have Freedom in Your Rest

One of the extraordinary abilities of the human race is that we can totally mess things up. With perverse ingenuity, generations of people from all sorts of cultures have managed to turn this command from being a liberating gift of God into a wearisome, day-long obstacle course. As I mentioned earlier, this happened at the time of Jesus. The religious leaders had invented a list of things that must not be done on the Sabbath. You couldn't prepare a meal, sew on a button, light a fire or walk more than 3,000 feet from your home. There were, in total, 1,521 of these rules to try and prevent this commandment being broken. Ensuring that no work took place on the Sabbath had become very hard work indeed!

Jesus' rhythm with the Sabbath was fascinating. Time and time again his actions got him into trouble with the religious leaders. Jesus felt free to heal, to pick corn and to cast out demons. These were all actions that, in the opinion of the religious leaders, broke their rules on what could be done on the Sabbath. The fact that there were so many controversies about Jesus breaking these Sabbath rules may suggest that they were a religious abuse about which he felt very strongly. When criticised about his lax attitude to such rules, he replied, 'The Sabbath was made to meet the needs of people, and not people to meet the requirements of the Sabbath' (Mark 2:27 NLT). The religious leaders had taken a blessing and turned it into a burden.

Such attitudes can occur even today and we need to beware of them. This commandment was given to set us free, not to enslave us. *That* you rest is essential; *how* you rest is up to you.

Enjoy Others in Your Rest

Sabbaths are also given so that we spend time with those to whom we are closest. God's day of rest should be used to develop and extend our relationships with family and friends. Not just in brief moments but with quality (and quantity) time. Jewish people have the practice of gathering the family as one of the central focal points of their Sabbath, and central to that family time is a shared meal. One of the casualties of the last few decades has been the family meal. We have less time for meals than we once did and they are frequently snatched or interrupted by the phone. Even if this is our pattern for living for six days of the week, on our Sabbath day of rest it is important to rediscover leisurely, uninterrupted family mealtimes. One thing that has helped our family is our rule that the phone is out of bounds during a mealtime. We just ignore it; phone calls can wait and emails can most definitely be postponed. In all the years, I can hardly ever recall an occasion when being instantly accessible was a necessity. We need to learn to master our communications rather than let them enslave us. This allows us to give our full attention to those nearest to us, those for whom we have primary responsibility. We need to remember that actual friends around us take precedence over virtual ones at a distance.

And let's remember: 'M' doesn't stand for 'Maid' but 'Mother'! The family can also help to prepare the meals and clear up afterwards together!

Enjoy God in Your Rest

God's day of rest is a day to worship. It is not the *only* day to worship and not the *only* day to pray, but it should be the day when we have time to focus on God and our life in him. It is a day to tune in again to God, to refocus and to reprioritise all that we do and are, in the light of the reality of God.

Normally, one part of our day of rest should involve worshipping with other members of God's family. If we can take our Sabbath rest on Sunday, then giving God the first part of the first day of every week serves to remind us that he is first in our lives.

Christians have always set time aside to be together, to listen to God's word spoken into their lives, to remember Jesus' death for them in the breaking of bread, to pray together for the world and to praise God for his goodness. To meet with God and his people nourishes and feeds us spiritually. Ceasing to meet together is bound to have a negative effect on our Christian lives. An old image is that a fellowship is like a burning coal fire: if you take a burning hot coal out of the fire and place it somewhere in isolation it will soon go cold. Experience over centuries has shown that this is what happens if individuals are isolated from a church community. Of course, if your day of rest is not a Sunday, using it for both rest and worship is not easy and you may have to make other arrangements. But whenever we take our Sabbath rest, we should spend time with God and the church.

'Remember the Sabbath day by keeping it *holy*.' The Sabbath day was created holy, and God wants it to be holy to you. The Sabbath is not just about time off; it is about sacred time. Sunday does not belong to business, it does not belong to industry, it does not belong to the government. It belongs to God.

So many people now have no room for God in their thoughts, in their schedules, or in the fabric of their lives. Let me ask you this: do you keep going along with the flow of the world and let it erode your relationship with God? Does God have an opportunity to look into your heart? Do you give him time to do so? If not on Sunday, then when?

Stand Up for the Right to Rest

Rather quaintly to modern ears, this commandment includes the instruction that God's people were to ensure that their sons, daughters, servants, animals and foreigners (visitors) were also to keep the Sabbath. The principle is clear and very up to date: we are to do all we can to make sure that others can have the right to rest too.

This is not easy in a society that is driven by 'market forces' (often used as a polite synonym for 'greed'). The suggestion that the problems of the economy can be resolved if only shops could open all day, every day, is ridiculous. The reality is that because there is only so much money to go around, Sunday trading merely spreads it more thinly. The battle to 'Keep Sunday Special' is far from over and we need to support efforts to give anyone who wants to, the right to a day of rest without being pressured into work.

I have a good friend, Gary Grant, who is the owner of The Entertainer chain of toyshops. Gary knows the challenge of keeping God's day of rest. What he said to me about how he had responded to the pressure for Sunday trading is so helpful that I want to share it.

We started our business in 1981 with one shop in Amersham and for the first ten years worked exceedingly long hours, seven days a week, to build the business. In 1991 I became a Christian and then had a new set of parameters within which to run my business. This changed many aspects of our business, from product selection, to the way we treated our staff, to the hours that we worked, especially Sunday trading.

In 1994, Sunday trading became lawful and I was really concerned about how it fitted in with my Christian belief of having a day of rest. I prayed as to whether I should open my stores on a Sunday. I was annoyed that God hadn't answered my prayers but, one night, God said to me, 'Gary, you've had the answer, but you've been praying for the answer "yes".' And to this day, we have not opened our shops on a Sunday. God says, in the Bible, 'I will honour those that honour me,' and it is absolutely true; I can testify that God has prospered our business as we have gone from strength to strength. We have grown from three stores back in 1991 to over one hundred today.

It hasn't been easy, we have been barred from a number of the sites that we would like to have opened in, as the landlords are only leasing to companies who are a seven-day week. However, we have found that our staff of 1,000 are pleased that having a Sunday off gives them the opportunity to be at home with their family and their children. As the owner of The Entertainer I am in a very privileged position to be able to make the decision not to trade my business on a Sunday. We only trade for six days and our business is financially viable.

God has honoured Gary's decision, even through the downturn in the global economy which has seen many retailers close and leave our high streets. If you have to make similar decisions then I am sure God will honour them too.

THE CHALLENGE OF GOD'S DAY OF REST

While we like the idea of the Sabbath, we resist the reality of actually observing it. We have become Sabbath-phobic. But ignoring the Sabbath carries a heavy physical, psychological, emotional and spiritual price tag. Unless we start to change now, there will come a time when it will be too late; others will have already suffered too much. Times will change for the better only when we change.

We need to follow the pattern that God has established for us, not as a dry and wearisome ritual but in a way that liberates us and rejuvenates us. This is not selfishness. The effects of observing the Sabbath principle are wider than just our own lives; they ripple out into wider society. As one Jewish rabbi taught, 'It was not Israel that kept the Sabbath, so much as the Sabbath that kept Israel.' It is true today: a society without Sabbaths is a society that is heading for trouble.

Let me end with this point. This commandment addresses a fundamental issue: who controls our time? It is not simply a question of legislation on trading hours or cultural practices; it is about the lordship of our lives and of our culture. By keeping God's day of rest we proclaim to ourselves – and to the world – that God runs our lives. We need to set an example and, by our use of our precious time, show that Jesus is Lord of all.

1   https://www.newsweek.com/recession-mental-health-depression-anxiety-585695

2   In the United States this many vary from state to state.

3   They are still doing a good job preventing the complete erosion of the value of Sunday. See http://www.keepsundayspecial.org.uk

4   http://www.keepsundayspecial.org.uk/Web/Content/Default.aspx?Content=91

5   Stephen R. Covey, *Seven Habits of Highly Effective People* (Simon & Schuster, 2004).

6   Diane Fassel, *Working Ourselves to Death: The High Cost of Workaholism and the Rewards of Recovery* (iUniverse, 2000).

7   https://www.theguardian.com/world/2017/oct/05/japanese-woman-dies-overwork-159-hours-overtime

8   Dorothy Bass, *Practising Our Faith: A Way of Life for a Searching People* (2nd edition, John Wiley, 2010), p. 79.

8

HOW TO TAKE GOD SERIOUSLY

COMMANDMENT THREE: YOU SHALL NOT MISUSE GOD'S NAME

'You shall not misuse the name of the LORD your God, for the LORD will not hold anyone guiltless who misuses his name.' (Exodus 20:7)

SO, WHAT'S THE PROBLEM?

One fascinating aspect of the way that our societies on either side of the Atlantic are changing can be seen in the choice of children's names. In the US in 2011 the top five most popular names for baby boys were Jacob, Mason, William, Jayden and Noah; and for girls, Sophia, Isabella, Emma, Olivia and Ava. Fast forward to 2019 and we find an almost total change, with the top names for boys being Milo, Jasper, Atticus, Theodore and Asher; and for girls, Posie, Isla, Olivia, Aurora and Maeve.[1] Britain has seen similar changes. In 2000 the top five girls' names were Chloe, Emily, Megan, Charlotte and Jessica; and the top five boys' names were Jack, Thomas, James, Joshua and Daniel. But here, too, by 2019 everything had changed and the top five girls' names were Amelia, Olivia, Emily, Isla and Ava; and the top five boys' names were Oliver, Jack, Harry, George and Jacob.[2]

I have a vested interest in the name John and am saddened by the fact that in both the US and Britain what was once a popular name is now rare (thirty-fifth in the popularity stakes in the US and ninety-third in Britain). Clearly there are fashions in names, just as there are in clothes.

Yet names are important. We can all remember when someone who should have known our name forgot it, or when we were mistaken for someone else. We feel awkward when our name is forgotten, and there is an uncomfortable sense of feeling insignificant. Equally, think about what happens when you see your name misspelled. What do you do? You correct it, of course. Not because it makes any difference to how it is pronounced but because we feel it is important that people get our names right.

In fact, we go to great lengths to protect our names. An entire branch of the legal profession exists to govern the use and abuse of names. Our newspapers are full of accounts of libel and slander cases; 'I need to clear my name' is the cry of those involved. One of the concerns of the new millennium, arising from the awesome power of the internet, is that of 'identity theft', where a fraudster manages to accumulate enough information about a person to pose as them. When our identity is at stake, we are protective of who we are and what we are called. And rightly so.

The reason we are so protective is because a name stands for something. Just mentioning a name can bring to mind a whole set of images. Take the name Adolf. Even without a surname attached, it conjures up images of indescribable cruelty, concentration camps and murder.

Having a 'good name' is synonymous with having a good reputation. 'A good name is more desirable than great riches; to be esteemed is better than silver or gold' (Proverbs 22:1). We all want people to have a positive impression of us and feel offended if there are malicious stories or unfair criticism going around about us.

It is not just our own names that we are sensitive about but the names we represent. School children are warned about their conduct on the bus home – any bad behaviour brings the school's name into disrepute. We have all watched embarrassed football managers on television trying to distance their clubs from some act of urban devastation wreaked by their drunken fans. Not only can our names be misused, but also those of others with whom we are associated.

This third commandment is about the disturbing fact that we can – and do – misuse God's name. The use and misuse of God's name involves far more than swearing or blasphemy. It concerns the very nature of who God is. And for us to understand who God is, we need to do some serious thinking.

THE HEART OF THE MATTER

Names Are More Than Words

Names are far more than collections of syllables and vowels. They have meaning, conjure up associations of images and have power and prestige that can even be transferred to a third person. I'm sure many of us can remember using the name of a friend in order to get into a party. At an even higher level, ambassadors serve in foreign countries as representatives of the government and people of their entire nation.

The fact that we know that authority and status can be transferred with a name is behind a lot of advertising. The attraction of expensive brand names is that people believe something of the power of the name is transmitted to the owner or wearer.

For many of us in both Britain and the United States, the origin of our names may mean very little. In fact, the naming of children today often seems to be quite frivolous, with infants' names of obscure flowers, entire football teams or pieces of fruit!

For many people in other cultures, the process of naming a child is still important because of what the name means. Nelson Mandela wrote:

Apart from life, a strong constitution and abiding connection to the Thembu royal house, the only thing my father bestowed upon me at birth was a name, Rolihlahla. In Xhosa, Rolihlahla literally means 'pulling the branch off the tree', but its colloquial meaning more accurately would be 'trouble maker'. I do not believe that names are destiny or that my father somehow divined my future, but in later years, friends and relatives would ascribe to my birth name the many storms I have caused and weathered.[3]

In the Bible, naming a person was a serious event. Some of the names are physically descriptive. In Genesis 25 when Isaac's wife Rebekah had twins, the firstborn was red and covered in hair, while the second came out holding his brother's heel. As a result, they called the first one 'Esau' which means 'hairy', and the other 'Jacob' which means 'he grasps the heel'. Other children in the Bible were given names which didn't describe them physically but which spoke about what God had done, or was going to do. When Hannah, a barren woman who had prayed to God for a child, was blessed with a son, she called him Samuel, meaning 'God heard me'. The prophets Isaiah and Hosea both gave their children names that referred to what God was going to do. The best example of all is the name Jesus, the Greek form of the Hebrew 'Joshua', which means 'the Lord saves'.

Names in biblical times signified something important about a person and communicated what they stood for; to use a name was to say who that person was. God's name was no different.

The Privilege of Knowing the Name of God

I would love to have been in the Garden of Eden just after Adam had been given the task of naming all the animals (Genesis 2:20). It must have been a fascinating exercise; I wonder how he came up with them all! It established the fact that Adam – 'one who names' – had dominion over the creatures that he named. Yet there was one being that Adam did not give a name to. That being was God.

God does not let human beings name him. Why not? One reason is that in the Bible, the inferior do not name the superior. Another reason is that no human being could name God properly. We wouldn't have a clue what to call him. Any name of God would have to describe him; that would be far too much for us, and our language is inadequate for us even to try. When the twentieth-century philosopher Ludwig Wittgenstein came to discuss the nature of God in lectures, he would bring a cup of steaming coffee into the room. He would then ask volunteers to describe the smell of coffee, a task that always proved impossible without saying something meaningless like 'it has a coffee-like smell'! Wittgenstein would then make the point that if human beings were not capable of describing the distinctive aroma of coffee, how could they cope with someone like God?

Thankfully, however, we read in the Bible that God has already revealed both himself and his name to us. We don't have to try and imagine what he is like or make up some name that we hope might do him justice. And it is vital for us to understand that what Christianity says about God comes not from vague human speculations but directly from God himself. Throughout the pages of the Bible we read that God is not a *something*, but a *someone*: a loving, personal God who cares for us and who has chosen to make himself known to humanity.

In fact, when God did reveal his name he did it in a very personal way. In Exodus 3 we read how Moses, having fled from Egypt where the Israelites were in slavery, was looking after his father-in-law's sheep in the wilderness when suddenly he came across a bush that, although covered in flames, was not burning. From the bush, Moses heard God call him by name. God announced that he was going to liberate his people who were in slavery, and told Moses to go back to the ruler of Egypt and bring the Israelites out of captivity. When Moses protested that he wasn't up to the task, God promised that he would go with him. Moses, still reluctant, then raised another objection. 'Suppose I go to the Israelites,' he told God, 'and say to them, "The God of your fathers has sent me to you," and they ask me, "What is his name?" Then what shall I tell them?' The answer is both powerful and mysterious. God said to Moses, 'I AM WHO I AM. This is what you are to say to the Israelites: "I AM has sent me to you"' (Exodus 3:13–14).

Two verses later God uses a name for himself, YHWH, which is a form of I AM and is translated in most English Bibles as 'the LORD'. This word, effectively the personal name of God, occurs 6,800 times in the Old Testament. Each time, it refers back to this great promise, 'I AM WHO I AM.'

But what does 'I AM WHO I AM' mean? It means 'I am the Living One' or 'I am the One who exists' or 'I am the One who will be who I will be'. Behind these words lies the concept of a being who is quite unlike anyone – or anything – else. God's name of I AM suggests that he is independent of everything else that exists and cannot be contained. With that comes the idea of God being absolutely trustworthy and unchangeable; when he makes up his mind to do something, he will do it. Furthermore, it suggests that rather than being some remote, philosophical abstraction or a vague force, God is the one who *is* someone. The rest of the Bible reveals who that 'someone' is, so that by the end of it, God has said to us, 'I AM your Creator, Saviour, Sustainer, Leader, Protector, Healer, Helper, Judge and Comforter.'

Now in revealing his personal name, God reveals his identity to us. It is quite extraordinary that God should do this, because by revealing his name to us he leaves himself open to us misusing his name.

In Old Testament times, people appreciated that knowing the name of God as 'I AM' was a great privilege. In fact, they treated the name with such high regard that they tried to avoid using it in speech or in prayer, just in case it was misused. When the scribes came to write out the name of God, they never wrote it out in full but only the four consonants. And when they did come to write the Hebrew letters 'YHWH' they would wash, put on new clothes, use a new quill, write the name and then throw the quill away. When they came to read the word aloud, rather than pronounce it, they substituted the word 'LORD'.

However strange and ritualistic to us, the decision not to use God's name at all was to ensure that, at all costs, this commandment to treat God's name with reverence was kept. I think it would be misunderstanding Jewish tradition if we felt that God's name was viewed as some sort of unexploded bomb that had to be handled with care. It was God's holiness that they did not want to presume upon and so his name was held in 'holy' reverence and awe. Knowing God's name was a great honour and a joyful privilege. The fact that God had made himself known to his people was at the centre of their existence as individuals and as a nation. They were God's people and he was their God.

Jesus and the Name of God

The coming of Jesus brought a whole new era of knowing God better because, in Jesus, God has fully revealed himself. In fact, through Jesus, God now invites us to be on first-name terms with him.

The names that are used for Jesus point to what he does for us. As we have seen, the name 'Jesus' means 'the Lord saves', but Jesus is also called Immanuel (Matthew 1:23) which means 'God with us'. God for us and 'God with us' sum up all of who Jesus was and is. The awesome gulf between humanity and God which had existed since Adam and Eve, is now bridged. That is why Jesus is also called a mediator (1 Timothy 2:5), someone who can intervene to resolve differences between two parties.

In God coming to us in Jesus, there is an extraordinary closeness and intimacy. A young girl was crying in her bedroom one night and her mother came in and asked her why she was so upset. 'Mummy,' she answered, 'I'm scared because I feel all alone.'

'You're not alone, darling,' said her mother. 'God's here with you.'

'But Mummy, I don't want a God I can't see; I want a God with skin on.'

Jesus is, if you like, God with skin on. He is the God who was touched and held, who ate and drank and who, finally, was tortured and strung up. You see, he doesn't issue some prayer formula or a series of rules for us to follow. Instead, he comes himself as a human being to whom we can relate personally; Christianity is not a religion but a relationship.

Jesus himself models how we are now to treat God's name. As an observant Jew he would have known all the rules about how God's name was to be carefully revered. Despite this, he introduced a new name for God that shocked those around him. Jesus referred to God as 'Abba'; the word that a young child might call their father. His use of this term, similar to our 'Daddy', displays the intimacy and confidence of a child with a parent. Yet Jesus never played down God's majesty or holiness, or signalled in any way that God's name should be treated with any less honour than it had been before.

Jesus makes this point at the very start of the model prayer that he gives his disciples. We call it the Lord's Prayer and it begins, 'Our Father in heaven: May your name be honoured' (Matthew 6:9 GNB). In those two phrases, Jesus perfectly balances an intimate familiarity with a profound sense of honour and respect. In Jesus, God has become accessible instead of remote. He is not just Lord; he is now also our Father in heaven. Yet these new privileges give us even more reason to honour God's name.

Respect: An Endangered Attitude?

Although western society increasingly marginalised God at the end of the twentieth century, it largely avoided direct attacks on him. The twenty-first century has proved to be very different. Apparently spurred into action by the events of 9/11, a small but noisy group of people known as the 'New Atheists' have spent a lot of time directly attacking the idea of God. The title of one of their books, *God is Not Great* by Christopher Hitchens, expresses well their contempt for traditional religion. One interesting feature about 'New Atheism' is that its emergence is not the result of any new evidence against God whatsoever; it simply appears to be a cultural mood whose time has come.

Another cultural shift is the rising tide of disrespect for authority that has become a hallmark of modern western civilisation. Today, few, if any, authority figures or institutions generate respect. Government is no longer revered – we barely blink when we hear of politicians' indiscretions or scandals surrounding their taxes or expenses. Any senior police officer will tell you that public attitudes towards the police have changed within little more than a generation from courteous respect to sceptical contempt. Teachers will tell you how 'Parents' Evening' has changed: within living memory it was the children who were concerned about what might be said; now it is the teachers who find themselves on the defensive. And in the classroom the most vital skill for schoolteachers seems not to be the ability to teach but the ability to retain control. Sadly, even when church leaders speak out, their words command little attention and even less obedience. In Britain, while the Queen may be honoured (and rightly so), the monarchy in general attracts less respect. Given this trend, I find myself unsurprised that a tone of mockery and scorn can now be found in comments made about God. While a nation may survive being sarcastic and sceptical about its leading public figures, I am not so sure it can survive giving God the same treatment. He deserves respect.

TREAT GOD WITH REVERENCE

My wife's name is 'Killy'. That name is, for me, most precious. If I were to hear someone pouring scorn on her name, abusing it, treating it flippantly or using it when they were annoyed or angry, it would hurt me very much. This is because Killy is the woman whom I love and respect more than any other. Such abuse would show that they didn't really know her, that they didn't have regard for her and that they did not respect her. I would, of course, be annoyed and try to put them right. My wife deserves respect. I am sure that I am not alone in having such attitudes and responses. Now, if this is true in our relationships to other human beings, how much more should it be true for how we relate to Almighty God?

Respect God's Name Because of His Actions

God deserves respect because of what he has done and continues to do. The Bible tells us that God is the creator of the universe, and that he continues to sustain it moment by moment. If God stopped his actions for even a fraction of a second, then everything – all the stars, all the cells in our bodies, every atom and molecule – would vanish into nothingness. There would just be nothing at all. When we think of that, we should realise that God is worthy of the highest respect and honour we can give.

God makes a similar point, only using pictorial language, in the Old Testament book of Job. Job has suffered greatly; everything and almost everyone he has loved has been taken away from him. Although Job keeps his faith in God, eventually he complains to God about the unfairness of his suffering. He demands answers. God's reply comes with thunder.

> *Who is this that questions my wisdom with such ignorant words? Brace yourself . . . because I have some questions for you, and you must answer them.*
>
> *Where were you when I laid the foundations of the earth? Tell me, if you know so much. Who determined its dimensions and stretched out the surveying line? What supports its foundations, and who laid its cornerstone as the morning stars sang together and all the angels shouted for joy?* (Job 38:2–7 NLT)

In the two chapters that follow, God challenges Job with more questions. As a result, Job realises both how great God is and how small he himself is. It is a lesson we badly need to learn today.

God's name should be honoured because he is powerful. We have learned to revere power when we can measure it in volts or horsepower. No one, unless they are very naive or stupid, tries to play with a high-voltage electricity cable, or go for a swim in a sea of storm-driven waves. We have a wise fear of what will happen to us. Yet people play around with the name of God, the one who is more powerful than any force we can imagine.

Think of the power of the most common name, 'Mum'. The children are in their bedroom playing and all of a sudden there is screaming and crying. What happens next? One of them comes running out crying, 'Mum, he keeps hitting me!' And Mum says, 'You go and tell your brother that I said to stop fighting.' The child runs back, and what's the first thing you hear? 'Mum said . . .' The child has gained power. How? By using Mum's name. How much more power exists in God's name.

In the Bible we are told there is power in God's name because behind the name stands the one who is all-powerful, all-seeing and all-knowing. God is the one who started the entire creation, who holds it all together and who will, one day, reshape it. God has power over all things, over the laws of nature, over life and over death.

Calling on God's name brings salvation; 'everyone who calls on the name of the Lord will be saved' (Acts 2:21). In God's name evil is rebuked, healing is given and people are commissioned and sent out for service. His name should be revered. One day it will be. We are told that, in the future, at his name every knee will bow and every tongue will confess that Jesus Christ is Lord.

There are lessons here for all of us, not just with regard to blasphemy or swearing. In the 1992 movie *Leap of Faith*, Steve Martin plays a travelling revivalist preacher touring round the United States with a large tent and all the trappings. He offers healings, encounters with God and life-changing miracles.

The man is actually a fraud and the film cynically portrays the whole thing as a moneymaking sham where everything is staged and manipulated. At the end of the film, though, the real healing of a young boy on crutches occurs. The preacher is left bewildered and frightened and the fear of God falls upon him and his team. As the Bible says twice: 'the fear of the LORD is the beginning of wisdom' (Psalm 111:10; Proverbs 9:10).

God is a powerful God; to misuse his name is dangerous. Those who play with God's name in an attempt to use him for their own benefit, are playing with fire. And they are likely to get more than their fingers burnt.

Respect God's Name Because of His Character

We worship God not just because he is powerful (after all, a dictator may have power), but because he is perfect and holy. What we find admirable in other people – their love, wisdom and thoughtfulness – we find in God to an unlimited extent. People may sometimes be kind, truthful and holy but God is always love, truth and holiness.

All human beings are sinful. If our names are misused then we may well deserve it. There may even be some truth in some of the abuse that is said about us. But there can never be any grounds for misusing God's name. God is free from sin and full of everything that is good and right.

To misuse God's name is foolish because of his mighty power; it is also immoral because of his perfect character.

HOW TO HONOUR GOD'S NAME

Let me now give you three ways in which we can honour God's name.

Don't Swear

If you are anything like me, the first thing you think about regarding this commandment is swearing. Most people understand swearing to be either blasphemy or vulgarity.

Increasingly, we find that 'Jesus!' is heard more often as a common expletive than as the personal name of the founder of Christianity. On both sides of the Atlantic there is enormous discussion about how films should be classified. In Britain, great care is taken over such categories as 'drugs', 'horror', 'sex' and 'violence'. The use of blasphemous language that might offend Christians is not a major issue. It is not surprising that, in this environment, the majority of people have just become numb to the way that God's name is so widely abused in our society.

Let me suggest some ways in which we can counter this. First, we can watch our own language and make sure that we don't use God's name in a way that is dishonouring. Secondly, we can be prepared to take people to task for it. There are imaginative and sensitive ways in which we can make others aware of the language they are using. In fact, in most cases people do not realise that what they are saying is offensive. For instance, if I hear someone reply to a question with 'God knows!' I often respond with something like 'Yes, he does.' If people say 'Jesus!' as a swear word, I will often ask 'Who?' or 'So you know my Lord, do you?' When they realise that you take God and Jesus seriously, it may even create an opportunity to a very interesting conversation. Thirdly, we can let our voice be heard about the misuse of God's name in the media, especially on radio and television. A letter or a phone call is treated with some weight in these media organisations and if you see or hear something that offends you, then make it known. You might point out that we are only demanding equal treatment with Muslims; after all, no scriptwriter would use the word 'Mohammed' as a swear word!

Decide today not to use the name of God in an irreverent, frivolous and disrespectful way. If you would not call yourself a Christian, then, on behalf of those of us who would, can I ask you to respect our God's name? Having read what I have written above, you will see why we find it hurtful.

Don't Name-drop with God

This commandment addresses far more than open blasphemy, and there are ways in which even those who would never dream of swearing can break this commandment.

One subtle temptation is to name-drop with God. Now name-dropping is perhaps one of the most common human traits. We let people know subtly that 'X' is a friend and we imply that X really values our friendship. X may be a politician, a film star, a sports personality or a church leader. By name-dropping, we are boosting ourselves by hanging on to the coat tails of someone else's reputation. In borrowing glory from them, who *we* are and what *we* say becomes far more important. Now, when we do this with human personalities we merely expose our insecurity, but when we do it with God we run far greater risks.

Misusing God's name this way has been distressingly common at a global level. In history there have been far too many 'holy crusades', 'sacred struggles' and 'wars in defence of Christian values'. God has been used to justify apartheid in South Africa, concentration camps in Nazi Germany and, under such titles as 'our mission to bring civilisation', any number of greedy imperialistic ventures. We need to be wary of thinking that such things are in the distant past; God's name has been invoked on both sides in Northern Ireland. To invoke God or Christianity to enable us to oppress, intimidate, hurt or exploit others surely involves a breach of this commandment. Those who do this will have to give an account of their words.

Our leaders would do well to learn from President Lincoln's wisdom. Shortly after the fall of Atlanta during the American Civil War, a woman exclaimed to President Lincoln at a White House function, 'Oh, Mr President, I feel sure that God is on our side . . . don't you?'

'Ma'am,' replied Lincoln solemnly, 'I am more concerned that we should be on God's side.'

This sort of abuse can even occur within churches. We can use God's name to further our own projects. We name-drop God to give ourselves credibility. Sometimes we use God's name to confidently underwrite something that is no more than our own wish, with words like 'the Lord showed me that . . .' The problem is that God *may* have spoken to us as an individual or as a church, or he may not. There is often a temptation to bring him in to justify our plans (especially when they need a helping hand). This type of name-dropping can also be used to manipulate others, as in 'God told me that you will marry me!'

Please do not misunderstand me; I am not saying that God does not speak today. That would contradict the Bible and does not honour his name. I believe that God speaks to the church, he speaks to me as an individual about my life and work, and I believe he speaks through other Christians too. But I do not think we should immediately believe everything that is claimed as being from God. Both as individuals and churches we must realise the seriousness of claiming that God has given us something specific for a situation or person, especially when it is likely to have significant implications for others.

The apostle Paul is helpful in this area. In his first letter to the church at Corinth he distinguishes clearly between what is his own advice and what he knows is from God. In 1 Corinthians 7:10 he says, 'To the married I give this command (not I, but the Lord) . . .' and then two verses later he says, 'To the rest I say this (I, not the Lord) . . .' Elsewhere he emphasises the need for discernment. 'Do not quench the Spirit. Do not treat prophecies with contempt but test them all; hold on to what is good, reject every kind of evil' (1 Thessalonians 5:19–22).

In the normal world, when you take someone else's name and use it for your own ends it is called forgery. When, either unconsciously or consciously, we attach God's name to something he has not said, it is like writing a cheque and forging God's signature. Because God makes real promises, he is not pleased when we invent them and pass them off as his. We must beware of spiritual forgery.

Don't Dishonour God

We can misuse God's name by not mentioning him at all. All too often when we do something praiseworthy, we personally receive all the honour. This is sadly true even if it is in answer to prayer. Often God doesn't even make it onto the credit screens of our lives.

We need to honour God by crediting him with all that he does. To do this requires the much-neglected virtue of humility. Humility means that when it comes to any sort of award ceremony, we step back and wave God forwards into the spotlight. After all, everything we have, we have been given by him. Even what we are inclined to think of as our own talents are nothing of the sort; they have been given to us – or more properly loaned to us – by God himself. Humility is to receive praise, and to pass it on to God untouched.

Again, the apostle Paul can teach us a lot. Not long after the church at Corinth was founded, some men who considered themselves 'super-apostles' began to boast of what they had done. As a result they were able to exert a harmful influence. In 2 Corinthians 1 Paul addresses this problem and actually boasts of his sufferings, not his strength.

At one point (2 Corinthians 12:1–7), Paul talks about 'a man I know' who had the most extraordinary vision of heaven, seeing things that 'no one should tell of'. Later, Paul lets slip that it was him, but because he is trying to be humble, he tells it as if it wasn't him. He goes on to say that he prefers 'to boast about my weaknesses, so that the power of Christ may work through me' (2 Corinthians 12:9 NLT). It is all too common to hear people boasting of the wonderful visions and experiences they have had, as if they had earned them. In contrast, Paul had a stunning vision but then refused to talk about it and instead changed the topic to his own weaknesses! Paul was anxious that God got the glory; he was honouring God's name, not his own.

How do we adopt an attitude like Paul's so that we give glory where glory is due? I think the best solution is not to lower ourselves, but to elevate God. And we elevate God by worshipping him. The best antidote to the misuse of God's name is to ensure its proper use, and the best way of using God's name properly is through praise and prayer. I believe that if our worship was more God-centred, the temptation to break this commandment would be drastically reduced.

There is a danger today that our worship revolves around *us*, when its true focus should be God. I said earlier that the temptation to name-drop was that it made us look good. We must be careful that something similar does not creep into our worship. Neither prayer nor worship is meant to exalt us. There is wisdom in the story of two people who were coming out of church and one asked the other how they had found the service. 'Oh,' came the reply, 'I didn't get anything out of the worship.'

'I'm sorry,' was the response, 'I didn't realise it was for *you*.'

Worship is for God's benefit, not ours. Frequently when listening to songs and prayers, I have wondered whether we have it all the wrong way around and we're making ourselves the centre and expecting God to circle around us. We must be careful to give glory to God alone.

Let me ask you to review those things that you are most proud of, the things that you count as your achievements. Are you giving God adequate credit for all he has done and is doing? Have you ever thanked God for them? If not, why not do it now?

What about your spiritual life? When you pray your prayers, are they God-centred? Or are they self-centred? Believe me, these are hard questions for all of us, but if we are going to take this command seriously we need to respond to them. We honour God by crediting him with all that he does and is.

Don't Live an Inconsistent Life

Finally, we can dishonour God's name if the lives that we live do not match up to the words we speak.

We need to live lives that show that the words we say are true. Now that's difficult, but it is essential. I believe one reason why the church's reputation has suffered lies here. Too many people have heard 'religious' people say one thing and then seen them do another.

When Jesus ascended to heaven, his followers on earth became his body and continued his work and witness. Very soon they became known by his name: 'Christians'. Interestingly, it does not seem that this was a name they gave themselves. Instead, outsiders who saw how central Jesus Christ was to what these people did and said, decided that *Christ*ian was a good term for them. His followers bore his name then; they still do today.

Now, as Christians, we are called to live lives that are worthy of the name of Christ, as if we go through life with his name marked on us. Paul often encourages us to be worthy of the name; of some false believers he says, 'They claim to know God, but by their actions they deny him' (Titus 1:16). We are urged not to bring disrepute on the family name by our behaviour. We must always ask ourselves whether there is a gap between our beliefs and our behaviour.

The whole issue of names is at the heart of our relationship with God. In Jesus, we can be on first-name terms with God. Jesus, in turn, tells us that God cares for us so much that he knows every detail of who we are. Yet this is just the beginning of the relationship, for the amazing thing that happens when we begin to honour God's name is that he honours us back. The nearer we draw to him, the closer he comes to us. The more we call him by name, the more we hear him calling us by name. As we do this, we learn one of the most wonderful truths about God: you can never out-give him and you can never out-love him. To honour God's name is to put in process a chain of events that, one glorious day, will result in us seeing God face to face.

1   http://nametrends.net

2   http://www.babycentre.co.uk/c1053850/baby-names-2019

3   Nelson Mandela, *Long Walk to Freedom* (Little Brown & Co, 1995)

HOW TO KNOW GOD

COMMANDMENT TWO: YOU SHALL NOT MAKE IDOLS

'You shall not make for yourself an image in the form of anything in heaven above or on the earth beneath or in the waters below. You shall not bow down to them or worship them; for I, the LORD your God, am a jealous God, punishing the children for the sin of the fathers to the third and fourth generation of those who hate me, but showing love to a thousand generations of those who love me and keep my commandments.' (Exodus 20:4–6)

SO, WHAT'S THE PROBLEM?

A Confused World

Our journey into the Ten Commandments started by looking at topics that dealt with how we relate to those around us and our family. Then we examined those commandments that focused on God himself. At first it was indirect as we looked at how we remember God and look after ourselves by keeping a Sabbath. Then, more directly, it was how we honour God's name. Now, as we come to the heart of the commandments, we will be focusing more on who God is. This second commandment deals with a vital and related issue – not so much who God is, but who God is not. Idolatry is the giving of worship to things that are not God. We need to talk about idolatry because there's a lot of it about.

There now exists an unprecedented confusion about who (if anybody) we worship. In Britain you would probably have to go back over fifteen hundred years to find a similar period of religious turmoil. The United States bears witness to a similar general consensus: until the last few decades, discussions about faith have been almost entirely about which brand of Christianity should be followed. In both countries there have been many religious debates and disputes, but all were basically about how we worship God of the Bible. They were not about who or what we worship – that was taken for granted. Not anymore.

There is now an extraordinary bewilderment about whether we should worship one God, many gods or no gods at all. The best definition of national religious belief in Britain is the almost totally meaningless statement that we are now 'post-Christian'.

This commandment deals with who we worship, so we must briefly consider where we stand. In Britain there has clearly been a decline in traditional or institutional Christianity. Although there are some splendid and encouraging exceptions, most churches have found that the number of people attending services has declined dramatically from the 1950s.

The most recent faith survey (2017) suggests that UK church membership has declined from 10.6 million in 1930 to 5.5 million in 2010 or, as a percentage of the population, from about 30 per cent to 11.2 per cent. By 2013 this had declined further to 5.4 million (10.3 per cent). If current trends continue, membership will fall to 8.4 per cent of the population by 2025.[1] This suggests that for many people in England and Wales, their Christian faith is little more than a label of identity.

A similar trend is appearing in the United States, but perhaps delayed by a generation. So, as recently as 1990, 71 per cent of the adult population were certain that God exists, but by 2014 that figure had dropped to 63 per cent.[2]

However, as in Britain, claims and reality are very different. It is appropriate to term this 'nominal Christianity'. After all, 'nominal' means 'in name only' and these are people who, while they claim to wear a Christian badge, are failing in at least one key respect to live that faith out. Nominal faith is perilous: it makes no disciples, changes no lives and not only is it not often transmitted to the next generation but it tends to do the exact opposite, because children (quite understandably) rebel against something that they see to be superficial. Nominal Christianity doesn't last. It is a hollow husk of faith, all too ready to crumple under the pull of the world or the hint of persecution.

In addition to the troubling state of the church, let me point out three other relevant phenomena in the area of worship.

1. The rise of 'non-belief'

According to the 2011 UK Census, those of no religion are the second largest belief group, at 26.13 per cent of the population, about three and a half times as many as all the non-Christian religions put together; 16,038,229 people said they had 'no religion' with a further 4,406,032 not stating a religion.[3]

A poll in the United States found that the number of Americans who say they are religious dropped from 73 per cent in 2005 to 60 per cent in 2019.[4] This has been claimed to demonstrate the rise of atheism, but it is not quite that simple. After all, to say you have 'no religious affiliation' is nowhere near the same as saying 'there is no God'. In the most recent US survey, only 9 per cent of the population called themselves atheists, a 4 per cent rise in recent years.

Unbelief, on the other hand, is sometimes presented, particularly by New Atheists, as being a neutral position on religious matters. It is actually nothing of the sort. It delivers a verdict on the basis of faith about the existence of God and so it is as much a religion as the belief systems it condemns.

2. The rise of other faiths

Both Britain and the United States now have sizeable but varying populations from other religions, notably Muslims, Jews, Sikhs and Hindus. Some followers of these religions are zealous for their faith and rigorous in seeking to live out their lives in light of their belief, while others are nominal. Nevertheless, the way these faiths have changed the spiritual landscape is significant. You only have to go back a generation or two to a time when many Britons and Americans could spend their entire lives without ever knowingly coming across someone of a different religion. The variety of faiths we now encounter has added to the confusion.

3. The rise of 'New Age'

So flexible in belief and practice this is less a religion, more a mood. Apart from where it is clearly a form of Hinduism or Buddhism, New

Age is hard to classify. It is, after all, a very informal, do-it-yourself, pick-and-mix thing; one of its attractions is that it allows you to do what you want. Whether it's meditation, feng shui, Gaia, reincarnation, astrology, crystal therapy, tarot or rebirthing, it's all on offer today and you can adjust to taste. New Age is a cocktail that can be made of many ingredients and at any strength.

These factors have combined to produce a confused, misty and constantly changing spiritual landscape of almost infinite varieties and combinations of belief and unbelief. In this intellectual and spiritual muddle three attitudes can be widely detected.

The first is the rejection of any sort of authority in the religious area. 'I'll believe what I want,' people say proudly. Although the majority of the population might well say they 'believe in God', if you asked them to describe the God that they believe in, the answers would be as varied and different as the people you asked. The fact that the Bible speaks with authority on such matters really does not make it – or Christians who believe it – popular. Certainly, if belief was once a virtue, it has now become a vice.

A second common feature is the preference for spiritual beliefs that are undemanding. Religion today is presented as just another lifestyle option, like keep-fit or gardening. It is simply the 'spiritual dimension' to life; if you need real, deep-down fulfilment, then you tack some spirituality onto your life. Here, too, Christianity finds itself out of favour. It is, people protest, too narrow and oppressive. It denies so much and it demands too much. Besides, it makes ethical demands: it says 'do this' and 'don't do that'. That is not popular; people prefer to separate morality from spirituality. Much religion today is something that we are supposed to *feel*, it is a matter of mood. And doing what is right can often get in the way of feeling spiritual. In the supermarket of New Age beliefs, the big sellers are labelled 'low in moral demands'.

A third feature of modern religion is the widespread belief in the sort of tolerance that wants nothing ruled out. 'It may not be for me,' people say, 'but we better not knock it.' This goes for beliefs and for morals. One of the few New Age commandments is 'Thou shall not say "thou shall not".' The thing that irritates many people about Christianity is not so much what it affirms, but what it denies. They can probably be persuaded that Jesus was good and wise, but to say that 'he is the only way to God' is too narrow and restricting.

The upshot is that traditional Christianity is not the flavour of the age. It is seen as too inflexible, too dogmatic, too restrictive and too demanding. People want a religion that they can tailor to suit their circumstances. God should fit in with us, rather than us fitting in with him.

The blunt reality is that in a religious world that seems to offer no fixed ground, people prefer to make God in their own image. In the past we accepted God's description of who he was; now it is we who define who God is. He is *my* God and I can create him (or her, or it) to be whoever and in whatever form I want. We now worship anything that suits us. The problem is that this 'anything' is idolatry.

Idolatry Today

One of the biggest issues with idolatry is that we don't see what it really is. When we think of idols and idolatry, our minds conjure up pictures of statues in exotic Far Eastern temples. For most of us, bowing down to some carved piece of wood or stone seems rather ridiculous. We smile at the thought. No, we say, that's one commandment you will never see me breaking!

This is a dangerous view. It obscures the extent, variety and subtlety of the idolatry that we face today. Idolatry does not just involve ancient sculptures and carvings; it has always been there – the only thing that changes is the nature of the idols.

Idols do not have to be figures made of stone or precious metal; they are just as likely to be high-tech and made of silicon and metal alloy. Some idols can be without physical form. In fact, I suspect that some of the most powerful idols exist only in the mind.

What is an idol? There are so many idols, and they are so subtle that a simple definition is difficult. Let me try to express it this way. A Christian could make the following statements about God:

- *God* gives purpose, meaning and fulfilment to my life.
- *God* governs the way I act.

- *God* is the focal point around which my existence hangs.
- *God* is often in my thoughts and I get enthusiastic about *God*.
- Thoughts of *God* comfort me when I am down.
- I read about *God*, I talk about *God*, I make friends with those who are also committed to *God*.
- I desire more of *God*.

You've got the picture? Now idolatry is where something – anything – takes the place of God in this central position in our life. An idol is anything that you could replace the word 'God' with in statements like those above. Try it with *money, possessions, my career, holidays, sport, music, sex* or almost anything else. An idol is what people live for. An idol is what consumes our thoughts when we lie awake at night; an idol is what our minds drift to when in neutral. Idols are what we buy magazines about, idols are what we read websites on, and idols are what we spend our time, money and energy on. Idols are the centre of gravity of our lives. Idolatry occurs when we hold any value, idea or activity higher than God.

THE HEART OF THE MATTER

So, why are we so prone to idolatry? And are idols that bad anyway? I believe that if we can answer these questions we will have come a long way to understanding what the problem of idolatry is.

The Attraction of Idolatry

Why is idolatry so attractive?

The first thing to say is that idols are not fundamentally evil.In fact, the most dangerous idols are actually good things that have been twisted. Think of the things listed above as being potential idols: money, possessions, career, holidays, sport, music, sex. Not a single one of them is bad; they are all good, and all gifts of God. And as good things, they are attractive to us. In fact, it is the very best things that make the most tempting idols.

Let me give an example of how this works with one very dangerous modern idol: nationalism. God made different peoples, ethnic groups and races. God obviously appreciates diversity and he delights in such differences. I have no doubt that it is a good thing to celebrate our culture, to love our nation and to be proud of it. It can give us worth, purpose, value and a sense of significance. Yet it is all too easy for those attitudes to slide over into something far nastier. If the race or the nation that we belong to starts to become the central feature in our lives then we must be careful. Once we start saying that we are better than our neighbours, or that any means justifies us beating them in sport, then we are in trouble. It is not hard to see where nationalism can lead to: you only have to look at Hitler's Germany, Rwanda in the 1990s or the simmering unease of the modern Balkans.

Sadly, even churches are not exempt from idolatry. Organs, music groups, preaching and theology are all good things and there is no reason why we can't take pride in them. But it is all too easy for them to acquire a distorted prominence. When they become the focus of what we are and what we stand for as churches, they cease to be good and start to become idols. At this point, God leaves quietly by the back door. He will not share his worship with any idols. And let's not be fixated with who is leading worship rather than the actual worship of God.

The other attraction of idolatry is that idols make fewer moral demands on us than the real God. The one true God is so uncompromising that idols present something of an attractive alternative. For a start, they rarely insist that you give up adultery, lying or theft. God does.

The classic example of the attractions of idolatry can be found in the Bible. Even as God was giving this commandment to Moses on Mount Sinai, the Israelites were breaking it. Why? Moses, we are told, had been up the mountain for some days and the people were frustrated and impatient with waiting for God. They wanted something instant and immediate. So, Aaron melted down all their jewellery, cast it into a golden calf and presented it to the people as a substitute focus for their worship. Idols offer the possibility to men and women of making their own controllable god, one whom they can deal with on their terms, not his.

It is because we cannot picture God in our minds that we are tempted to create an idol. Throughout history, people have made symbols to represent the things they cannot see. People have argued that if images help us to worship God, then they have some value.

The problem is that aids to worship can easily become objects of worship. God knows that any image we might use to portray him would depict him as less than he truly is. Eventually, we would begin to conceive of him in ways that mirror the image we constructed. It is so nearly right – but it is wrong. To fill God's place with an image is like blotting the sun out and substituting a 60-watt bulb in its place.

It is not wise to underestimate the subtle attraction of idols. The story of King Solomon is very sobering. He was the wisest man of his day, a constructor of the temple and a man to whom God had appeared twice (see 1 Kings 3 – 10). Yet we read (in 1 Kings 11) how, in his old age, he turned to the worship of foreign gods and incurred God's anger. If a man like Solomon can fall into idolatry, then you and I ought to be very careful.

The Adultery of Idolatry

But so what? Does it matter that modern Britain or the United States is awash with a thousand varieties of formal and informal religion? Does it matter that, for many, sport, shopping or 'stuff' is what is at the heart of their lives?

Isn't God big enough to handle these and other religious beliefs? Does God really mind whether he is called 'Krishna', 'Gaia' or 'Great Light of the Cosmos'? Can't he just say, 'Well, I know what they mean. They may have the wrong address on their prayers but I'll just redirect them to me.' And if people worship rocks, trees or crystals does it really matter? I mean, no one's perfect. Besides, shouldn't the church (and God) be glad of any devotion, whatever form it may take?

Surely God doesn't mind if hobbies and pursuits become the core of our lives? After all, he made these things. God can't seriously be threatened by someone's devotion to their garden, fishing or sport?

To answer these questions, I need to talk about adultery again.

I love my wife Killy very much. We were married in 1983 and I am more in love with her today than when we married. But can you imagine how she would feel if she noticed a photo of another woman in my wallet, alongside the one I have of her? Do you think that she would say, 'Well this is interesting, but my husband is entitled to his freedom and privacy so I won't ask any more?' Isn't it far more likely that she would immediately find me and demand to know who this other woman was and what her picture was doing in my wallet? What do you imagine her reaction would be if she learned that I had developed a friendship with this woman and that I turned to her when I felt especially in need of support, affection or encouragement? Do you think it would upset Killy? Do you think she would continue to believe me when I whispered in her ear that I loved her with all my heart? Could you blame her if she confronted me, tore the photograph into pieces and demanded that I never see this other woman again? Could you fault her for feeling jealous, hurt, betrayed and angry about having to share my love and devotion with another?

These are obviously absurd questions. In such a context you can't love a person and be tolerant of other loves. You can't love someone and be indifferent about them having an affair. Killy is my wife; she has every right to expect and insist that I keep myself for her, and her alone. And I want to live up to those expectations because I love her, I need her and because our relationship is the most important earthly thing I have. Even the idea that there might be 'someone else' is terrible to both of us. A scenario like this goes to the heart of the issue that is addressed in this commandment.

Surely though, you protest, this commandment is about idols? In fact, this commandment is about how we love God, a relationship for which the nearest parallel we have is marriage. In marriage there is no room for any other person. It is a unique and exclusive relationship between two people. That exclusivity is at the very heart of what a marriage is all about. And our relationship with God is to be similar.

The idea of using marriage as an image for how we relate to God is not mine. It is God's, and we find it used several times in the Bible. There are many similarities between a relationship with God and a marriage. Both are personal relationships that are bound by pledges of faithfulness and priority. In fact, the concept of a covenant – a mutually binding treaty of one party to another – lies at the heart of both relationships. As the husband and wife make promises exclusively to each other, so God and his people make similar promises: he to protect and bless us and we to trust and obey him. A key element of any covenant, ancient or modern, is its restricted nature; it is *only* between the named parties. There cannot be any sort of heart-to-heart intimacy between two individuals unless all third parties are ruthlessly excluded.

Idols tempt us away from our exclusive bond to God. They strike at the very foundation of this relationship with him by introducing 'someone else'. God is as uncompromising about the purity of his relationship with us as any partner in a marriage – in fact, even more so. He uses strong language in the Bible about what bringing idols into this relationship means. It is adultery, unfaithfulness, a breaking of a sworn agreement, the very deepest breach of trust and devotion. God wants sole rights to our worship.

CONFRONTING IDOLATRY TODAY

I want to look now at how we combat idolatry. First, I want to give you some strategies and then I want to look at some specific areas where idolatry needs to be confronted.

Recognise a Double Danger

Let's look at two dangers that exist when confronting idolatry.

The first danger is that of simply giving in to idolatry. Faced with overwhelming pressure from our culture to worship such things as sex, power and possessions, we could just shrug our shoulders in defeat. It is all too much, we might say. The only hope, we conclude, is that we can preserve an idol-free hour in our churches on Sunday. This is wrong. If we realise how serious idolatry is, and how much of an affront it is to God, we cannot simply give in. Besides, for how long would our holy hour survive?

A second danger is more subtle. It is to look at what the idolatry centres on and to reject that completely. Is sex being worshipped? Then the response is to be against sex. Is meditation being made a god? Then the response is to reject anything in our own worship that remotely resembles being contemplative. Is sport becoming an idol? Then the response is to preach against it and to be suspicious of anyone in the congregation in trainers. Is being green replacing being godly? Then the response is to ostentatiously drive to church rather than walk.

At the heart of almost all idolatry is something good, so complete rejection hurts us more than it hurts idolatry. When we reject what is good for us, simply because it has been abused by others, it makes Christians seem joyless and negative, and appear as though they are always against something.

It is easy to find ourselves trapped between these two positions of defeatism or unconditional rejection. Let me suggest a more profitable strategy.

Plant the Flag for God!

My friend theologian Tom Wright talks about a discovery he made which helps us in confronting idolatry. He explains that when the first Christians arrived in Britain and started to build places of worship, they chose to build them on sites the pagans had used for worship. This was not because these places had something special about them. Rather, it was a conscious decision to say something about Christianity – that the call to us is to worship God in places where idols are worshipped. It is to plant the flag for God in hostile soil, to claim the good things of God for him, to proclaim that only under the loving and gracious gaze of God can everything be held in the right balance and with the right perspective.

I find this a very helpful concept. Instead of running away scared or rejecting anything contaminated by idolaters, this gives us a better alternative. It's harder work, of course, but then most good ideas are.

Some Current Confrontations

With these things in mind I want us to look at five areas where there is currently a struggle against idolatry. I believe that the principles we see in them can be applied elsewhere.

1. Preserving the natural world

As I suggested earlier, the best things make the most tempting idols. It is when God's handiwork is at its best that we are most tempted to worship it, instead of its creator. Nowhere is this truer than in the area of the environment.

Just a few decades ago humanity's attitude to the natural world was straightforward. Life was a hard struggle for existence against the elements, the seasons, predators and pests. For most people nature was something that you battled against because, if you didn't, you starved. Only the rich had the luxury of contemplating the majesty of nature in the grandeur of the mountains; the poor were too busy bent over their ploughs to look up. The idea that we could do harm to the natural world did not enter many people's minds. In the past few decades there has been a growing realisation that our species is capable of doing permanent harm to the world. Indeed, as the ever-growing list of extinct species demonstrates, we have already done so. The result has been a great deal of interest in the environment, something which is good, right and long overdue.

However, some New Age views hold the idea that the earth, living things and indeed Nature (always with a capital letter) are actually to be worshipped themselves. Some people, digging around in old mythologies, have revived terms such as Mother Earth or Gaia for the planet and have credited her (feminine deities are currently fashionable) with being the creator. People recite mantras to life, invoke the spirits of winds and atmospheric energies and protest that all life, whether plant, animal or human, is of equal value. Some wild places have become sacred sites, mystical glades or focal points of spirit power.

Now, as Christians we actually have some sympathies with people who hold such ideas. They have rejected the atheistic view that there is nothing but cold, sterile biology, physics and chemistry in our world. So have we. They recognise in woods, animals and countryside something wonderful, something far greater than anything that time, chance and natural selection could produce. So do we. Where we must disagree is over what it all means. They see nature as so wonderful that it is to be worshipped; we see it as the wonderful craftsmanship of God the creator who alone is to be worshipped. The splendour of the natural world is to us a mirror in which God's glory is reflected. The distinction is important; I know that Killy would think me very strange if I paid more attention to her reflection than to her!

So, what should we do when we see this good thing being turned into an idol? As I suggested earlier, the answer is not to simply shout 'Idolatry!' and run away with our eyes closed. The solution is to 'plant a flag for God' in this area. To do that means first, the hard work of thinking and praying through how we should treat the natural world, and then the even harder work of getting out there and doing it.

In fact, there are an increasing number of Christians involved in conserving the environment and there are some remarkable projects underway in the name of God. Incidentally, it turns out that the worship of Nature is not actually a very good basis for conservation. After all, there are often hard decisions to be made. For example, if rats threaten rare seabird colonies, can we take the life of the rats when they are a sacred part of Nature? If all life is holy, how dare we intervene at all? The Christian view – of us holding a delegated responsibility for the natural world and of being God's stewards – is actually a far safer one.

2. Sex

Eroticism continues to entice us with the promise of bliss, fulfilment and escape. Although this is not new – after all, eroticism has always existed – the grip it has on today's society is particularly strong. This is a classic case of idolatry. How do we deal with it?

Again, there is a temptation to adopt a simplistic solution and reject the good that is being abused. This has led in the past to enforced celibacy or denial. Here, problems arise. When sex is not talked about, sexuality becomes something to be wary of and to avoid. The trouble is that sexuality is too potent a force to be neutralised by pushing it below the surface of our lives. Some people are so afraid of facing up to their problems in the area of sex that they try to pretend they have no past or present struggles. This can be the recipe for future disaster.

Again, we must be those who 'plant the flag' for God. It will not be easy. The middle of a battlefield is never an easy place to plant any flag and I have no doubt that both sides will misunderstand us when we try and set up God's ideal standards and claim this whole area of human life for him. We will need to be patient and gracious with those who are victims of the god of sex, an ever-increasing number of whom are cast aside, hurting people who need the healing of the God of life.

3. The body

Another major god of our age is the perfect body. The second commandment could read 'Do not make "yourself" an idol.' 'How do I look?' has become a question that haunts both sexes, especially from adolescence onwards. We are surrounded by examples of those who appear physically perfect: the super-thin supermodels; the lean and muscular footballers; the glamorous and immaculately groomed rich. In a million air-brushed and digitally manipulated glossy pictures, human perfection is laid out before us. 'Are you like this?' ask the advertisements, leaving us depressed as we stare at ourselves in the mirror and try to tug in our waistlines. We bow to what our scales say about us, and let their verdict determine how we feel about ourselves. It is idolatry.

We pile up sacrifices on the idolatrous altar of the perfect body. In order to try to live up to the impossible standards held before us, we sacrifice wealth, time and health. We feel the need to stave off age at all costs, whether by beauty treatments or surgery. Women especially feel this enslaving compulsion to fit the mould. The victims are everywhere. Low self-image is common among young people who feel that they just don't look right, and the number of people suffering from eating disorders such as anorexia and bulimia has never been higher. If this is something you have struggled with or you are concerned about someone, then I urge you to seek professional help. Your doctor will be able to recommend people to talk to.

Here we see a familiar pattern. Once more, it takes what God made good and fatally distorts it by making it everything. To state that one look or one physique is superior to another denies the truth that we are all made in God's image. It also hides the fact that God made us all different and that he is far more concerned with who we are than what we look like. Again, we could respond by being negative about health, fitness and beauty. But we need to come up with another flag-planting alternative that affirms what is good about the body by pointing out some truths.

Healthy bodies are important, and it is good to pursue bodily health for ourselves and for others. Our bodies shouldn't be mistreated, neglected or discarded; we are to take good care of what God has given us. However, we should remember that our bodies, even the fittest, are not going to last for ever; we are all finite and fragile. We should also remember that we are all made in the image of God and given his breath of life. The God who created us values each and every one of us, whatever we look like. In fact, God loves us all so much that he put the highest value on us: the life of his Son. Beautiful bodies are fine, but what God seeks most of all is not outward good looks but an inner spiritual beauty. Only that is of eternal value.

4. Power

'Power' is a word that makes us sit up and listen. On the international stage, there is weekly posturing by 'political powers' and frequent discussion of the 'balance of power'. The media talks about global military power and economic power. We talk about power in our offices, councils and governments. We read of politicians and governments 'coming to power', when we had thought they were being 'elected to serve'. In today's world, power of every sort is important and is worshipped. Power has become an idol.

As with the natural world, sex and the body, we see the same pattern of the good gift mutated into the tempting idol. There is nothing wrong with power; used correctly and responsibly, much good can be done. God has given humanity power and we are called to exercise it for the sake of his world and his people. The trouble occurs when power turns into an idol and is pursued as an end in itself, to control and influence others. It is all too common for people who started off seeking power for all the right reasons to end up becoming corrupt and betraying their original principles just to stay in power. They have been seduced into worshipping the idol of power. We see the same pattern repeated throughout history at every level. Not even the church is immune to the idolatry of power. Power seems to become an idol very easily.

So how do we react? The temptation here is the same as before. We could make it a point of principle that all Christians automatically refuse promotion and deliberately seek jobs at the bottom of whatever ladder they are perched on. It is also wrong. Never having power is too easy an answer. If we opt out of society, we can hardly complain when things go wrong. We are told to be salt and light in society and this means that we must be where we can have influence. There are numerous examples in the Bible of men (Daniel, Ezra) and women (Esther, Deborah) who used their power for good, even within corrupt systems.

We again need to plant a flag for God. We need to watch our motives. If we want to gain (or keep) a position of authority and power, we must ask ourselves *why* we want it. The only really safe answer is 'to serve God and to do good to others'. If we are in power, we need to have wise and honest friends who will tell us if they think our authority is adversely affecting us. Another principle is to ensure that there are outside checks and balances on our power. It is so tempting to abuse power that we need to be accountable to others.

Above all, we need the example of Jesus. Here was a person with unlimited power (after all, he was God), who spent time doing the lowliest of jobs and finally died a shameful death for others. He sets *the* example of humility and of selflessness. All the power that he wielded was entirely for others. Furthermore, we read that Jesus spent most of his time with those outside the structures of power, those who were stripped of respect and dignity.

We need to ask ourselves how our exercise of power at home, work or church matches up to that of Jesus. Do we have the same attitude as he did? Do we have the same concern for the poor and powerless as he did?

We have no excuse for worshipping power when we have the greatest possible example of someone rejecting its attractions. Jesus totally rejected the corruption and idolatry of power – so should we.

5. Possessions

I talked earlier of the greatest of all our modern-day temples of worship: the shopping centre. Both in the UK and in the US we are driven by the desire to amass yet more possessions. This is an ancient trait: human beings have always accumulated things and been strangely obsessed by them. In fact, much of what we know about the ancient world is because people were so strongly linked to their possessions that they had them placed with them in their graves. But there has never been a time in history when so many things have cried out for us to possess them, whether houses, cars, computers, jewellery, gadgets or clothes.

Again, the temptation is to react by a drastic outright rejection of all possessions. Throughout the history of Christianity there have been individuals or groups who have renounced all ownership of private possessions. It neglects the fact that creation is good. (However, I do respect and esteem those nuns and monks who have renounced all ownership of private possessions to be part of a monastic community to serve God and the poor.)

In planting the flag here, let me sketch out some guidelines. We must hold possessions lightly. We need to be able to look around at all that we have – our cars, our music, our books and our clothes – and say, 'Well, God, if you asked me to, I could give them away.' If we can say that, we are on the right track. An even better practice is to get into the habit of giving things, even good things, away. Nothing insults idols quite so much as giving them away.

These are just some examples of where idolatry is being confronted. What you and I need to do is to look at our own lives and see where we need to challenge the idols. Where in your life do you need to plant the flag for God?

REMEMBER THE COST OF IDOLATRY

It is worth remembering that the Ten Commandments are given for our benefit, not God's. He is against idolatry, not just because it robs him of his rightful worship but because it is hurtful to us. This commandment reminds us that God is jealous of anything that would take his place. This is not because he is some wicked dictator who wants to stop us from enjoying ourselves. On the contrary, it is precisely because he loves us so passionately that he urges us to stop being involved in anything that would hurt us. If God did not react like this, it would show that he did not care what sort of mess we got ourselves into.

Idolatry is harmful in two ways. The first is that it cheats and destroys those who practise it, and the second is that it steals from us the most precious thing we can have: a knowledge and experience of the living God.

Idolatry Cheats and Destroys the Idolater

The whole basis of idolatry is a lie. We take things that are not God and pretend that they are. The results are catastrophic. Think of the examples above.

- The idol of the natural world whispers that if we serve it, it will show us truth and meaning and give us purpose in our lives. But it never does.

- The idol of sex murmurs to us that if we serve it, it will give us a permanent state of ecstatic joy, delight and intimacy. But it never does.

- The idol of the body tells us that if we serve it, it will make us the gods and goddesses that we want to look like. But it never does.

- The idol of power thunders at us that if we serve it, it will give us the freedom to do whatever we want, whenever we want. But it never does.

- The idol of possessions announces that if we serve it, it will make us fulfilled, complete and content. But it never does.

They all lie; they never – except for the briefest moment – ever deliver. Many years ago, an Old Testament prophet said, 'All who make idols are nothing, and the things they treasure are worthless' (Isaiah 44:9). It is hard to argue with that. These idols promise the world but cannot deliver. And it is hardly surprising; the world is not theirs to give.

It gets worse. Idols also enslave their followers. In an effort to find what the idols have promised we get lured in ever deeper. Devotees of the idol of sex spend their lives in a futile, dangerous and ever more draining hunt for sexual fulfilment. But it is a mirage; as real as the pot of gold at the rainbow's end. The idol of possessions exerts the same hold; you may 'shop until you drop' but even then you will still want more. Idolatry is as satisfying as drinking saltwater.

The reason why idols grip us in an ever-tighter embrace is simple. When we give some part of the created world the worship that belongs to the creator God, that idol acquires power over us. When we worship things, we offer them our service. We may think they serve us, but it is the other way around: we serve them. And idols are cruel masters.

Some of the most profound words on idols are found in the psalms, the worship book of God's people.

Our God is in the heavens, and he does as he wishes. Their idols are merely things of silver and gold, shaped by human hands. They have mouths but cannot speak, and eyes but cannot see. They have ears but cannot hear, and noses but cannot smell. They have hands but cannot feel, and feet but cannot walk, and throats but cannot make a sound. And those who make idols are just like them, as are all who trust in them. (Psalm 115:3–8 NLT)

The psalm writer is making the point that the idols of men and women are not real, they are not living and they are not lasting. If you are in trouble, they are useless. They have feet, but they can't come to you; they have hands, but they can't lift a finger to help you; they have eyes, but don't see what's going on in your life; they have ears, but they don't hear your cries when you are lonely, frightened or in despair. They are useless.

What is more, the writer says, what you worship you end up resembling. So when people worship idols, they become like them: more and more unreal, more and more false, and more and more dead. The trouble with idolatry is that it makes us less than human.

Idolatry Cheats Us of the Living God

There is still worse news about idolatry. Around sixteen hundred years ago the wise Saint Augustine opened the account of his conversion with the following statement to God: 'You made us for yourself and our hearts find no peace until they rest in you.' There is a 'God-shaped void' in our lives that only God can fill.

Now, I must remind you that God is very different from idols. Above all, he is the living God, the one who is above everything, the one who cannot be controlled by us. 'I AM WHO I AM' is how he defined himself. Psalm 115 said of the true God, 'Our God is in the heavens, and he does as he wishes.' Another danger of worshipping idols is treating the true God as simply another but bigger idol. In coming to the real God, we are coming to someone who will never be at our beck and call.

C.S. Lewis alludes to this in his children's story, *The Lion, the Witch and the Wardrobe*, when Mr Beaver talks about Aslan, the great lion.

'Who is Aslan?' asked Susan.

'Aslan?' said Mr Beaver. 'Why, don't you know? He's the King. He's the Lord of the whole wood . . .'

'Is he – quite safe? I shall feel rather nervous about meeting a lion.'

'That you will, dearie, and no mistake,' said Mrs Beaver; 'if there's anyone who can appear before Aslan without their knees knocking, they're either braver than most or else just silly.'

'Then he isn't safe?' said Lucy.

'Safe?' said Mr Beaver; 'don't you hear what Mrs Beaver tells you? Who said anything about safe? 'Course he isn't safe. But he's good. He's the King, I tell you.'[5]

Lewis's description of Aslan is, of course, also of Jesus. This idea that the living God is free, active and cannot be manipulated by us comes over in the life of Jesus. There is an independence about Jesus that we can – and ought to – find disturbing. Jesus can never be controlled or made to say what we want him to say, he will never 'toe the party line' and he never marches to our tune. Yes, he keeps his promises, but in his way and in his time. He wants us to pray to him, but we can't tell him what to do.

Now this has exhilarating consequences for those of us who are followers of Jesus. You see, I made the point earlier that we become like the things we worship and that dead idols produce enslaved idolaters. But in contrast to the idols, God is alive and free; he does hear, does see, does feel, does speak and does know. The Bible tells us that we were made in the image of God; therefore, if we worship him we become more human, more like the people we were made to be. To worship God is to become liberated.

Oddly enough, we need to remember this especially in our churches. One of the dangers in the Christian faith is that we can acquire a certain view of God and how he works and cling on to it. These images or ideas are often formed through experiences or teaching, and are often good and right. The trouble is that we let them set the agenda for how God must work in the future; we hold on to past experiences and just look for repeats. We look back to wonderful times in the life of a church and use them as the criteria for whether God is working today. If something doesn't fit the pattern, then we reject it. I travel a lot and meet many people who have made past experiences, past churches and past ways of doing things into idols. Because of this idolatry, new and good things can be rejected. Now, of course, I am not saying that new things are always the best or that novelty is a proof that God is working in a situation. What I am saying is that we need to remember we are dealing with a God who is living, who is more real and alive than we can ever imagine. We must allow God to be God and not treat him as a tame idol.

KEEP YOURSELF FROM IDOLS

The apostle John wrote, 'Dear children, keep yourself from idols' (1 John 5:21). It is advice we need to remember.

Let me ask you, what are the 'photos in your wallet' that could gradually steal you away from a relationship with God? Are there any things to which you have been, perhaps secretly, offering sacrifices? What do you talk about the most? What does that reveal about what is at the centre of your heart? How free do you feel to give things away or to give things up?

We must all confront these idols, otherwise they will hold us captive. And it will not just be us whom they enslave. Did you notice that this commandment talks about the children of those who bow down to idols? That is not because God is vindictive or wants to punish innocent people; it is because idolatry has repercussions that, unless God intervenes, roll on for years. Whole families and generations get taken into captivity. What the parents worship, the children will too. The stakes are high.

There is room for only one woman's photo in my wallet: her name is Killy. There is only room for one Lord in my life: his name is Jesus. What about you? We may reject God's warning by neglecting this commandment. But as Jonah in the Bible learned the hard way, 'Those who cling to worthless idols turn away from God's love for them' (Jonah 2:8).

Now let me conclude with an encouragement. One of the exciting things about times like these is that we find ourselves in the world of the Bible again. The atmosphere in which Christianity was born and grew was full of idols and worship of other gods. Christians knew that not only did those idols hurt those who worshipped them, they set them on a collision course with the true God. With great skill and courage, churches in cities and towns around the Mediterranean took on these gods who held men and women captive. They called people to worship Jesus as Lord, as the God who was not created by us and who is not controlled by us.

It is this call that our world, dominated by idols, needs to hear again, needs to see lived out again and needs to experience. The apostle Paul, when he wandered around the city of Athens just under two thousand years ago, was 'greatly distressed to see that the city was full of idols' (Acts 17:16). He then proclaimed the true God, and many 'turned away from idols to serve the living and true God' (1 Thessalonians 1:9 NLT).

God knows that the 'images' offered by the world are bankrupt. He knows that if we pursue them, in the end we will find ourselves disappointed and devastated. False gods will only take, take and take again. The true and living God gives, gives and gives again.

Now, as we come to the first commandment, it is this living and true God that we must consider.

1   https://faithsurvey.co.uk/uk-christianity.html

2   https://www.pewforum.org/2015/11/03/u-s-public-becoming-less-religious/

3   https://humanism.org.uk/campaigns/religion-and-belief-some-surveys-and-statistics/

4   https://en.wikipedia.org/wiki/Irreligion_in_the_United_States

5   C.S. Lewis, *The Lion, the Witch and the Wardrobe*, copyright © Lewis Pte. Ltd, 1950. Extract reprinted by permission.

HOW TO LIVE BY PRIORITIES

COMMANDMENT ONE: YOU SHALL HAVE NO OTHER GODS

'You shall have no other gods before me.' (Exodus 20:3)

SO, WHAT'S THE PROBLEM?

Finally, we have arrived at the beginning, at the heart of the commandments: the great rule that we are to have no other gods but the one true and living God. If the second commandment dealt with idols, those make-believe gods, this concentrates exclusively on the true God.

This is the commandment that underpins all the others and is the reason for everything we have already looked at. As the sun lies at the centre of the solar system and has planets orbiting around it, so all the other commandments revolve around this first one. God himself lies at the heart of the commandments and holds them all in place.

It is vital we understand that we cannot remove God from the commandments. This is something that people often try to do. In fact, I could have written a book on the Ten Commandments without so far mentioning God at all. In it, I could have argued that not murdering, coveting or stealing were good ideas because they were the best way for a stable society to exist. I could have argued that not coveting leads to less stress, having a day off a week makes you feel better, and that not committing adultery keeps your marriage intact. I would not have been lying, all these things are true. I could have justified all the previous commandments without bringing God in at all. I could even have called them the 'Common-sense Commandments'. I think I could even have justified a 'no-idolatry policy' on common-sense grounds, by interpreting it to mean 'thou shalt not get things out of proportion'. Such a set of commandments would probably be very popular and might find wide support across the diverse religious and spiritual landscape of modern Britain and America. But this first commandment makes such an interpretation totally impossible. These are God's commandments and his name and character are stamped through them.

These commandments only make sense when we see God as being behind each of them. Murder is wrong, primarily because it takes from another person what was given to them by God – life itself. Lying is wrong because God is a God of truth. Adultery is wrong because God is a God of faithfulness. And so on. God is the foundation on which all the commandments stand. You cannot take the God of the Bible out of the Ten Commandments any more than you can take the steel frame out of a skyscraper. All the commandments refer to God and it is only possible to obey them when we are in a proper relationship with the God who gave them.

Christianity isn't just about obeying some rules for life. It is not about 'the best way to act', or having a 'moral code to guide us'. In fact, to think of the Christian life as a matter of dos and don'ts is to make a catastrophic mistake. To say that Christianity is only about keeping the Ten Commandments is like saying that driving is all about keeping the traffic regulations. The Ten Commandments have a similar relationship to the Christian life: they are the guidelines for life; they are not the life itself. Fundamentally, Christianity is about having a right relationship with God. And that is why this first commandment is so important. It puts God first.

God is central to the Ten Commandments. He is the kind and loving being who proclaims them as the best way to live and the one whom we increasingly come to know and love as we let them guide our lives. God is both the giver and the goal of the commandments.

THE HEART OF THE MATTER

Who is God?

God declares who he is at the very start of the commandments. We mislead ourselves if we start the commandments by simply saying, 'Number one: you shall have no other gods before me.'

The commandments really start with the two previous verses: 'And God spoke all these words: "I am the LORD your God, who brought you out of Egypt, out of the land of slavery. You shall have no other gods before me"' (Exodus 20:1–3).

The way the commandments are set out is actually very similar to a legal agreement or treaty. Like most legal documents, they start with the name of the one who makes the agreement. It is not quite *'I, John Smith, the undersigned, do hereby . . .'* but it is not far from it. In this brief introductory sentence, the one who makes the treaty with its commandments sets out who he is. In it, God defines himself.

In these opening words we find four descriptions of God. He is *God*, the maker of all things; he is the LORD, the one who reveals himself to humanity; he is *King*, the one who is our God; and he is *Redeemer*, the one who saves his people.

Using these four pointers as guides, I want to sketch out what the Bible tells us about the one who gave the Ten Commandments to us.

The One Who Creates and Sustains – God

'And God spoke all these words . . .'

The one who gave the commandments is the God who created and sustains the universe. The Bible opens with the declaration that God is the maker of the cosmos, of all living things and of us. There is no suggestion in the Bible that God *had* to make the universe. No one can make God do anything. It must have been because he wanted to, because that's the kind of God that he is. God is the one behind all the breathtaking beauty and astounding intricacy of the world that we see. He is the one who is both powerful enough to create vast star systems and delicate enough to make a butterfly's wing. All the rhythms of days and seasons, all the cycles of life with their complex interdependency that we will never get to the bottom of – they are all God's handiwork.

God has not finished being God either. The Bible teaches that he continues to work in the universe by sustaining it and keeping it going. The 'laws of nature' are simply God's normal working patterns.

In everything that happens, from the sun shining to flowers blossoming, we see God's powerful but gentle hand.

Jesus, as God made flesh, was also a creator. We see this in the miracles where he turned water into wine, multiplied fish and bread, and stilled storms. He did things that only a creator God could do. But Jesus' main work was in the area of 're-creation'. In a world where God's good creation had been damaged, Jesus brought a healing and restoring touch: the blind received sight; the paralysed were given working legs; and even the dead were raised back to life. Now in heaven, Jesus continues that work and one day, we are promised, he will return in power to restore this ravaged world and make a new creation.

Now such a view should fill us with awe and reverence and ought to move us to worship him. It should encourage us to treat these commandments seriously. They are not the product of some human 'Working Party on Ethics'; they are a statement of God himself. It should also inspire us with confidence in them. These commandments are indeed 'the maker's instructions' and we would be well advised to follow them. We need to be sure that the only god we have is this true God.

The One Who Reveals Himself – LORD

'I am the LORD your God . . .'

In this opening to the commandments, God states that he is *the* LORD. I said previously that this name is an attempt by our English translators to represent the personal name of God, which is written in Hebrew as YHWH but was probably pronounced 'Yahweh'. This four-letter name means something like 'the one who brings into being all that is'. Behind this term lies the vital truth that God is not simply a maker or creator; he is also one who reveals himself to people.

This is of critical importance. If God had not spoken to us frail and finite people, we could never have found out about him. He would have remained a distant mystery, someone who could only be speculated about. But we see throughout the Bible how God spoke repeatedly to humanity about who he is. In giving his name, and in stating 'I AM' (in Hebrew 'I will be who I will be'), God is allowing himself to be found by us. As God reveals in the Bible that his name is 'the LORD' or Yahweh, he also lets us know that this is his covenant name. It is this name under which he makes – and keeps – his promises to the human race.

In the Old Testament we see how the LORD revealed himself to people in many ways: through words, visions, actions and by rare, brief and mysterious appearances. There is a distance between humanity and God, a distance caused not just by him being the eternal, infinite God but also by him being holy and us being sinful. In Jesus, though, God reveals himself fully to us. We see in Jesus as much of God as we can take in. God is no longer elusive, appearing only rarely to the very holiest of people, he stands before us in the flesh.

I was once faced with an incredibly hostile school assembly. To try to break the icy atmosphere, I began my talk by introducing myself as a Christian and asking if anyone had any questions about God. A hand shot up at the back and one of the obvious 'characters' of the final year asked sneeringly, 'Have you ever seen God?' I said, 'If I had lived over a hundred years ago in London, I would have seen Queen Victoria – one of the longest-ruling monarchs this country has ever had. If I had lived over four hundred years ago in Windsor, I would have seen Henry VIII, one of the most immoral monarchs this country has ever had. If I had lived over two thousand years ago in Palestine, I would have seen Jesus Christ. I wasn't around two thousand years ago so I didn't see him, but many people were around then who did see Jesus, so they did see God.'

In Jesus, we see what God is really like. In the film *The Wizard of Oz*, Dorothy and her friends follow the yellow brick road and eventually get to the Emerald City to see the great Wizard. There they get ushered in for an audience with him and find themselves standing in front of a huge and awesome face from which comes a booming voice. Just then the yappy dog Toto nips behind a curtain and reveals the real wizard: an old man who projects his face onto a big screen and speaks through a microphone. The whole thing is a fraud and a big disappointment. It's important to realise that the God of the Bible isn't like that. In Jesus, he meets us face to face and openly. There is no projection or screen, no booming voice or curtain. We see God as he wants us to see him.

Not only was Jesus like 'the LORD' of the Old Testament in revealing God to his people, he was also like him in making promises to them. In fact, he announced a new covenant, one that was to centre on his death on the cross and which was to be commemorated by a shared meal of bread and wine.

Jesus' role in showing who God is did not end with his death, resurrection and return to heaven. Jesus said that he would never leave his people and promised that when he had gone back to heaven God would send his Holy Spirit to live in us and be with us. True to that promise, God still comes to his people, now no longer a nation but instead spread worldwide as the church, by the Holy Spirit. The Spirit reveals to us his love and his care, speaks to us his truth and helps us pray and know him.

The God who gave these commandments is not a distant, aloof God. He is a God who, through Jesus, has come down alongside us, to show us who he is and make it as easy as he can for us to enter into relationship with him.

The One Who Rules Humanity and History – King

'Your God'

This little but significant phrase points to the bond that already existed between Yahweh and the people of Israel. They are his people and he is their God. This is the language of a king and his subjects, and much of the setting and the structure of the commandments is similar to the sort of treaty that kings made.

People in Britain can get themselves into trouble with the word 'king'. They tend to imagine a modern British monarch: a man or woman who is little more than a figurehead or national emblem, with very little real power or authority. Americans, in contrast, can tend to look back to the eighteenth century and think in terms of some kind of tyrannical monarch from whom they must declare independence. Yet the 'king' of the Bible is not like either stereotype. He is far greater and better, and we must define him on his terms, not ours.

God as 'king' is a theme that occurs throughout the Bible. God, it declares, is king over humanity. He is king over individuals in that he sets laws for us, and he is king over nations in that he orders their rise and fall. He is also king over history in that he makes all its tangled events work out to serve his purposes. These commandments were given that God himself might be king over the nation of Israel and that they would be his people. Later in the Bible, we see that this idea was rejected by Israel who decided they would rather have a human and visible king than a divine but invisible one. After a brief time under King David, the earthly kings failed, but the hope remained: one day the Messiah, the godly king, would sit on David's throne.

When Jesus came, he came as that true and long-hoped-for King of Israel. His kingship, though, was not the sort that his contemporaries wanted. Jesus avoided any open and direct claims to being king and spoke instead of a Kingdom of God that was far from the political notion favoured by the nationalists. However, those who observed him with open minds saw in his words and miracles undeniable evidence that he was indeed the Messiah King. Yet he was rejected and he was crucified under the Roman governor's ironic (but prophetic) placard: 'This is the King of the Jews'. Three days later he rose from the grave and appeared to his disciples. Within weeks, the message was spreading out from Jerusalem: Jesus was risen – he was Christ (the Greek for 'Messiah') and he was Lord.

The kingship of Jesus is not yet fulfilled; he is now the hidden king over a world that still rebels against him. That will not last forever. The Bible is full of promises about the future and how, on a day unknown, Jesus will return in unspeakable glory and majesty to be the crowned ruler of this world. King Jesus will exercise a final and full act of judgement and all those who have turned to him will live with him forever. All evil, along with all those who practised it, will be eternally destroyed. In the new heaven and earth, eternal wholeness, joy and life will replace all the pain, mourning and dying of this present age.

The God who is king gave the Ten Commandments and if we are to be the king's people then we must follow them. To keep his commandments is the best possible investment for our future.

The One Who Saves His People – Redeemer

'. . . who brought you out of Egypt, out of the land of slavery'

Finally, God reminds his people that he has acted on their behalf. He is not just God the creator, God the Lord and God their king; he is the God who has taken them out of Egypt and brought them out of slavery. In the world of slavery there was – and is – a word to describe the release from bondage. It is the word 'redeem', which according to The Concise Oxford Dictionary means 'to free (oneself or another) from slavery or captivity by paying a ransom'. God was saying to the Israelites, 'I, Yahweh, am your redeemer. I have set you free; I have brought you out of slavery.'

This is another great theme of the Bible: God is our redeemer, rescuer and deliverer. Almost as soon as humanity had fallen into sin and rebelled, God announced that there would be a deliverer. The entire history of the Old Testament is that of God working out his purposes to create a people of his own from whom the great deliverer could come. He called Abraham and made promises to him, brought his descendants out of Egypt and put them in the Promised Land. Then, through wars, famines and exile, under judges, prophets and kings, God taught his people that he accepts no rivals. God also taught them that he was holy and that the only way a sinful humanity could come to him was by rigorously and repeatedly obeying a system of animal sacrifices.

Throughout these centuries of discipline and learning, God continued to show that he was a loving redeemer, constantly reaching out to rescue his people and forgive them.

Finally, just over two thousand years ago, a baby was born into a family of the kingly line of David, in David's own city. The child was given the name Jesus, which means 'the Lord saves'. This child, Jesus, grew up to start his ministry acclaimed as 'the Lamb of God that takes away the sin of the world'. Throughout his ministry of preaching and healing he made a number of references to his death. He would, he said, 'give his life as a ransom for many', have to 'drink the cup' of God's judgement and wrath and be 'the good shepherd who lays down his life for the sheep'. Finally, on the night of his betrayal, Jesus explained the meaning of his imminent death to his followers. Using the language of sacrifice, he told his followers that the broken bread and poured wine of the Last Supper represented his body and his blood.

The next day, after a series of hasty, sham trials, Jesus was executed on a cross. What happened there is something so momentous it is difficult for our minds to comprehend. Somehow, in dying on the cross, the totally innocent Jesus took upon himself the guilt and sin of all human beings. There are many pictures for what happened there. Some of them come from the New Testament (he 'became sin for us', 'made peace for us', 'paid a price', 'made atonement for sin' and 'was the slain lamb'). Other images have come from twenty centuries of imaginative preaching. For instance, we might think of Jesus on the cross as becoming the lightning rod upon which the force of God's judgement is expended, or as a ladder between heaven and earth. Others have come up with stories where someone sacrifices themself for the good of others. In the film Saving Private Ryan, one man is saved from death by the sacrificial death of another.

But all of these images are inadequate in some way or another. The death of Jesus on the cross is too big for any images. The fact is, on the cross Jesus became one of us and took our place. In that awful death lies our forgiveness, our freedom and our future hope. Through it, those of us who were guilty rebels are now able, if we choose, to become the sons and daughters of God.

It is no accident that God referred back to the way that he saved his people from Egypt before giving them the commandments. He wanted to remind them that he was their redeemer. We have a far greater privilege than they had. The Israelites merely knew that God had redeemed them out of Egypt. We know that, in Jesus, he has redeemed us from hell.

The One Who is More Than We Can Imagine

This is just a thumbnail sketch of some of the things we know about God from the picture he paints of himself in the Bible and the words at the very start of the Ten Commandments. One night, Saint Augustine had a dream in which he saw a little boy on a beach. The child was at the water's edge scooping up the ocean in a thimble and pouring the water out onto the sand. In his dream Augustine heard an angel tell him that this boy would have emptied out the ocean long before anyone could possibly have exhausted what could be said about God.

All other gods are finite and will fail; they are not worth worshipping for a moment. Only the true and living God – God the creator, God the Lord, God the king and God the redeemer – is truly worthy of worship, and he is worth worshipping both now and for eternity.

GETTING RIGHT WITH GOD

The commandments are about ensuring that we are in a right relationship with God. That is what I would like to focus on now.

We Need to Recognise God

Sometimes after a war or a power struggle in another country we read that our government has 'recognised' the new leadership. We need to do that with God.

First, we need to recognise *who God is*. Many of us have an inadequate understanding of who God is. I have tried to explain something of the nature and character of the God who speaks to us in these commands. He is not an unknown mystery; he is the God who reveals himself clearly in order that we might know that we can trust him. Can I encourage you to think over what you know of him? Maybe you now realise that you have had an inadequate idea of who God is and that it needs changing. Perhaps you need to admit for the first time in your life that God really does exist.

Second, we need to recognise *God's concern for us*. The Bible tells the story of a God who cares for men and women even though they have rebelled against him. He cares for them so much that he has personally and painfully intervened in history in order to pay the price for their wrongdoings. He wants us to get into a right relationship with him. God desires us. He wants to be friends with us, for us to know him in this life and throughout eternity, and for us to have abundant life. In short, he loves us.

Third, we need to recognise *God's demands*. It is God who has given us these commands. He has given them to us because he made us, he knows what we are like and he knows the best way for us to live. They are not given to become a weight around our necks, but to give us boundaries within which we can live safely.

Fourth, we need to recognise that God *wants the fullest possible relationship with us*. He wants first place in our lives, and he wants to rule over every area of who we are and what we are. There is sometimes a danger of thinking that God is just interested in the spiritual side of us. This is not the case. On a plane journey to the Atlanta Olympics a journalist asked President Clinton what his favourite event was. Without hesitation he said, 'The Decathlon.' He went on to explain that this event, with its ten different sections, was so like life because there were separate disciplines which all had to be concentrated on with equal determination. Many people compartmentalise their lives: work, home, family, friends, leisure, hopes and loyalties. These things are often watertight compartments that are kept entirely separate from one another.

The God of the Bible won't put up with being kept in a little compartment marked 'spiritual'. He isn't a one-day-a-week or a special-occasion God. In this first commandment, God communicates what he expects, which is everything. Let's face it: he deserves nothing less than that. God is *God*. He is not applying for a job or bargaining for a position. Giving God the number-one spot in our lives is not us doing him a favour, it is simply us recognising the position that is rightfully his.

We Need to Review Our Lives

Having recognised all that God is and all that he demands of us, we need to review our lives. Imagine your life is like a car. Where is God? Is he actually in the car? Good. If so, where is he positioned? You may feel that he is there, but you try to hide him; it's as if he's in the boot or the trunk. It might be that he is in the back seat like a passenger, or in the front passenger seat like a companion. Or is he, as he should be, in the driving seat? But if he is in the driving seat, are you a backseat driver, instructing him where to go? Jesus will settle for no other place than one in which he takes full control, in the driving seat of our lives. That's what we mean when we call him Lord. Jesus must be resident and President of our lives.

It is worth taking time to do some stocktaking of our life as one of God's people. Let me remind you about some of the issues that we have looked at in this book.

Coveting: what is it that we aspire to? Who sets our desires? Do we desire what God desires or are we getting caught up in chasing after the things of this world? Do we trust him to provide all we need?

False testimony: does the fact that God hears every word we say give us any cause to be concerned? Are we truth-tellers? Could we say that the words we use are always truthful?

Stealing: are there things that we have acquired through dishonest means? Are all our dealings in order and above board? Does our life speak of the honesty of God? Do we put God first in our finances?

Adultery: in our relationships is there ambiguity or secrecy? If we are married, are we faithful to our partner in all our actions, thoughts and desires? Is God honoured by our sexuality?

Murder: are there people whom we refuse to forgive? Are our relationships, at work and at home, healthy and free from malice and resentment? Are we prone to violence or harming other people in any way?

Honouring parents: does our family life, whatever shape that is, honour God? Is there respect and gratitude, commitment and care?

If our friends could see us in our home environment, would they be surprised by how we treat those closest to us? Is God the head of our family?

Day of rest: do we take regular time off each week? Do we trust God enough to take a whole day off? Do we use that time wisely? Do we treat the day as holy and worship God?

The name of God: do we live consistently? Do we swear? Do we ever justify our ideas by saying God is behind them? Do we bring honour to the name of Jesus?

Idols: are there things that have us in their grasp, such as money, sex or power? Do we have divided loyalties? Does anything else claim the number-one spot in our life?

I don't know about you, but I barely get past the first of these before being challenged about what God wants for my life. None of us can keep the Ten Commandments. In fact, there is only one person who has ever kept them and his name is Jesus. It is because he was able that he could pay the price for our lives, which fall short in so many ways. Falling short of what God requires of us is called sin and it's something that we are all guilty of.

Fortunately, we are not left simply under the judgement of God. We may have broken the commandments, but God has intervened in Jesus to help us.

We Need to Respond to God

It is quite amazing that God, rather than leaving us in the dark, gives us instructions so that we can be the people we were made to be. Far from despairing of us, God himself comes and pays the penalty for our rebellion from him and his instructions. Jesus, the only one who ever lived by the maker's instructions, chose to take our place. We are told in the Bible that 'God made him who had no sin to be sin for us, so that in him we might become the righteousness of God' (2 Corinthians 5:21). A great exchange takes place. He gets what we deserve, and we get what we don't deserve: forgiveness, a new start, the promise of eternal life with God for ever.

God does this because of his love for each one of us, not because we earn it or have to show ourselves worthy of it. We do, however, have to accept it. Admitting our wrongdoing, we must say 'yes' to him and all that he has done for us. In grateful response to him we must now seek to put him first in everything. He knows how weak we are, so he forgives us when we repent and fills us with his Holy Spirit so that we are able to do what he asks of us.

God has saved us in Christ. The first thing we need to do is accept it with gratitude. The second thing is to work at relating properly to God as a result. It's easy to think that, even if we are forgiven, we are no more than God's servants. In fact, he wants us to be his children. It isn't that he just wants us to do the right things; he wants us to have a right relationship with him.

What should characterise our relationship with God? Let me suggest that, as in any relationship, one of the ways we keep God at the centre of our lives is to give him time. There is no better habit to get into than spending regular time with God. I would encourage you to carve out time, as busy as your schedule is, every day and set this time aside just to be with him. I try to spend a proportion of my time with God on each of these areas:

Praise: giving time to praising God, as a response to all he has done. This is one of the best antidotes to this generation's biggest problem: our obsession with ourselves. When we turn to God and put him at the centre of our lives, we take the focus off ourselves and put it onto him. Focus on him – worshipping and thanking him for all he has done.

The Bible: reading his word and listening to what he says to us. This prevents us from listening either to our own words or to all the advice and opinions in the world around us. Jesus himself said, 'People do not live by bread alone, but by every word that comes from the mouth of God' (Matthew 4:4 NLT). In this day and age we have more access to the Bible than ever before. We have study aids and commentaries to help us understand the Bible. There is no excuse for how little we know of God's word. A very godly man called John Henry Newman once said, 'I read the newspaper to know what people are doing and I read the Bible to know what people ought to be doing.'

Confession: laying our lives open to him and asking him to show us where we haven't put him at the centre or when we have lived in ways which have harmed our relationship, then asking for his forgiveness.

Prayer: bringing our needs and concerns to him and asking him to establish his ways in the world. This helps us to take our hands off the things that are tempting to hold onto, and give them over to God.

These four – praise, reading the Bible, saying sorry, praying for ourselves and others – have been the main elements of time spent with God by Christians for two thousand years.

However, being with God isn't just an individual thing. The Bible leaves me in no doubt that God wants me to meet with other people who love and honour him. Attending church is not some optional extra that is only for Christians who are particularly sociable. Church is where we can meet with others who are seeking to live their lives completely for God, so that we can worship him together, learn more about him, remember his death with bread and wine, and seek together to serve the world about us as well as celebrating his life among us. God made us for relationships. When we are close to others who are seeking to put him first in their own lives, then we receive encouragement to live for him. In such an environment of trust we can be open about how difficult it is sometimes. We all have blind spots and other people can point out areas of our lives that we aren't aware of, that may be displeasing to God. We can then receive support, wisdom and encouragement.

I want to conclude practically by encouraging you to pray the following prayer. In some churches this prayer is prayed by the whole congregation at the beginning of each new year. It is a prayer of commitment to God, giving him everything and trusting him with all we are and all we have, from this day on. It is not a prayer that can be prayed lightly. It is a prayer that transforms our lives.

Holy God, I am no longer my own, but yours. Put me to what you will, rank me with whom you will; put me to doing, put me to suffering; let me be employed by you or laid aside for you, exalted for you or brought low for you; let me be full, let me be empty; let me have all things, let me have nothing; I freely and heartily yield all things to your pleasure and disposal.

And now, O glorious and blessed God, Father, Son and Holy Spirit, you are mine and I am yours. So be it. And the covenant which I have made on earth, let it be ratified in heaven. Amen.

To pray this is only possible because we know that the God to whom we pray knows us and loves us. Therefore, we can trust his promises and give ourselves to obeying his commands, relying on his endless forgiveness, grace and strength.

And I pray for you, that you will experience the peace of God the Father, the presence of God the Son Jesus, and the power of God the Holy Spirit now and forever.

See, I set before you today life and prosperity, death and destruction. For I command you today to love the LORD your God, to walk in obedience to him, and to keep his commands, decrees and laws; then you will live and increase, and the LORD your God will bless you. (Deuteronomy 30:15–16)